How
6 *Psychological Factors for Success*
can affect your life . . .

"I am excited to be a part of Steve's project. People in all areas of life can use these ideas to become more successful. All of us are curious how to become winners. You don't have to reinvent the wheel. Find out what these highly successful coaches are doing and shape their ideas to your situation."

Cindy Book, Director of Athletics and Head Volleyball Coach
Saint Olaf College

"Dr. Brennan's book is a valuable resource for anyone in a leadership role. The lessons contained inside can be applied in the workplace as well as the sports world."

Scott Downing, Assistant Head Football Coach
Purdue University

"There's an old coaching cliché that says, 'You better stand for something, or you'll fall for anything.' Simply said, establish priorities in life and commit to living by those priorities. Steve Brennan's book is about mind games, and it can provide genuine guidance towards personal and team success."

Rick Moody, Head Women's Basketball Coach
University of Alabama

"The ideas and concepts contained in Steve's book are excellent guidelines to energize and motivate an athletic team, small business, sales group or corporate leadership to new heights of competitive excellence in Today's world."

Don Klosterman, Head Women's Soccer Coach
University of Nebraska-Omaha

6 Psychological Factors for Success

America's Most Successful Athletic Coaches Reveal the Path to Competitive Excellence

Stephen J. Brennan, Ph.D.
with Bill Donaldson

Peak Performance Publishing
Omaha, Nebraska

Other books by Stephen J. Brennan:

Competitive Excellence: The Psychology and Strategy of Successful
    Team Building
The Mental Edge: Basketball's Peak Performance Workbook
Inside Recruiting: The Master Guide to Successful College Athletic
    Recruiting
The Recruiters' Bible
Basketball Resource Guide (3rd ed.)

Other resources: *The Recruiters Library*™-Audio and video recruiting materials for coaches, parents and student-athletes.

Library of Congress Control Number: 2001093512
International Standard Book Number: 1-893353-13-3

Printed in the United States of America

10 9 8 7 6 5 4 3 2 1

Published and distributed by
Peak Performance Publishing
A Division of Peak Performance Consultants, Inc.
14728 Shirley Street
Omaha, Nebraska 68144 U.S.A.
(800) 293-1676
www.peakperformanceconsult.com

Dedication

*To all the architects of athletic, academic and corporate
teams worldwide.*

Table of Contents

Foreword

We all love to win and want to find ways to gain an edge over our opponents. In Dr. Brennan's book, *6 Psychological Factors for Success*, he has put together a fascinating publication for coaches and those in corporate leadership positions. He shows you how successful coaches from various sports have gained an edge over their opponents by utilizing six psychological tools.

Steve has researched the fundamental principles of creating and maintaining a winning organization in today's highly competitive work environment. The coaches eagerly share their most successful approaches and techniques. Each chapter explores detail-oriented aspects of championship programs, written by the coaches themselves, which describe organizational strategies that only insiders to the program would recognize.

As coaches, we tend to focus on the physical side of the game and spend most of our practice time preparing our teams physically. However, the mental discipline of the game has evolved into a major factor for success. As with any successful organization, it takes precise planning and delegation of time with those individuals who will make the organization successful. With part of that planning should come designated time spent on the mental aspect of competition. Steve's six psychological tools for success include motivation, team cohesion, discipline, mental toughness, mental preparation, and communication.

In essence, *6 Psychological Factors for Success* is a terrific book and unique resource for everyone interested in motivating and mentally preparing their team for success. Athletic coaches and leaders in industry and government will find this book by Dr. Brennan a valuable guide for building competitive excellence within their organization.

Caren Horstmeyer
Head Women's Basketball Coach
University of California-Berkeley

Introduction

I can truly say that I am thrilled when describing my feelings regarding the publication of this book. I think it was great that so many outstanding coaches agreed to share their trade secrets regarding their championship programs. They certainly didn't have to do it. But what I've found over the years, both during and following my high school and college coaching career, is that the coaches who are most psychologically and emotionally secure in their coaching philosophies and game strategies are the ones who are leading the most successful men's and women's athletic programs in the country . . . and the ones most eager and comfortable with sharing their ideas with others.

The premise behind the writing of *6 Psychological Factors for Success* was to identify some psychological concepts, when actualized both individually and collectively, could improve one's personal as well as professional life. There certainly can be compelling arguments that the six components I've chosen are not the only factors in making one's life more successful. But I believe there would be little disagreement that the six factors discussed by our esteemed group of coaches can be considered the "major players" when talking about guidelines for achieving competitive excellence.

Motivation, team cohesion, discipline, mental toughness, mental preparation and communication are primary principles for success in every endeavor in life. These six elements make up the blueprints for championship athletic teams as well as highly-profitable corporations. Players on athletic teams and employees on corporate teams need to exhibit these six psychological skills in order for their organizations to achieve success. That is why athletic coaches and corporate managers painstakingly search for individuals who possess these skills. When they are located, coaches and managers know they have found winners for their organizations.

Readers will appreciate the enjoyable flow of the book. Each championship coach is featured in his/her own chapter, with a cover page of biographical information and team and career highlights. Following a short introduction, the chapter concludes with the coach discussing team philosophy and strategy regarding the six psychological factors for success.

The last chapter in the book, *The Final Analysis*, is a brief overview linking current published research on the topic with the coaching methods employed by our coaches. It is an attempt to scientifically validate whether championship coaches actually practice what is preached in the research literature, or they whistle to their own tune. The findings make for interesting reading.

Another valuable element of the book is contained in the special appendix section. Bill Donaldson, my esteemed co-author with no history of athletic coaching in his background, has written a very insightful response to whether the coaching strategies employed in the book are applicable to today's corporate management teams. Bill's chapter is must-reading for the business leader.

In conclusion, *6 Psychological Factors for Success* should not be considered the definitive study for achieving competitive excellence in our lives. It can, however, be considered a simple attempt to pragmatically share success-building strategies with leaders in the athletic, academic and corporate worlds. Finally, I hope the book can be a valuable resource to assist researchers in the fields of sport psychology, coaching education and corporate management.

Steve Brennan

Acknowledgments

I want to sincerely thank my "team," whose efforts made the successful completion of this book possible: Bill Donaldson for his professional approach to contributing to all aspects of the book; Arnie Fencl for his patience and expert knowledge in designing the superb front and back covers; Dee Fogarty for her expert and creative typesetting; the pleasant and helpful personnel in the college sports information departments and athletic offices; and my family, Lorna, Anne, Bradley and Stephanie, for their support, encouragement and patience in allowing dad to finish this project.

Finally, I want to offer my sincerest thanks to all the coaches who agreed to participate in this valuable book project. Their contributions in giving their expertise, time and energy are all deeply appreciated.

CINDY BOOK

Saint Olaf College

- - - - - - - - - - - - - - - -

Position
Director of Athletics
Head Volleyball Coach

Career Record
524-234 (19 seasons)

Education
B.A.   Springfield (MA) College
M.Ed.   Keene (NH) State College
Ph.D.   University of Minnesota

```
┌ ─ ─ ─ ─ ─ ─ ─ ─ ─ ─ ─ ─ ─ ─ ─ ─ ─ ─ ─ ┐
```

Team and Personal Highlights

➢ NCAA Division III Regional Coach of the Year.

➢ MIAC Coach of the Year.

➢ Surpassed 500 career victory mark in 2000.

➢ Coached program's first All-American players.

➢ Conference and regional championships.

➢ NCAA Tournament appearances.

➢ Winningest volleyball coach in Saint Olaf history.

CINDY BOOK

Introduction . . .

Cindy Book is the winningest volleyball coach in Saint Olaf school history. She has elevated the volleyball program to a nationally-recognized level since her arrival at the small, private Minnesota school in 1991. Her enthusiasm is contagious, and her love and knowledge of the game has provided her teams with winning records in all but one of her 19 years of coaching.

She surpassed the 500 career victory mark early in the 2000 season, and now holds a 524-234 overall record. In the past nine years at Saint Olaf, she has chalked up a 278-91 record and received NCAA Division III Regional Coach of the Year and MIAC (Minnesota Intercollegiate Athletic Conference) Coach of the Year recognition. She has also coached the program's first All-American players.

Cindy earned her Ph.D. from the University of Minnesota and a M.Ed. from Keene (NH) State College. A graduate of Springfield (MA) College, she has been a featured speaker nationally at volleyball and recruiting seminars. In addition to coaching volleyball, Cindy became the Director of Athletics and department chair in the Department of Physical Education in 1998. She has also taught biomechanics, measurement and evaluation, and activity classes for the physical education department, in addition to coaching track and field teams in the past.

Let's begin our exploration into the six psychological factors for success with Cindy's thoughts . . .

. . . on Motivation

Coach Book uses a series of words and phrases to define motivation: "drive, excitement, willingness, work ethic, focused on goals, will sacrifice, want it so bad you can't stand it." She says that it's important to talk about goals almost constantly to keep them uppermost in the athletes' minds. And to motivate, she wants to paint mental pictures of what new experiences will be like. "Matches will be different from practices. They will be loud. What is a picture of a team like, compared to just a group of individuals? What is our gym like? Is it more than just a structure?"

She organizes the goals in a step-wise fashion. It's like a high jumper's raising the bar after each successful jump. First develop skills and teamwork. Then come the regular season matches. And then the post season, with that NCAA championship as the ultimate goal. "As you make progress, it's important to monitor the progress and keep talking about how the Oles are progressing and accomplishing things," Cindy says.

"This is a 'we' thing—not an 'I' thing." According to Cindy, "It's not 'me,' 'mine,' or 'yours'. It's 'we' and 'ours'. I need to find out, by whatever means is appropriate, what the athletes, as individuals and as a team, want to do and what they are willing to do. I may be able to change what they want to do—make it a bigger challenge or a bigger goal than they originally had in mind—but in the end, I'm limited by what they genuinely want to accomplish. Because their goals and desires are the limit to what we can accomplish, I must keep this in mind in motivating them to accomplish our mutual goals."

Sometimes Cindy uses some innovative stimuli. For example, she says, " I like to break the girls into pairs, eight weeks before they report for practice in late August. I give each girl eight postcards, with stamps on them and the address of the girl she is paired with. Each of them is to send her partner a postcard each week, telling the partner what she has done in preparation for the volleyball season." This practice accomplishes several things. First it makes them think and be creative, which is important not only in volleyball, but it's important in life. Next, it places them in a team environment, even though they are geographically separated. And it motivates them to keep up with—actually out-pace—their partner. It appeals to their competitive nature.

And what does Cindy feel are impediments to motivation? "Yelling at people is not motivating. I realize a lot of coaches do this, but I don't, because I think it's demeaning. College athletes are becoming adults, and civilized adults don't respond to humiliation and a coach's failure to respect them. Failing to make sure they know that I want what they want is an impediment. This program isn't for me. It's for the Oles. After losing nearly all of our 'Final Four' team in 1996, I had to be careful to make sure that the incoming freshmen knew that I wanted them to reach the Final Four too—maybe even go all the way—but not for me. I wanted them to want it. If they thought it was for me, they would feel exploited."

Cindy doesn't like punishment. "That's a bad word. It's a negative word. It has the same negative effect that yelling at people has. Coaches have to correct mistakes—both technical mistakes and personal mistakes—but that correction must be done in a positive manner."

◆　◆　◆　◆　◆

. . . on Team Cohesion

"My approach to team chemistry and team cohesion can be separated into two parts and then they have to be combined: working together and getting along together. You can't be a team just when you're in the gym. You can't interact effectively on the court if you have a subconscious—or maybe even conscious—dislike for your teammate. But there will always be some differences among teammates, so you have to put aside those differences on the court. And when you do that, it carries over to the off-court relationships" says Cindy.

"And then there's what I like to call 'court personality.' It's like another skill—the scowl on your face—what we look like to opponents. Players must be players—not coaches. Be excited; and if you can't be excited, act excited. And don't whine or complain. Whining and complaining are for losers; and regardless of the score, you can be winners in your demeanor. Make sure you know and the team members know how each person likes to be talked to after a mistake. How you respond to a mistake can be the difference in making it a positive, learning experience or a negative, discouraging experience."

Cindy says that laughing together is a tremendous bonding activity. But you must laugh with each other, and not pick on an individual. Being picked on stays with a person long after the act is over, and it hurts about as bad as anything that can happen to a person, because it says to you that someone doesn't like you. We all want to be liked. "I like to develop 'core groups' as role models and expand the size of the group gradually until the whole team is a core group," she says. "Maybe I'll start with 4 people and enlarge the group as the other team members begin to emulate the original core players. These are bonding activities inside the gym."

What does Cindy encourage outside the gym? "I encourage the team to do things together in their normal every-day activities. Go to the mall together, go to movies, go to other Oles team events. After the freshman years, most team members room with other members of the team. During bus and van rides, we like to tell stories about our experiences. Some of the most interesting ones are about embarrassing moments. We all have them, and it makes us feel closer to share them."

Cindy says that traditions are team building. "We like to have a 'Halloween Practice' on October 31, when everyone comes to practice in a costume." This serves two purposes: It adds some levity to the practices, which can become arduous, and it keeps the girls from feeling like practice is denying them an opportunity to participate in activities other students enjoy, because they actually participate in them, too.

Book 5

Don't take good performance or good attitudes for granted. Cindy says, "Stop and compliment players—often!" She likes to mix groups of players when assigning roommates in motels, just like she mixes the lineups in matches. This makes the on-court experience more natural.

Every coach worries about problems among team members that she doesn't know about. While you would hope that any team member would bring her problems to you, you also know that this doesn't always happen. Cindy says, "Ask your leaders for help in learning who's having problems so you can try to nip them in the bud. Learn about who's forming cliques. Cliques can disintegrate team cohesion."

. . . On Discipline

Cindy has no written rules other than those set forth by the college. And, as stated before, she doesn't like the idea of punishment. That's not discipline. She says, "I like to work with individuals when they seem to have a problem before it becomes a team problem. But if I have to, I'll step in and point out behavior we must stop and make sure it's stopped." She's learned that she can't do all of the discipline herself. "I need all the help I can get; and the seniors, team captains, and other leaders form a core group that I encourage and depend on to influence team behavior in a positive manner."

But she does let the team know that there are practices that enhance their performance and they are expected to pursue these on their own. "For example," she says, "everyone must understand that the only way to achieve their goals is through hard work. The team must look on hard work as something that is good, not bad. They must develop the attitude that 'I love hard work, do that to me again (if it makes me stronger), bring on the tough assignments.' When they are waiting in the gym, do sit-ups and push-ups. This gets in those repetitions without having to take time away from some other developmental activity, because they weren't using the time for anything else anyway."

While Cindy doesn't have a list of written rules, there are some well-understood un-written rules that she enforces. She doesn't tolerate talking in the gym about non-volleyball activities. While friendly chat and maybe even gossip (if it's not destructive) may be OK for one's free time, they have no place in the "workplace." And the gym is the volleyball team's workplace. This type of talk affects the progress of at least two people: the one talking and all those listening. Cindy may require a team member to leave the gym for non-volleyball-related talk.

Cindy doesn't tolerate lateness and encourages early arrival to practice.

And "Yes," she says, "there is a point where continued problems may lead to dismissal from the team." But with her leadership, that isn't likely to happen often.

. . . on Mental Preparation

"It's important to understand all of the details of a match—the situation, the opponents—in preparing for a match," according to Cindy. "I tell the team that they need to concentrate on momentum. We need to know how to find it, get it, and get it back if we lose it. We have to realize that momentum changes occur and that they swing both ways. Patience is paramount in looking for momentum." She says there are things the team can do to slow down the opponent when they have the momentum (a three-point run or more)—call timeout, substitute, stall, wipe off the floor, be slow in putting the ball in play, even go on a coughing jag. "To prepare the team for matches, we try to make practice as much like matches as possible—execute drills that simulate game conditions, be aggressive, not passive."

It's a long time between the beginning of fall practice and the Oles' first intercollegiate match. So Cindy has all sorts of "fun things" to mitigate the grind of pre-season. "We have 'dumb prizes' for various fun contests, like painting finger nails or toe nails all sorts of ways. I'm the judge of the fun contests. We have a 'K Mart' tourney with 4 teams of six players and prizes that are brought by the players. And half-way through the pre-season practices we have a game against the alumnae."

Some of the more "affluent" athletic programs have massage therapists who can work with various teams. Massages are a tremendous help in relieving pain after workouts and in loosening muscles before workouts. Cindy says, "We aren't that affluent at Saint Olaf, so the girls give each other massages. Some are quite skilled at being masseuses, and it's a great way to create a sense of helping each other accomplish goals."

Before the academic program kicks in, the team needs to have wholesome activities for the evenings. Whatever the activities—movies, board games, watching videos—many of the ventures are followed by ice cream at Cindy's.

In preparing for matches, whether at home or away, Cindy says that mental preparation is as important as the physical sessions. She says, "You must go back to the fundamentals to make sure the team stays focused. Review the 'game plan'—the goals, the plays we think will be most effective and how to know when they are likely to work. Don't concentrate on the score but on the next point. And remind them that showing their excitement and enthusiasm is intimidating to the other team and stimulating to them. We review scouting reports to help them know the characteristic movements of the other teams—to anticipate who's likely to attempt the spike, etc. But reviewing scouting reports also gives our team confidence. People fear the unknown, but they have much less anxiety if they know what they're up against."

Late-game strategy is a built-in part of the overall game strategy. Cindy reminds us, "It's always one point at a time, regardless of the situation. The other team has to get the last point to win, and as long as there's a point between them and victory, we have just as much chance at making it our point as they do of making it theirs. Sometimes we have to change our strategy at a timeout to intensify our concentration on the next point and to build a little more fire into our enthusiasm. Particularly when we are behind, we need to celebrate every positive step. And as we celebrate each achievement and concentrate on that next point—point after point—we might look at the scoreboard and see that WE are the team that is just one point away from a victory."

◆ ◆ ◆ ◆ ◆

. . . on Mental Toughness

Cindy defines mental toughness with a series of phrases, too: "Stay aggressive, a 'come-back-at-you' attitude after adversity, 'you got me once, but you can't do it again.' You must compete to the very end, go for everything, and never give up. Be fierce and scrappy."

"There are many pressures on a team and on each individual on the team. Each individual must remain fierce and scrappy and want the ball—without losing sight of the team concept of the game. Fierceness and scrappiness by individuals are contagious. Pretty soon the whole team is fierce and scrappy. In away matches, you must tune-out the crowd yelling against you. And remember that losing your temper is the worst thing that can happen to you. Regardless of how difficult the task of overcoming a lead may appear, a positive attitude is your best weapon in getting back into the match."

Cindy thinks a mentally tough person is pretty much like a leader. In fact you have to be mentally tough to be a good leader. According to Cindy, "A mentally tough person likes to take charge and lead her teammates. She is aggressive, isn't afraid to take chances, and likes to serve—taking responsibility."

. . . on Communication

"Staying positive," according to Cindy, "is the most important requirement for dealing with a losing situation. Stay focused on the fundamentals. They are what got us here, and they will get us past this obstacle. Review in your mind where to serve, and how you plan to execute blocks. Review the characteristics of the other team your coach reviewed in the game plan. It's still the same team."

"When the other team is 'hot', you must remember that hot streaks don't last forever. Be patient, and pretty soon you'll realize that the momentum has shifted and you're the hot team. If this sounds like a broken record, it's because I simply cannot over emphasize the importance of focusing on one point at a time. Remember the advice to the server in tennis: 'First serve in'. Then focus on return of service. In volleyball only the server has to be concerned with getting the serve to the right spot, so the rest of the team is focused on the return of service and how you will deal with it under various circumstances. But the game moves so fast that you hardly have time to think. Your actions have to be instinctive sometimes. That's why mental preparation even before the match is so important."

Cindy often will ask a particular player to "step up" during a game. Assigning additional responsibility to players who want to win gives them incentive and confidence. "So I like to ask different players to 'step-up' during the game. That way, the whole team begins to gain confidence. And when that confidence is gained, look out, the Oles are coming!"

There is not a team in any sport who doesn't lose sometimes. How does Cindy deal with a loss? "First of all, I find the things to compliment the team about. I've never coached a game yet when my team didn't do something to be proud of, whether they won or not. So I point those things out in a way that is sincere and credible. But the team is asking themselves, 'What went wrong?' They had a game plan. They did their best to execute it. They may be confused, and they may begin to lose confidence in themselves or in me. So it is equally important for me to point out what failed us. What mistakes did we make, and what did the other team do that we hadn't prepared them for? Maybe we were prepared, and the other team just executed better than we thought they would. Learning what failed us usually is uplifting, because it restores confidence that the coach has found a way to help the team and that they know what to do to correct the problems. All is not lost."

"There are times, after a loss when I sense that the team is not ready to accept losing, which we must do before we can discuss how we can improve. So I just wait until the next practice and let time be a factor in dealing with the loss. One of the most helpful and instructional tools in dealing with defeat—even in dealing with victory—is reviewing the game films. The mistakes are usually more easily defined and usually we look better on film than our image of what we looked like during the match."

In reviewing Cindy's remarks, a few axioms stand out: You must want to win. You must be willing to work and sacrifice. You must organize your journey to achievement of your goals into discrete steps. You must be a team player on and off the court. You must focus on one step (one point) at a time whether you're ahead or behind. And you must always, always, always, be positive.

BOBBY BOWDEN

Florida State University

- - - - - - - - - - - - - - - - -

Position
Head Football Coach

Career Record
315-87-4 (35 seasons)

Education
B.A. Samford University

Team and Personal Highlights

➢ Five-time National Coach of the Year.

➢ Winningest coach in Florida State football history.

➢ Two national championships.

➢ Teams have finished in Associated Press Top Five for 14 consecutive seasons.

➢ Only coach in history of Division 1-A football to compile 13 consecutive 10-win seasons.

➢ Teams hold NCAA record with 11 consecutive bowl victories and 14 straight bowls without a loss.

➢ Nation's second-winningest active head coach with 315 victories.

BOBBY BOWDEN

Introduction . . .

Bobby Bowden has made his mark on the college football world in grand fashion. His style, grace, class, humility and humor have made him one of the most revered head football coaches in the nation. His energy and enthusiasm is still visible as he begins his 26th season at Florida State.

To put the recent accomplishments of Florida State's football program into perspective, a college basketball analogy is most appropriate. Imagine a college basketball program advancing to the Final Four 14 years in a row. Even more impressive is the thought of a team playing in the national title game five times in the last eight seasons. That is what the Seminoles have done under Bowden. Florida State is on an NCAA record 14 straight Top Five finishes and the 2001 Orange Bowl was the Tribe's third straight national title game and fifth in the last eight years.

Bobby Bowden is a man so closely identified with the phenomenal success of his program that he, as Renegade and the war chant, is Florida State football. Gracious in both victory and defeat, Bowden is at peace with himself, a man with rock-solid character and firm coaching principles that date back 46 years. He is the calming voice in the face of the turbulence surrounding college football: a proud moral leader, a family man of the first order and a caring disciplinarian.

One of Bowden's greatest achievements revolves around bowl games. His 17-6-1 record and .729 bowl winning percentage rank first all-time. He is the second winningest active coach in the history of college football with 315 victories, trailing only Penn State's Joe Paterno. He is the winningest coach in Florida State football history. He is a five-time National Coach of the Year award winner. He has been inducted into the Florida Sports Hall of Fame and is considered a lock when his name becomes eligible for induction into the College Football Hall of Fame.

Bobby's credentials as a caring human being rise even farther above his coaching accomplishments. Always friendly and outgoing, he is a devoted Christian and family man. His ties with the Fellowship of Christian Athletes organization are deeply rooted. Because of his personality and charm, he has become somewhat of a folk hero in the South. Even though his busy coaching schedule curtails many speaking engagements, he is still highly-sought-after as a speaker not only at corporate and athletic events, but you may also find him in the pulpit of a church on Sunday morning somewhere in the South.

Bowden achieved impressive numbers at his previous head coaching stops at Samford University (31-6 in four seasons) and West Virginia (42-26 in six seasons). He met his future wife, Ann Estock, in Tuscaloosa while playing freshman football at the University of Alabama, fulfilling a lifelong dream of the Birmingham native to play for the Crimson Tide. They soon married and Bobby transferred to Howard College (now Samford University) in Birmingham.

Bobby's family has always been most important to him. His son Tommy is the head football coach at Clemson University and Terry, a former Auburn head coach, is ABC's top college football studio analyst. Steve is in private business, and Jeff is in his sixth season as an assistant coach on his father's staff at Florida State. The four boys, along with daughters Robyn and Ginger and 21 grandchildren, keep Bobby and Ann busy and active year-round.

Let's listen closely as Bobby Bowden discusses his success formula with his thoughts . . .

. . . on Motivation

Considered by many of his coaching peers as a motivational genius, Coach Bowden believes that motivation begins in the heart.

"Motivation is a state of heart and mind," he says. "You really can't be totally motivated unless both your heart and your mind are in it."

When the player is in the correct state of mind and heart, "he will have the courage and confidence and enthusiasm to give 100 percent effort all the time," Bowden says. Coach Bowden is a master mental technician when it comes to getting 100 percent effort from his players.

He has a simple theory when it comes to effective motivational techniques.

"I can tell you what doesn't work, and that's punishment for any kind of failure," he states.

Bowden believes that negative behavior from the coaches when a player makes a mistake only compounds the problem.

"Chewing the kid out won't make it better, for him or me," he says.

The most effective motivational technique that Bobby uses is reward for doing your best.

"We like to keep things positive all the time, so a reward might take the shape of less conditioning for the team or a helmet decal for great individual effort," he says.

The most important aspect, he points out, is that the players know they are loved and respected by the coaches.

In summary, Coach Bowden defines motivation as a state of heart and mind, a combination that gives the players courage, confidence and enthusiasm to give 100 percent effort at all times.

Least effective motivational techniques include any kind of punishment associated with failure, while the most effective tool includes rewards for individual effort.

◆   ◆   ◆   ◆   ◆

. . . on Team Cohesion

Team chemistry is a vital ingredient for ultimate team success, and no one knows that better than Coach Bowden. His philosophy concerning team cohesion is built around one word.

"Love is how I define team cohesion and team chemistry," he says. "The sacrifice, commitment, and pain involved with football is insurmountable, and without the players loving each other, you won't find cohesion and winning chemistry."

Building team cohesion, Bowden says, means involving everyone in all team activities.

"I try to build team chemistry by taking the boys to dinner together, to church together, even to banquets together. Wherever there is an easy, free setting where everyone can enjoy themselves is where we'll go."

Coach Bowden's strong Christian faith is also utilized in building team chemistry.

"I encourage the players to be a part of F.C.A. (Fellowship of Christian Athletes) so that they can realize the love of Christ in their lives," he says.

Bobby believes that Christian love has a tremendously positive effect on team building.

"It's mighty powerful in uniting a common bond of love between men," he professes.

In summarizing team cohesion, Coach Bowden defines team chemistry as a love among all the players. This love and respect for each other is the only way there can be winning cohesion on a team, he states.

Effective team building methods include taking the team to places as a group, such as dinners, church and banquets. He also encourages participation in FCA activities to help develop the common bond of love among team members.

◆   ◆   ◆   ◆   ◆

. . . on Discipline

Discipline is a trademark of all successful teams and individuals. Discipline is also a way of life at Florida State and many outsiders consider it to be the glue to the success of the Seminole program.

"I am a firm believer in discipline, on and off the field," Coach Bowden emphasizes. "We stress it here and we make a big thing out of it!" But Bowden also makes sure that it is done properly.

There are different ways to discipline a person, and Coach Bowden has his own way of doing things.

"Discipline is great, but you have to make sure that you don't push it too far, or that you don't over-do it," he says.

Too much or too little makes any kind of discipline less effective, he believes.

"Hold a bird in your hand too loosely and it will escape," he states. "Hold it too tightly and it will die."

Effective discipline methods again revolve around the concept of love," Bowden says.

"You must convince your squad that discipline is love," he says. Bowden continues with a story to illustrate his point.

"Your dad spanked you as a child when you disobeyed and told you that it hurt him more than it hurt you. He did that because he loved you and wanted to make you a better person."

Coach Bowden puts the finishing touches on that story by stating his philosophy on discipline in no uncertain terms.

"If you don't love the children on your team, then don't discipline them. If you do love them, then you will discipline them, because proper discipline is love."

In summary, Coach Bowden is a firm believer of discipline, both on and off the field. He makes it a big issue with the players, and will not hesitate to exercise his use of disciplinary penalties when they are needed.

He considers too much or too little discipline as ineffective, stressing that a consistent approach must always be utilized. Discipline will be most effective, he believes, when the team is convinced that discipline is another form of love.

Finally, he strongly emphasizes that if you don't love your players, then don't discipline them. Every person on the team must realize that proper discipline is a message of love and that accepting discipline is a way of becoming a better person.

◆ ◆ ◆ ◆ ◆

. . . on Mental Preparation

All successful coaches say that mental preparation is essential to team and individual success. Bowden believes that mental preparation is not only a responsibility of the student-athlete, it is a responsibility of the coach as well.

"Mental preparation is transferring the coach's mental attitude and knowledge into the heads of his players," Bobby says.

In Coach Bowden's thoughts, mental preparation also means increasing the powers of concentration.

"Mental preparation means focusing on the priorities of the game and shutting out all distractions," he says.

Coach Bowden thinks that there are no secrets to mentally preparing a team for the long grind of a football season.

"The kids already have a mindset even before they report for fall camp," he says. "We tell them they better show up in excellent physical shape, they better be goal-oriented, and they should expect pre-season practice to be rough."

Every game is important to the Seminoles because they are a national power.

"Every game is big to us because a loss is a loss, whether it's to Nebraska or Furman," he points out.

So mental preparation means getting ready for all games, not just a few.

"I want the kids to keep a level attitude and not have mountains and valleys mentally," he says. "We must be ready for 11 straight games once the season has started."

Mental preparation for late-game strategy is practiced thoroughly during the week of game preparations.

"We work on our two-minute offense every day," Bowden states. "So if we are behind late in the game, we can still win."

He adds that late-game strategy practice includes both the offense and defense.

"It's important that the kids understand that all late-game situations involve both the offense and the defense. It's a team game no matter how you look at it," he says.

In summarizing mental preparation, Coach Bowden stresses that mental preparation is the responsibility of the player and the coach. It is the coach's duty to get the student-athlete thinking like a coach and keeping a focus on the priorities of the game.

Mental preparation for the season begins long before the players report to fall practice. Coach Bowden communicates his expectations for the pre-season long before the student-athletes arrive on campus. These expectations include reporting in top physical condition, having team and individual goals in mind, and having an understanding that fall practices will be very rough.

Mental preparation for non-conference and conference opponents is identical because Florida State is a national power. This means that all 11 of their games are important, so mental preparation is ongoing right from the beginning of fall practice.

Finally, to ensure late-game success, the Seminoles practice their two-minute offense each day, incorporating the defense in the preparations as well. The "team" concept is always evident in Coach Bowden's philosophy, so mental preparation will involve all the members of the team.

◆　◆　◆　◆　◆

. . . on Mental Toughness

Mental toughness is a trait found in all highly-skilled athletes, and the team with the most mentally tough players is usually the team that wins. Coach Bowden is very aware of the need for mentally tough players on his teams.

"Mental toughness is also something you can't coach, but you hope that each of your players has it," he says. "I think that mental toughness means allowing the mental to overcome the physical pain associated with football."

Mental toughness is also an attitude, he says.

"It's an attitude that 'no opposing player can physically whip me' and 'no coach is tough enough to run me off.' That's mental toughness."

Coach Bowden believes that there are several traits evident in a mentally tough player.

"He definitely has to be able to play with pain," he states. "That's a critical point."

Reacting to criticism is also a mental toughness trait.

"The player must be able to accept criticism in a positive way," he says. "That is a difficult thing to do for some players."

The final characteristic of mental toughness is persistence.

"The mentally tough player absolutely will not quit at anything he attempts," Coach Bowden says. "Nothing can get in his way to stop him once he sets his mind to accomplish it."

In summary, Coach Bowden believes that mental toughness means having the mental strength to overcome any physical pain associated with football. It is also an attitude of never allowing anyone or anything to influence or intimidate you away from your goals.

Mental toughness traits include playing with pain, accepting criticism in a positive way, and never quitting at anything you do.

◆ ◆ ◆ ◆ ◆

. . . on Communication

A major responsibility of a head coach is the ability to effectively communicate with players, fellow coaches, administrators, the media, alumni and the community. Coach Bowden loves talking with people.

"I guess I've always been a talker," he says.

His ability to communicate with his team and coaching staff during critical times of a game puts him in the upper echelon of coaches.

"I very rarely yell or chew the kids out at halftime if the effort was good, but the execution was bad," he says. "But if the effort was bad, I may have a few things to say."

But as most successful coaches do, any inspiration comes from technical responses to adversity.

"There just isn't any time to be jumping up and down and getting emotional late in a close game," he points out. "I have to be able to have the right play called when the game is on the line. The kids expect that and I do, too." So keeping a calm, poised response to adversity is Bowden's way of inspiring his teams late in a close game.

Post-game comments after a tough loss or a poor performance are usually met in a positive way.

"I'm not afraid to tell the kids I'm disappointed," Coach Bowden says. "But no single player or official's call or botched play caused us to lose. It's always a combination of factors and I may touch on only a few of them."

The usual routine is to tell the players that they did the best they could, regroup, learn from our mistakes, and get ready for the next game.

"Now if I see something in the films that I didn't see in the game, well, we'll just have to talk to the team or player about it to get things straightened out," he says.

Always talking, always making sure that everyone understands what needs to be done is the master-teacher approach to communication that has made Coach Bowden one of the best in the country.

In summarizing Coach Bowden's approach to communication, it is apparent that he believes effective communication is an important psychological factor within the program.

Halftime talks will center around technical adjustments for the offense and defense. Only a short time period remains for general comments, and Bowden stresses the importance of effort and concentration during those moments before the team returns to the field.

Reacting to adversity late in a game makes communication vital for success. Coach Bowden takes a calm, poised approach because any kind of emotional scene would be counterproductive to the team. The players expect a professional response from the coaching staff and he makes sure that they get one.

Post-game comments after a tough loss or a poor performance are met in an upbeat tone. Bowden places the blame on no one, and makes it a point to mention the positive aspects of the game. Any additional comments are made to the team after the coaching staff has reviewed the game film.

Coach Bowden ultimately communicates the thought that every game should be a learning experience for the players, whether it is a win or a loss for the Seminoles.

FISHER DEBERRY
United States Air Force Academy

- - - - - - - - - - - - - - -

Position
Head Football Coach

Career Record
135-72-1 (17 seasons)

Education
B.A.   Wofford College

Team and Personal Highlights

➢ National Coach of the Year.

➢ 3-time Western Athletic Conference Coach of the Year.

➢ Winningest football coach in Air Force Academy history.

➢ 16th active coach in NCAA to win 100 games.

➢ 14 All-American players.

➢ 114 All-Conference players.

➢ 10 Academic All-Americans.

➢ 9 NCAA Postgraduate Scholarship winners

FISHER DEBERRY

Introduction...

Faith, family and the Falcons. These are the priorities in life for Fisher DeBerry, who enters his 18th season in 2001 as the Air Force Academy's head football coach. As successful as he is colorful and charitable, the 63-year-old DeBerry has become as much a part of the AFA landscape as Falcon stadium and the Cadet Chapel.

His teams have posted winning records 15 of his 17 seasons in Colorado Springs, and 11 teams have played in a post-season bowl game. He coached the Falcons to a share of the Western Athletic Conference championship in 1985 and 1995, with the 1998 team claiming the first outright Mountain Division championship. He received his third WAC Coach of the Year award following the 1998 season in which the team's 12-1 overall record helped complete the school's first back-to-back 10-win seasons in school history.

A native of Cheraw, South Carolina, Fisher graduated from Wofford College in 1960. At Wofford, he lettered three years in baseball, playing second base and shortstop. In football, he lettered twice as a flanker, defensive back, and linebacker. After six years of coaching in the high school ranks in South Carolina, he returned to Wofford in 1968 as an assistant coach, helping Wofford win 21 consecutive games and obtain a number one ranking in the NAIA.

Fisher served as president of the American Football Coaches Association in 1996, and five of his former assistant coaches are currently head coaches at Division I schools. Deeply religious, DeBerry and his wife, Lu Ann, are active in church, charity, and community affairs. The coach also gives motivational speeches to religious and corporate groups. Lu Ann's volunteer work includes the Ronald McDonald House and Sunrise United Methodist Church.

Fisher has strong ties to the Fellowship of Christian Athletes, and he and his wife have assisted fund-raising efforts for Easter Seals, March of Dimes, Salvation Army, American Heart Association, and the American Cancer Society. The DeBerry's have two children and four grandchildren.

Fisher was eager to share his thoughts on achieving competitive excellence, so let's take a closer look at Fisher's ideas . . .

. . . on Motivation

Fisher DeBerry places a lot of the responsibility for motivation on doing something to motivate—not just creating the right environment. He thinks the coach or other leaders should be proactive. Fisher: "Motivation is the direction and encouragement you give a person in seeking fulfillment of a desired goal. It's using techniques to get someone to do something they don't necessarily want to do and getting someone to succeed in something they might not have confidence they can succeed in. It's never, never giving up until—out of pride—he achieves the goals you and he have set together." Fisher assumes that motivation follows goal setting, and he refers to goals twice in his explanations of motivation.

"Positive reinforcement." That's high on Fisher's agenda for motivating. "The most effective means of motivation is the positive reinforcement you give a person on his journey to attaining personal and team goals. You need to salute, congratulate, and make a big deal of the mini accomplishments on the way to achievement of the ultimate goals. And the ultimate goal for our team each year is the 'championship ring.' To keep the team focused on that goal, we frequently pass around a ring for our players to touch and feel. We keep pictures in front of them to remind them that the ring is the ultimate goal for the team."

Fisher equates players to people in the corporate ladder in warning against negative criticism. "It's been my experience that neither players nor corporate ladder climbers respond positively to negative criticism. Being negative, profane, or overly critical is counterproductive in trying to help a player reach his personal goal or a team goal. You must be positive—never comparing players to their peers or putting them down. The picture you paint of a player's journey must be laden with images of success."

◆ ◆ ◆ ◆ ◆

. . . on Team Cohesion

To Fisher team chemistry is an attitude of putting the team first. He says, "Team cohesion or chemistry is every team member totally committed to doing whatever it takes to reach the team goal. All players must have this commitment. In successful attainment of team cohesion or chemistry, there can be no attitudes of individuality—no 'I' or 'me' or 'I come first.' In all considerations and decisions, the team accomplishments must be the only things that matter—not individual recognition.

"During the season some players will receive individual recognition. That happens with media coverage of any sport. But our attitude is that even individual recognition and awards would not occur if it wasn't for the team concept and commitment of the other players. Therefore we give few individual awards at our recognition banquets, emphasizing team success over individual success."

"Family is the foundation of our program, and brotherhood is our cohesion." Fisher says the family unit is the strongest organizational unit in this country. In relating the family unit to his team, he says, "It's the commitment each player makes to the others—that he truly loves, cares, respects, and totally accepts his teammates; and that he will do anything to keep from letting his brothers down! I learned a long time ago, growing up in a small country town, that brothers are hard to beat as companions. We had several brother combinations in our community. If you got in a fight and whipped one of the brothers, you'd better get ready to whip his brother."

"It may seem uncomplicated—and it is—but team chemistry or cohesion depends solely on brotherhood: a commitment from each individual not to let his brother down. This uncomplicated ingredient keeps the focus on team and not on individuality. I tell our players that there is no letter, 'I' in TEAM. On our best teams the brotherhood concept was strongest, with the attitude of 'we,' not 'me.' The concept of cohesiveness can only be fully appreciated when you've been a part of it on a day-to-day basis, as we strive to integrate cohesiveness and chemistry into our program at the Air Force Academy."

◆ ◆ ◆ ◆ ◆

. . . on Discipline

Fisher says, "Discipline is how you conduct your affairs. It's how you respond to different situations, on and off the field. It's not about rules. The only rule we have for our team is 'Do what's right.' When our players have a decision to make, we ask them to ask themselves, 'If I do this, will it make our team better?' If it will, do it!"

"Responses to stressful situations—how you act when we're on the goal line, for example—are the ones that reveal a player's level of discipline. Well disciplined teams handle adversity well. I remind our team before each game that there will be some adversity during the game. I can't tell them what form the adversity will come in or when it will come. I don't know. But I do know that how we respond will tell us a lot about the character of the team and whether or not we'll become champions."

It would be an understatement to say that Fisher's not big on a lot of specific rules. "The least effective disciplinary programs are those in which the coaching staff sets up a bunch of conduct rules for the team. The fewer rules you have, the fewer problems you'll encounter. Too many rules can encourage an attitude that rules are meant to be broken. If this is the antiestablishment attitude of your team, you're not likely to reach your goals.

"When players' decisions go outside the team concept, then their actions have to be dealt with. An effective way to deal with wrong decisions is to do something that will make the offender appreciate what he is risking by going astray. He should pay a huge price to remain a part of something much bigger than he is. And he should explain to his brothers where the breakdown in discipline occurred. Demonstration of sincere remorse should be a condition for his continued participation on the team. And if his conduct indicating his commitment to our team concept falls short of my expectations, I allow his teammates (his brothers) to decide whether they want him to remain on our team. He has put a crack in our foundation—our family."

"Elimination from the team is the last disciplinary action we want to take, however. The team and the opportunity to play belong to the players, and the team family grows and the individual players grow and mature through their participation. But we can't sacrifice our program by failure to handle player misconduct."

"Finally, I want to reiterate that consistency is paramount in team discipline programs, both in their development and in their implementation."

◆   ◆   ◆   ◆   ◆

. . . on Mental Preparation

Fisher says that everything you do involves mental preparation. But there are some things he likes to talk about that are totally mental. "I'm a strong proponent of visualization and repetition. We have a focus time every week when each player sits alone in the stadium and focuses on how he sees the up-coming game unfolding. He visualizes the plays he must make to execute the game plan so that the team is successful. He must understand his role in tomorrow's success. Repetition, repetition, repetition is the key to success. He must have already played the game in his mind and on the practice field before Saturday's game."

Elimination of surprises is critical to Fisher's preparation for the game. Surprises not only cost in physical aspects of the game, like breaking a big play on offense or sacking the quarterback on defense, they can demoralize the team. Conversely, being prepared and foiling your opponent's "secret plays" can demoralize the opponents. So elimination of surprises gives you a double whammy. "We pride ourselves in organizing our practices to cover every situation the players might find themselves in for the upcoming game. We practice, over and over, the responses to these situations."

"Bud Wilkinson used to say that he wouldn't run a play in a game until he'd run it a thousand times in practice. Once you have put together the plan for success, you must practice and perfect its execution until it becomes an attitude. We share with our players what is written in the 'Master Playbook' in Mark 9:23—'All things are possible to him who truly believes.' I truly believe that we will enter every game expecting to win; not just hoping to win. As a matter of fact, we will win every game this year! Time, however, might run out on us a couple of times. But the attitude is that we will never, never, never give up. This is Falcon football style."

Football can be a grind—especially pre-season practice. But Fisher says, "We don't ever want practice or the season to be a grind. We look continually for ways to make practice more fun. We shorten practice as we go through the season. Once you reach an optimum level of conditioning, it's counterproductive to overdo conditioning drills. You can maintain your condition through fast-paced drills and teamwork."

"We believe that the other team should not come to our field and win. But don't forget; half of our games are played at home. We make no distinction between home and away games. The football field is 100 yards at both places, and we will always have our fans who matter the most there. Our record shows that we're one of the most successful road teams in the country. Falcons love to play on the road. I attribute that to mental preparation. To help keep us from getting mentally stale, we like to make our road trips educational. There are educational sites every where we play. A lot of them are places we'd like to go anyway, so why not take advantage of the trip?"

"But we also make sure we don't drift too far from the game. Through our game plan, our situational practices, and our assimilation of information about our opponent, we want to anticipate every aspect of his strategy. Once the competitive season begins, we devote practically all of our practice time to putting the team in the situations they will face in the game. If our mental preparation is successful, the team's response will be second-nature, and we'll move one more step toward that ultimate goal."

. . . on Mental Toughness

When Fisher talks about mental toughness, one word keeps coming up—focus. "Mental toughness helps successful teams and players remain focused on their goals. Essential to successful performance is not allowing anything to cause you to lose focus. There are many distractions as you go through the season. However, you must remain focused and not allow the potential distractions to interfere with the achievement of team goals and dreams. That's where mental toughness comes in. And satisfying team goals will satisfy individual goals for the Falcons."

"When adversity comes, mentally tough players find a way to overcome and persevere and get themselves and their team back on track quickly. They are the ones who keep their focus. They let nothing chip away at the foundation of their team. They stand tall in defending the team and family concept. When there is a player behavior issue, the mentally tough players don't hesitate to take the bull by the horns and deal with it, even before the coaching staff learns of it. They put the team ahead of everything."

"Mentally tough players are the ones who respond instinctively or respond as they have been taught by their coaches to respond to critical game situations. They maintain their belief that we can overcome any situation if we doggedly respond as we have been trained to respond. They are the leaders of your team."

◆ ◆ ◆ ◆ ◆

. . . on Communication

When the game has begun, coaches are restricted in their communications. It's not like practice, where you can stop the action, give an instructive lecture, and then continue. You have to take advantage of official breaks in the game, and halftime is the only major official break. So communications at halftime are critical. When Fisher's team is behind at halftime, he is prepared. "I encourage the team to never lose the belief that we will find a way to win. Our consistent execution, in contrast to the mistakes of our opponents, will open the door for us to be successful. I tell them about previous Falcon teams who found themselves down big at halftime and came back to win. We were behind Utah 35-14 and came back to win 45-35—scoring 31 unanswered points. At Fresno, we were behind 30-10, but we won in overtime. I emphasize that they are never beaten until they, themselves, think they are. And I remind them of Mark 9:23—'All things are possible to him who truly believes."

"Dealing with the team in the locker room after a loss is critical. In our post-game meetings, there is no one outside our team family present, whether we win or lose. I make a distinction between disappointment and discouragement. I'm disappointed that we lost, but I'm not discouraged about our future. I reassure them that they are a better team than what we demonstrated in the game. Our staff knows this and has confidence in them. I reiterate that a champion is one who gets up one more time than he is knocked down. And I take aim at their pride and our tradition and expectations for Falcon football."

"I let them know that I know they will bounce back. And I tell the team to look at the good things they did in the game. Look at their personal pride and look at how each man fulfilled his responsibilities to his brothers on the team. I point out that nothing is ever as bad as it may seem at a bad moment—neither is anything as good as it may seem in a moment of exhilaration. We hug our brothers' necks after every game—win or lose. And I remind them that I'm part of this family: 'You can count on me, and I'm not going to let my brother down.' This is consistent with the basic philosophy of the Falcon football program."

◆   ◆   ◆   ◆   ◆

ROD DELMONICO
University of Tennessee-Knoxville

- - - - - - - - - - - - - - -

Position
Head Baseball Coach

Career Record
492-250 (13 seasons)

Education
B.A.   Liberty University
M.Ed. Clemson University

Team and Personal Highlights

- ➤ Winningest baseball coach in University of Tennessee history.
- ➤ *Baseball America's* National Coach of the Year.
- ➤ Two-time Southeastern Conference Coach of the Year.
- ➤ Two 50-win seasons; eight 40-win seasons.
- ➤ Two Southeastern Conference titles.
- ➤ Two College World Series appearances.
- ➤ Three SEC Players of the Year.
- ➤ 15 All-American players.
- ➤ 30 All-SEC players.
- ➤ Three Academic All-American players.

ROD DELMONICO

Introduction . . .

Rod Delmonico is considered one of the premier college baseball coaches in the nation. His success with the Volunteer baseball program over the last 12 years is unprecedented, as he has fashioned a career record of 492-250, while becoming the program's winningest coach in school history.   He is eight victories shy of becoming the ninth coach in Southeastern Conference history to reach the 500-win mark.

Citing former mentors Bill Wilhelm at Clemson and Mike Martin at Florida State, Rod's teams have posted eight 40-win seasons, two 50-win seasons, six NCAA regional appearances, two trips to the College World Series in Omaha, four SEC Eastern Division crowns, and three SEC Eastern Division tournament championships. For those efforts, he was named National Coach of the Year in 1995 and SEC Coach of the Year in 1994 and 1995.

Delmonico has seen 53 of his players selected in the major league draft, including four in the first round. He has coached 15 of Tennessee's 22 All-Americans, including three 3-time selections and the 1995 National Player of the Year in Todd Helton, currently a member of the Colorado Rockies baseball franchise. He has also recruited and coached three SEC Players of the Year in Helton, Jeff Pickler, and most recently, Chris Burke in 2001. Along the way, he became the winningest coach in Tennessee history, garnering his 409th career victory in 2001.

As the top assistant at Florida State from 1984-89, the Seminoles finished in the Top 15 nationally each year and played in three College World Series. Four of his freshmen recruiting classes were ranked in the top three in the country. Mike Martin at Florida State: "I don't think there is any doubt that Rod is the best recruiter in the country. Our success, especially our College World Series years, was a direct result of Rod's recruiting."

A native of Wilmington, North Carolina, he is the author of four baseball books and two teaching videos. He is a highly-sought-after speaker at national baseball clinics and recruiting seminars. He has three sons.

Here, now, are Rod Delmonico's success strategies . . .

. . . on Motivation

Motivation is a prime ingredient for success in all organizations, and Rod Delmonico believes motivation needs to be addressed on a daily basis.

"Motivation is like taking a bath," he says. "You need it daily."

Rod says that coaches need to understand their players and motivate to the individual personalities.

"Motivation is different for each player you coach," he begins. "Their buttons are similar in some respects, but in most cases, they are different."

Least effective motivation techniques surround any kind of negative feedback and response to the athletes.

"Belittling a player is seldom beneficial," he states. "Constant negative feedback can only do harm to the athlete and to the program. There are times when players need to be challenged."

Coach Delmonico lists several effective motivational techniques.

"All kinds of positive reinforcement is the key element," he asserts. "Being enthusiastic and positive with the players lays the foundation for success."

He continues: "You must teach the kids to believe in themselves. Our motto is 'You gotta believe!' and we are constantly sending that message to the players."

The success of the program helps build self-esteem in the players, he says.

"Success builds self-esteem," Rod says. "Great athletes believe in themselves and their abilities."

Rod cautions coaches about exposing inexperienced players to no-win situations.

"Don't put freshmen or other talented, but inexperienced players into a no-win situation," he states. "Lack of success at this point could have negative long-range effects."

In summary, Coach Delmonico believes that motivation needs to be addressed daily with his players. Negative feedback or belittling a player are least effective motivational techniques, he says.

Finally, Rod lists positive reinforcement, enthusiasm, teaching the players to believe in themselves, exposing the players to successful experiences and screening inexperienced players from no-win situations as the most effective motivational techniques.

◆ ◆ ◆ ◆ ◆

. . . on Team Cohesion

Coach Delmonico believes that team cohesion is the foundation for his success at Tennessee, and the coaching staff works daily to promote the team concept.

"We talk about the team concept all the time," Rod says. "You have to get the players to believe in it, and we promote it constantly."

Promoting the team as a family unit is the key, he states.

"The key is to treat your team as a family unit," he says. "The concept of 'a mind of one' is essential in building a team chemistry format."

Coach Delmonico suggests several methods to build team cohesion.

"We do a number of things on the field and off the field to build team unity," he begins. "On the field, we are always reinforcing the team concept. An example would be stressing the importance of sacrificing a player over during the game. We praise the players a lot when they do that and the team understands and appreciates the importance of that act."

Captains are chosen by team members, and the leadership demonstrated by the captains has much to do with team unity, Rod says.

"Our captains choose different players to lead our calisthenics and drills each day," he says. "We also make sure that we don't show favoritism toward a specific player. We really stress that no one player is bigger than the team."

Coach Delmonico also incorporates mottos and themes that magnify the team concept.

"The word TEAM stands for 'Together Everyone Accomplishes More'," he states. "That says it all right there."

Off-the-field methods for building team chemistry vary, Rod mentions.

"We try to do a lot of things together as a team," he begins. "For example, we'll attend football games as a group. We play basketball together and have team meals together, both at home and on the road. We sit together in study hall. In essence, we try to get the players to know each other not just as baseball players, but as students and human beings."

In summary, Coach Delmonico believes that team cohesion is built by treating your players as members of a family unit. He reiterates the concept of "a mind of one" as essential to building team chemistry.

Successful team building methods include reinforcing the team concept daily. Making players aware of the importance of team goals over individual goals must be stressed, he states. All punishment is based on a lack of team spirit, he adds.

Coach Delmonico utilizes mottos and themes that spotlight the team concept. Team captains are utilized in the team building process. Finally, off-the-field activities involving team members are the final link in building team chemistry.

. . . on Discipline

Discipline is a trait of championship teams and individuals. Rod Delmonico believes that today's athletes lack discipline and that the coach is responsible for establishing an atmosphere that stresses discipline in the program.

"Players in this day and age receive very little discipline," he states. "They are able to do and get away with more than in previous years. You must run a tight ship in order to develop a championship team."

Rod asserts that a least effective method of discipline with players is by not enforcing team rules.

"Yelling at a player after a discipline problem without taking anything away from the player will cause further problems," he states.

Coach Delmonico believes that the most effective method of discipline is taking something important away from the player.

"Taking away some privileges from a player has always been an effective discipline method for me," Rod says. "And you can establish a sequential order of discipline, if you wish."

He continues: "Benching a player always has an effect," he begins. "Taking him out of the lineup or banishing him from practice can be effective. The bench is the great equalizer.

"Suspension and dismissal from the team is really a final act to take, but sometimes that is the only answer.

The team and the program come before any one player. Finally, reducing or eliminating a player's scholarship may also be beneficial at the moment."

Rod stresses that communication with the player is critical when disciplinary measures are being pondered.

"You must pull the player into your office and discuss the entire situation," he says. "Always put all the cards on the table for the player. Let him know all the consequences of his behavior."

In summary, Rod Delmonico believes that coaches need to run a structured program regarding discipline because today's athletes receive very little discipline in their lives. You must have the same set of rules for everyone.

Finally, he states that the most effective method of discipline is taking away some privileges of the player.

He mentions benching, suspension, dismissal, and reduction or elimination of a scholarship as some examples of action a coach can take when disciplining an athlete.

. . . on Mental Preparation

Mental preparation is essential to team and individual success. Coach Delmonico places a high priority on mental preparation within his program.

"Every day I give my team some mental coaching," he states. "I give it to them before, during and at the end of practice. The game is 90% mental preparation."

Rod defines mental preparation as a combination of positive reinforcement and visual imagery.

"I think that mental preparation is a constant bombardment of mental thoughts that the player can visualize seeing himself doing in order to enhance his skills," he says.

Mentally preparing for a long season is critical to the overall success of the program, Rod mentions.

"Our mental preparation is built from a strong work ethic," he begins. "We run at 6:30 in the morning during fall camp. We believe strong conditioning has a lot to do with mental preparation."

He continues: "We practice in all bad weather—rain, the cold, snow. We want our players to feel confident late in a game in bad weather, knowing that we deserve to win because of all the preparation we've had for this kind of game situation. We believe this kind of practice experience prepares our team mentally for all game conditions."

Coach Delmonico believes that non-conference games are important to mentally prepare the team for conference play.

"We work very hard in preparation for non-conference games," he says. "We also work harder during winning streaks because we believe that, from a mental preparation standpoint, the players gain a lot of self-confidence which we will need when conference play begins."

Mental preparation for conference games takes on a singular focus, Rod says.

"During conference games, we simply want to stay on top of things," he states. "We want no mental mistakes."

Mental preparation for late-game strategy is a season-long process, he asserts.

"We practice every late-game scenario we can conceive," he says. "We have also been preaching to the players from the first day of practice, that if the game is close in the 7th, 8th or 9th innings, that we will win because we are better conditioned both physically and mentally."

Another motto that Coach Delmonico believes has a positive effect on the mental preparation of his team is "In a world of give and take, not enough people are willing to give what it takes."

"We tell our players how we can beat the other team," he states. "We teach our players to execute all facets of the game correctly. We show our players how we epitomize that motto. We are committed to giving what it takes to be successful, not only on the field, but in life as well."

In summary, Coach Delmonico believes that mental preparation is extremely important to the success of his program: "The game is 90% mental preparation." He defines mental preparation as a constant bombardment of mental thoughts that a player can visualize seeing himself doing to enhance his skills.

Hard work beginning with pre-season conditioning is the beginning of mental preparation for the team, he says. Rod's teams will practice in all weather conditions, including inclement weather, to mentally condition themselves for identical playing conditions during the season.

Non-conference games carry a special significance because they prepare the team mentally for the coming conference games, he asserts. Making no mental errors is the focal point for conference play.

Finally, late-game strategy is practiced from the beginning of fall camp. Coach Delmonico preaches to the players that they will win every game that is tied going into the 7th, 8th or 9th inning because they are better conditioned physically and mentally. He says he wants his players to have a statistically better chance of winning every time they play.

. . . on Mental Toughness

Mental toughness is a trait found in all highly competitive individuals. Coach Delmonico believes that a mentally tough player handles winning and losing in a consistent manner.

"I define mental toughness as a player being able to handle defeat and winning and stay on a level that remains constant during preparation," he states.

Rod lists several characteristics of a mentally tough player.

"A mentally tough player rises to the next level in all big games," he begins. "He wants to be the man in crunch time. He wants to be the main person hitting or pitching."

He adds: "A mentally tough player can fight through a slump or when he's struggling. He's very aggressive in his actions. He always hustling, going 99 mph all the time."

Coach Delmonico mentions that he believes that a passive individual can not be mentally tough.

"To me, passive kids just aren't mentally tough," he says.

When asked to identify a player he thought was mentally tough on his teams, Rod didn't hesitate.

"This player may not mean much to someone other than our team and the teams we played in 1993-94. But James Northeimer, who was a catcher for us during that time and signed with the Phillies, is the mentally toughest kid I ever coached.

"He wasn't big by any means, 5'9" and about 170 pounds. But he just would never give up. He always worked hardest of anyone and his attitude was great.

"Let me put it to you this way: I would want this guy going to war with me. If I had one guy that I would want in a foxhole with me before I engaged the enemy, it would be Norty. Otherwise, I would just kill myself because no one else would be mentally tough enough to handle the situation."

In summary, mental toughness is a trait that Coach Delmonico holds close to his heart. He defines mental toughness as the ability to handle defeat and victory in a level-headed manner and to remain consistent in all preparation.

He lists several characteristics of a mentally tough person, including rising to the highest level of competitive spirit, wanting to be the main person in crunch time, being aggressive in all actions and having the ability to fight through slumps. Finally, he used James Northeimer, a former Volunteer catcher, as an illustration of the mentally toughest player he ever coached.

. . . on Communication

Communication with staff and players and effectively handling adversity are important psychological factors for the success of any program.

"There are different ideas, but you can't always push the same buttons each time you try to motivate," he says. "Each player has a unique way of being coached or motivated."

Communicating with the players and staff during the late innings of a tied game is important, but the foundation for late-game communication has been present all season, he states.

"We always talk with the kids late in a game," he says. "What we do, basically, is repeat what we have been saying all season: We're better conditioned mentally and physically than our opponent. We also go over the mental plans we had discussed in the outfield prior to the start of the game."

Post-game comments after a tough loss or a poor performance are handled the same way, Rod asserts.

"After a loss, we generally try to build the players up," he begins. "If we won, but played poorly, we will probably get on them a little more. We will also allow the peer pressure to come into play. Sometimes when the players say something to a teammate, it has more meaning than when a coach comments."

In summary, Coach Delmonico believes that communication is important at all times. He also comments that a coach cannot use the same type of communication with all players because each player is different and reacts differently to certain motivation techniques.

Late-game communication is a method of recall for the players to remember what has been preached all season long regarding superior mental and physical conditioning. Finally, post-game comments after a loss will carry the tone of building up the players, while post-game talk after an "ugly" win will include more critical comments and the use of peer pressure.

SCOTT DOWNING

Purdue University

- - - - - - - - - - - - - -

Position
Assistant Head Football Coach

Career Record
85-50-2 (12 seasons)

Education
B.A.   Sterling (KS) College

Team and Personal Highlights

➢ Assistant Head Football Coach: Purdue University and University of Wyoming.
➢ As special teams coach, his teams at Purdue and Wyoming have set school records.
➢ Coached running backs currently playing in the National Football League.
➢ Wyoming teams won three Western Athletic Conference championships.
➢ Purdue and Wyoming teams have participated in eight post season bowl games.
➢ Head freshmen football coach at the University of Nebraska-Lincoln.
➢ His Sterling College teams were ranked in the NAIA Top 20.

SCOTT DOWNING

Introduction . . .

Scott Downing is on the fast track to a Division I head football coaching position. Under the tutelage of his mentor, Joe Tiller, at Wyoming and Purdue, Downing is considered one of the top assistant football coaches in the country. His recruiting skills and coaching savvy have produced NFL, All-American, and All-Conference players at the schools in which he has coached.

Before coming to Purdue in 1997, Downing spent 10 years at Wyoming, serving as assistant head coach, defensive coordinator, linebackers, running backs, and special teams coach during his tenure in Laramie. The Cowboys went to four bowls, and were Western Athletic Conference champions three times.

Scott was the head freshmen coach at the University of Nebraska-Lincoln, and his Sterling College teams were ranked in the Top 20 in the NAIA for the first time in school history during his time as head coach at the small Kansas school.

A native of Kansas City, Scott graduated from Sterling College in 1979 with a degree in history. He and his wife, Karen, have three sons and reside in West Lafayette.

Let's listen to this future Division I head coaching candidate relate his philosophies and strategies for success . . .

. . . on Motivation

Coach Downing believes that there are different types of motivation and different levels of intensities of motivation. It's certainly logical that motivation to exert all the energy an offensive lineman can muster in trying to move out a heavier defensive lineman is different from the motivation to study the play book, both in what the stimulus may be and in the recognition of reward. He defines motivation as "that which stirs people into action." That definition seems to fit both of the examples listed above, even though the types and intensities of motivation are quite different.

In leadership in business, one has to convince employees that the goals are the proper ones. Similarly, Scott believes that in athletics, you also have to convince the athletes to "buy into whatever it is you want them to do." Another business analogy can be taken from Scott's belief , "The more you give the athletes 'ownership' of the process, the more motivated they become, and the more ingrained in them the goals of the program become."

A major incentive in business is employee ownership. Business leaders have found it to be one of the strongest incentives for employees to pursue goals on their own. He says, "Including them in the plan to achieve goals is motivating." Often they contribute ideas for achieving objectives that extend and augment the original plan a coach develops. They are closer to the process and experience things from being in the middle of the fray that a coach cannot experience from the sidelines. But this valuable contribution can't be recognized if you don't include the players in planning.

Scott says the worst impediments to motivation are threats "to do something—some sort of punishment—if the team doesn't play well. Worse yet is a threat to do something if the team doesn't win." Did you ever see a team that didn't want to win? Of course not. So why suggest that they would lose on purpose. Scott says, "I have found that these threats usually fall on deaf ears or—or maybe worse—reverse any type of mental momentum that may have been building in the team."

◆ ◆ ◆ ◆ ◆

. . . on Team Cohesion

Scott defines team cohesion as "a feeling of togetherness that arises in a group of people with a common goal who have genuine affection for each other." What does that sound like—a family? That's how Scott puts it: "I prefer to use the word, 'family,' when referring to team chemistry; because, in essence, that's what we're trying to build: a feeling of family togetherness."

"Our methods for building a feeling of togetherness are very simple. We try to have the players spend as much time as possible in situations that are different from the playing field." Cohesion is not something that can be turned on when you walk on the field or turned off when you walk off, so being together off the field is essential.

"We like to encourage the team to participate in team 'outings,' such as bowling, basketball, and softball—competitive activities in which the best performers may be different from the best performers on the football team. This shows the worth, as people, of those who may not make the starting lineup. Each team member is gifted in someway other than his ability to play football, and the other team members need to see this so they get to know them and respect them as people, not just as football players.

Athletes are naturally competitive, so competitive sports other than football may not only be relaxing, but also entertaining. The coaches participate too. It makes the team look on us as human beings, not just 'drill sergeants'." For coaches to lose in extracurricular competition lets the team know that the team knows that coaches realize athletes can't perform perfectly on every play.

"We involve our seniors in leadership roles as much as we can. This helps in several ways. It shows the underclassmen that they can expect to get better as they work hard each year. It lets them see the feeling of 'ownership' the seniors feel and enhances their own feelings of ownership in the team. And it shows them that there are people other than just the coaches who will be there for them when they need them."

◆   ◆   ◆   ◆   ◆

. . . on Discipline

Coach Downing considers two standards in administering discipline. "No player is worth losing the respect and discipline of the entire team for— no matter how great he may be athletically. I would not bend the rules just to keep a 'star' on the team," says Scott. "Many outstanding athletes are given special privileges in high school, and they expect the same in college. We are here to teach young men the 'lessons of life.' Young people need to know that they don't live in a vacuum. Their choices affect the people around them. The world does not revolve around them." Scott thinks there is no better place to learn the choices of life than as a member of a team. "They must be held accountable for their actions."

Scott's other standard is that each disciplinary case is different and must be handled according to the circumstances regarding the case. He says, "For example, I would not expect a freshman to know some of the things I would expect a senior to know. The freshman may make a mistake because of his inexperience, whereas the senior has been around long enough to know what's expected of him. Even though each case must be considered individually, there are some infractions that carry mandatory actions, regardless of who commits them or what the circumstances are. Players need to know what's expected of them, to help them avoid getting into trouble out of ignorance. It's my job to see that they know."

In deciding on what action to take, Scott says, "You have to know what values each player holds important. A person on the scout team isn't likely to be concerned with taking away playing time, because he only gets to play when the outcome of the game is not in doubt. But starters and other players who get a lot of playing time usually treasure playing time. So cut playing time if it is something that the player really values." One good thing about cutting playing time is that it doesn't result in physical abuse, which should never be a part of discipline. And for the "star," it lets him know that the team can play without him.

Restricting "free" time is a positive means of discipline, because the assignments a player gets when his free time is limited are things that should help him, either academically or in physical conditioning. "For example," says Scott, "Saturday night study table may make the difference between a grade of C and one of B. Getting up early to run or perform other stamina and strength-building activities can improve endurance in a game. It may result in the extra strength or endurance to lay a key block or run down a runner who has broken free." These are positive steps that players may look back on and actually appreciate someday.

Scott describes two actions to avoid in administering discipline: "Never prescribe an action that is unreasonably harsh for the act committed. At the same time, make sure that the action is sufficient to be effective. In other words, you have to tailor the punishment to the offense."

The other problem in some disciplinary programs is inflexibility. "You want to be fair. But dealing out prescribed punishment for an offense without taking into consideration the circumstances surrounding the offense isn't necessarily fair."

The judicial system has found this to be a problem in dealing with crime among the general public. Mandatory sentencing was put into play because some judges were too easy on some criminals, but not all crimes that fall under the same technical charge are the same in terms of the attitude of the criminal or the degree of damage to the victim. Scott repeats: "You must tailor the corrective action to the offense, considering all relevant circumstances. The discipline can serve two purposes: (1) it corrects the behavior of the athlete and (2) if done properly, it can prove a positive learning experience for the athlete."

◆ ◆ ◆ ◆ ◆

. . . on Mental Preparation

According to Scott, "Mental preparation deals with all of the steps or processes an athlete goes through that allow him to focus entirely on producing his best physical performance on the field." Notice that he's linking mental preparation to physical performance. In athletics, the mental and the physical really can't be separated.

While physical and mental preparation are linked, the ratio of emphasis placed on them varies as the season goes on at Purdue. "The longer the season goes on, the less physically strenuous and the more mental our practices become," says Scott. "We've found that this approach helps the team stay 'fresher' during the season. It keeps their minds off the aches and pains and on the task of executing the play we are working on.

The players always enjoy the fast-paced workouts during the end of the season when there is little physical contact."

"Conversely, early in the practice season it is essential that we concentrate on the more physical aspects of the game: timing, movement patterns, etc. Placing too little emphasis on these fundamentals and too much on mental preparation early on would be detrimental to the team's performance."

"When we travel, we try to stay as close to the routine we practice at home as we can—workout times, mealtimes etc. The players don't like to be surprised. Even at home, we try to get the players away from fans and from concentrating too much on football on the Friday night before a Saturday game. We'll go to a movie together or rent a video of their choice. This diversion helps relax them mentally, rest better, and be fresh for the game the next day. There is an optimum degree of mental 'looseness' that enhances physical performance in the game. Mental stress can actually drain you physically."

But there is also a "technical" side to mental preparation. Players have to feel comfortable with their knowledge of the game plan and the characteristics of the opposing team reviewed in scouting reports. Scott says, "We try to present to our players every kind of situation that could occur during a game. Some situations require responses that a player has to have thought about before, so that he can react almost instinctively. If the clock is running out and we need to kick a field goal, with no time-outs left, our players could come apart mentally if we hadn't practiced dealing with that situation and reviewed it with them prior to the game. We create 'pressure situations' like that in practice, and the more we go through them, the more comfortable the players are in dealing with the stressful situations in a game. Without a doubt, the team who is better prepared mentally for that last-second critical situation will win the game."

. . . on Mental Toughness

Scott believes mental toughness is important in all aspects of a person's life, because all of us face taxing situations other than those on the athletic field. So developing mental toughness is one of the most valuable lessons an athlete learns.

Scott: "Mental toughness is the ability to sustain your effort at the highest levels when the situation is not working to your advantage. If you are mentally tough, you can overcome obstacles and setbacks that occur during contests on the field, and you can deal with obstacles and setbacks in your day-to-day activities."

"A mentally tough athlete keeps working and playing hard even when the odds are against him—even when the outcome of the game is no longer in question. He will overcome the results of small injuries to keep on contributing. He'll 'bust it' to make the play that can change the outcome of the game. He'll want to do anything to help his team win."

"Characteristically, a mentally tough player is also a smart player. He'll understand what's at stake in various situations, whether it's a critical third-down situation in football or a last-second shot in basketball. And a mentally tough player thrives on stiff competition. He wants to know just how good he is, and the only way he can find out is to go against the best. But he'll give his best effort against every opponent, regardless of how good the opponent is. You must practice mental toughness consistently, to the point that it is an integral part of your character."

◆ ◆ ◆ ◆ ◆

. . . on Communication

Scott describes two circumstances in which effective communication is paramount: the half-time meeting and the talks with the team after the game. "We have to be well organized at half-time. There is a lot to go over and not much time to do it. The players are physically tired, so it's critical that we communicate in a way that accommodates their physical fatigue. A person can't concentrate mentally if he is hurting physically so bad that everything but the pain is blocked out of his mind. So we give them time to take care of their physical needs while the coaches discuss the adjustments and game plan for the second half."

"It's also important that the atmosphere is business-like. You can't concentrate when there is confusion and yelling. Within this atmosphere, the organization of half-time comes forth. First the position coaches get with the players they coach and discuss changes that need to be made. Then the offensive unit and the defensive unit meet separately, to lay out the plan for the second half. Finally, the head coach will address the whole team, other coaches, and support staff to remind them of their goals established before the game, and lay out what we have to establish in the second half to accomplish those goals."

"The half-time is efficient and well-organized. It's conducted in the same format every game. This puts the players in their comfort zone and reinforces their confidence in themselves and in their coaches. It reminds them that the coaches know what they are doing and can help them improve in the second half, whether they are winning or losing."

"A well-timed 'fire-up' speech is sometimes effective, but it has to fit the situation. Sometimes the situation calls for such a speech, and other times it doesn't. More often, positive remarks—an encouraging word—at half-time go a long way in helping us win a game. You must always be positive, regardless of the score."

After a game, the coaches at Purdue become instructional. That's how they can help the team most. "Berating the team or individual members of the team is never productive after a tough loss," in Scott's words. "They understand the effect of the loss on our program. They certainly didn't lose on purpose. So we try to let them know why they lost. And if we feel that their performance wasn't up to their capabilities or their effort was lacking, we don't hesitate to tell them. But this isn't necessarily a condemnation. Sometimes teams just weren't mentally ready. It's our job, as coaches, to make sure the team is mentally ready. If we have done our jobs as coaches, the team already knows what they need to do to move in the right direction to win the next game, and they are already moving in that direction."

Scott reiterates: "It is essential that coaches stay consistent in their preparation techniques as well as in their reaction to situations. We must stay focused on the long-range goals that we and the team have set at the beginning of the season and on the intermediate goals for each game. Always stay positive, and make sure the players 'take ownership' in the team—in the victories and in the losses."

PAUL GIESSELMANN
College of Saint Mary

- - - - - - - - - - - - - - - -

Position
Head Volleyball Coach

Career Record
193-76 (8 seasons)

Education
B.A.   Wayne State (NE) College

Team and Personal Highlights

➢ NAIA National Coach of the Year.

➢ Three-time Regional Coach of the Year.

➢ Six-time Midland Collegiate Athletic Conference Coach of the Year.

➢ Two-time Omaha Sportscasters Association Special Recognition Award winner.

➢ Six-time MCAC regular season and tournament champions.

➢ Winningest volleyball coach in College of Saint Mary school history.

PAUL GIESSELMANN

Introduction . . .

Paul Giesselmann has taken the volleyball program at the College of Saint Mary from obscurity to national prominence. Recruiting mainly from Nebraska high schools, he has fashioned an enviable program that proudly displays the Midwestern work ethic on the court.

After a sterling high school coaching career, Paul entered the collegiate coaching ranks as an assistant coach at the University of Nebraska-Omaha, a perennial NCAA tournament qualifier and a past national champion. Under the watchful direction of his mentor, Rose Shires, Paul quickly acclimated himself to volleyball life in the tough NCAA Division II North Central Conference.

After one season, he took the helm of the lowly volleyball program at the College of Saint Mary, a small, private liberal arts school in Omaha, Nebraska. He started quickly, winning the Midland Collegiate Athletic Conference championship in just his second season, and the Flames have won it every year since 1995.

He not only is the winningest coach in College of Saint Mary school history, his teams hold the school records for most wins in a season (39), and MCAC and school records for conference wins (80) and consecutive conference wins (42). Nationally recognized for coaching excellence, he speaks often at clinics nationwide. His teams also are heavily involved in community service projects off the court.

Paul is honored to have the opportunity to discuss his success strategies . . .

. . . on Motivation

Paul Giesselmann calls motivation "the driving force behind a person's action." Sometimes we tend to forget how universal motivation is in our daily lives. Paul's definition brings this home.

Paul recognizes the difficulty of maintaining motivation through a long volleyball season: "A college volleyball season can be a long grind, physically and mentally. For the players and the coaches to perform at their best throughout the season, they must understand why they do what they do. And they must understand that motivation must last throughout the season."

According to Paul, motivation has to be managed: "You have to sit down with each player and find out what motivates her. Successful teams have coaches who understand how to motivate each individual and how to point the team toward a common goal."

And Paul thinks the players must help define those goals, too. "I believe team and individual goals set by the athletes will be more effective at motivating them than goals forced on the athletes by the coaches. But a group of highly motivated individuals does not always make a successful team if the individuals' motivations are self-serving." It's all about team.

"We believe in the long-term focus. No match is more important than the next one. Remember, motivation should last the whole season. It's not an up and down thing. And praise and rewards are among the more important aspects of motivation."

What doesn't work? According to Paul, "Constant yelling and intimidation by the coach don't motivate. I don't use gimmicks, like mounting quotations from opponents on our bulletin board. And as I said, we don't pick out one opponent to focus on as the biggest match of the year."

In summary, Paul focuses on the long term, he sets individual and team goals with strong team input, and he praises his team for their accomplishments.

◆　◆　◆　◆　◆

. . . on Team Cohesion

Paul defines team chemistry as "the ability of individual athletes to help each other work through stressful situations."

He says that some coaches don't place a great deal of importance on team chemistry and their failure to stress chemistry shows up in the post season, when more is on the line. Talent and execution alone can carry you just so far. "When faced with adversity, a team either grows stronger together or it falls apart. Team chemistry is what makes the difference," says Paul. "And you can see the difference on the court. Players on teams without good chemistry will begin to yell at each other when mistakes are made and they fall behind—not yelling encouragement, yelling criticism."

"I don't think that players necessarily have to be best friends off the court, but they do have to trust and respect each other. But you never fully know whether you have developed good chemistry or not until you see the team's reaction to a stressful situation. That's why I try to put my team in stressful situations during the regular season, so that they can learn and grow from the stressful experiences."

Paul's not high on "orchestrated togetherness"—like weekend retreats, social gatherings, and team dinners before games. He says, "At the College of Saint Mary's, I've tried to implement a philosophy instead of conducting a retreat. We focus solely on the team. When we talk, we talk about team accomplishments and team goals. We never discuss individual successes or individual honors. And the goals we set for individuals never include post season awards for the individual. It's rare for an individual to be on the cover of our media guide. I believe stressing team versus the individual helps avoid the jealousy that can destroy team chemistry."

But doesn't Paul think it's important for players to know each other as individuals? "Of course, it's important for players to know each other as individuals, and our normal activities provide plenty of opportunities. One of the best ones is the long road trips. They spend the nights together. That's real togetherness—not manufactured. And I don't force the girls to live with other volleyball teammates. It's good for them to get to know other people and get their minds off volleyball. If they are naturally good friends with a teammate and, as a result, they want to live together, that's fine. But I don't dictate who lives with whom. I've found that the girls appreciate each other more when they do things together on their own initiative."

Paul gives us an example of really finding out how strong his team chemistry was in the year, 2000. "Just four hours before the Round-of-Eight game at the national championships, one of the assistant coaches learned that her mother had passed away suddenly. Everyone on the team knew the mother, and was deeply affected by her death. Instead of getting a game plan together, I was busy getting both of my assistants on a plane home. I didn't want my assistant to fly home alone after such shocking news. After I told the players of the tragedy and we ate a team meal, it was time to go the competition arena. I had no idea how the team would respond."

"I tried to do everything the same for this match that we had done all season. We lost the first game 14-16—to the number 4 team in the country. I was proud of the team's effort, but I was concerned, after a big disappointment, that they were emotionally spent. Then they showed their mental toughness. They came out and dominated the next three games: 15-6, 15-9, and 15-7. The victory advanced us to the Final Four. The next morning, the team gave another inspired effort, in a five-game, three-hour loss to the two-time defending national champion. The girls rallied around the adversity and grew closer, because they trusted each other and were focused on a goal they had all season. There were no rah-rah speeches. Just a group of girls, focused on a goal that bound them together.

"When the team is really stressed or faced with adversity, that's when you find out their true chemistry."

. . . on Discipline

Paul thinks that discipline must be balanced: "A lack of team discipline can bring you down, just as too much discipline can choke a team.

"The most important thing to me in team discipline is to be consistent. Most athletic departments have department-wide discipline policies regarding major offenses. But it's the minor offenses—like being late for practice—that can break a team apart if handled wrong.

"I believe in letting the team have a say in what should happen to a player if she is late, etc. Many times, the corrective action prescribed by the players will be tougher than what the coaches would have prescribed. I expect the captains to handle internal grumbling. Leaders with great character and peers who set good examples can play a significant role in establishing a good program of discipline."

Paul says there are some pitfalls that coaches must avoid: "I think one of the biggest mistakes coaches make is failing to put closure to a disciplinary action—continuing to mention a problem to a player long after it's past, and holding a grudge because a player committed an infraction of team policy. My players know that once the punishment is completed the situation is over. A player who's been punished one day can come into my office the next day and expect to be treated just like any other player. I treat people fairly and move on."

◆ ◆ ◆ ◆ ◆

. . . on Mental Preparation

"Developing a mind set for success." That's Paul's definition of mental preparation.

Paul has become sold on what a good team psychologist can do for a team. "We're fortunate to have a good one at The College of Saint Mary. Few volleyball teams have a team psychologist available. The psychologist works with our players every week—as a group and individually. All teams with high national rankings have good talent. There isn't a great deal of disparity. So the mental aspects of the game become more and more important. A good program of mental preparation, with the coach and psychologist working together, can add 3% to 5% to a team's performance, and that can make the difference between winning a game 15-13 and losing 13-15.

"Goal setting is a big part of mental preparation," says Paul. "The grind of pre-season practices and conditioning can take a toll on athletes physically and mentally. Two-a-days can wear them out. But if they fully appreciate why they are going through this grind—why they are expected to report to fall camp in great physical condition—it helps them understand that a reward is ahead."

"We try to approach the grind in a positive way. We don't say to them, 'Are you ready for two-a-days?' That's not very motivating. Instead, we say, 'I'm excited for the season to start. Are you ready to make another run at the Final Four?' That's motivating."

Another point in Paul's approach to mental preparation for the season is treating every game the same, from the standpoint of mental preparation. "It doesn't matter if it's a conference or non-conference game, if it's a Top-10 team or one that went 3-20 last year, at CSM we approach every match the same way. This gives the players a mental balance and helps them avoid the emotional peaks and valleys." That valley can come at the wrong time, if the coach puts too much emphasis on the importance of one game over another. And besides, shouldn't all the games be fun? That's why players come out for the team."

"At CSM, we put our players in stressful situations in practice so that they are accustomed to the stress in competition. For example, we'll require a player to serve 10 balls in specified zones. Each time she serves to the wrong zone or makes some other error, her teammates have to run. Having your teammates running because you make a mistake puts a lot of pressure on you. But the biggest gain from this exercise is that it prepares the server mentally. It teaches her to master the concentration techniques that the team psychologist may be working on with her. And I have no doubt that if she masters serving the ball in the designated zones in practice, when she is serving for the match point in a game, she'll be totally prepared mentally to meet the task."

Situational drills are a big part of Paul's program of mental preparation. "For example, we'll simulate in practice a situation where our team in down 12-14 with the opposing team serving—one play away from losing the game. If our team loses, we have a penalty. Most of our situational drills focus on winning and losing, with consequences for losing."

There are circumstances over which the team has no control that must be prepared for as well. "We know that we're going to get some bad calls by the officials. Whether it's real or not, most teams think the bad calls go against the visiting team more than against the home team. That just adds to the home-court advantage. Players can't let bad calls distract them. Distraction can cost points, games, or even matches. To help our players prepare to deal with bad calls, we'll intentionally make terrible calls in practice to try to provoke our players. The players know they have no control over these calls, and they look past them to the next serve. Then, when they get bad calls in a game, they look past them, too, maintaining their composure and focus. "

"As I've mentioned before, there is close parity in talent among the better teams. A team or a coach can blow a match in a hurry if they aren't prepared to deal with bad calls. Because of the mental preparation drills, I don't believe we've ever lost a match because of a bad call, while equally talented teams who are not mentally prepared probably have."

Another distraction that can cost a serve or point is getting upset with yourself for making a mistake. "We tell our players to look to the next serve after a mistake, just like they would after a bad call. And if we see a player from another team show any sign of frustration, we'll go after her like sharks smelling blood. The success we have at this reinforces our determination to not get vulnerable by losing composure."

"Our team psychologist talks to the team on a regular basis about some key psychological factors:

1. Focusing on the immediate task at hand.
2. Recognizing and taking advantage of opportunities our opponent gives us.
3. Putting a team away when you have the chance.
4. Relaxing and enjoying the moment instead of getting keyed up.
5. 'Resetting the score.' If we're way ahead, reset the score to 0-0 in your mind so you won't relax. If we're way behind, reset to 0-0 so you won't give up.
6. Communicating among the players, regardless of the situation. Some teams fall into the trap of not communicating positively when they're down. That just assures defeat."

Paul sums up his feelings about mental preparation: "Mental preparation is the whole philosophy by which you train your team and run your program. The team is a reflection of the coach. If the coach is out of control because of his frustration with bad calls, or if he panics and quits coaching when his team is way behind or discouraged near the end of a match, you can expect the players to react the same way the coach does. That's why I believe that mental preparation begins with the coach."

. . . on Mental Toughness

"Mental toughness is the ability to perform when stressed—from the pain of injury, from the hype about an important match, or from the antics of a hostile crowd." That's what Paul calls mental toughness.

Mentally weak players will demonstrate their mental weakness sooner of later. The coach would like to identify them before the team is far into the competitive season. Paul: "I've seen a lot of players whose performance is great at 3 o'clock in the afternoon, when there are no opponents on the other side of the net and no fans in the stands. If they are not mentally tough, these same players will wilt at 6 PM, when there is a talented opponent across the net and the stands are filled with loud fans. The mentally tough player wants the ball served to her at match point when the Final Four is on the line. She demands that the setter give her the ball at crunch time—knowing full well she could be the goat if she doesn't deliver. Mentally tough players are not afraid to be put on the spot. They crave responsibility, and they usually deliver."

"I mentioned the pain of injury. Let me tell you about Julie Trouba. She was an All-American right side at CSM. We were playing away from home against the defending national champion, Columbia College, who had not lost a home match in five years. In the first rally of the match, the outside hitter for Columbia lost her balance and fell to the floor under the net. Julie was in the air. When she came down, one foot landed on the Columbia player, and Julie rolled her ankle. It was obvious that she was in severe pain, but she insisted on staying in the game. When she rotated to the back row, we took Julie out. After examining Julie's ankle the trainer said, 'The ankle's sprained, but if she can tolerate the pain, playing shouldn't do serious damage to the ankle.' Julie played during the remainder of the 2.5-hour, 5-game match. And she played exceptionally well. After the match her ankle was severely swollen. How's that for mental toughness!

"Mental toughness is displayed by players and teams who put it on the line when their season is on the line."

◆ ◆ ◆ ◆ ◆

. . . on Communication

Paul integrates much of his philosophy into his communications with his team. And he says much of his philosophy is patterned after his role model. According to Paul, "I think many coaches model other coaches. They pick up ideas and philosophies from successful coaches and use them in molding their own style. My model is Coach Tom Osborne, former head football coach at the University of Nebraska, now serving in the U.S. Congress."

"Coach Osborne stressed that no game is more important than the next one. He tried to avoid the emotional peaks and valleys. This has been the foundation of the volleyball program at CSM. The 'rah rah speech' might work occasionally, but it won't work consistently. I think you need to be more consistent in communicating with your team."

Honesty is paramount in Paul's book. "Always be honest with your team. And being consistent and predictable is part of being honest. Be consistent in preparing the team for competition. Be consistent in preparing them for road trips. Being consistent will build trust and maintain a constant positive attitude—as opposed to the sporadic 'rah rah speech.' Suppose you give the big 'rah rah speech' and lose. How does your team come back for the next match? And how do your players respond to the next big 'rah rah speech?'" There is one sure thing about Paul's philosophy: He is not a fan of the "rah rah speech."

Honesty is also a part of Paul's next admonition. "We try to get better each match. If you lose, be honest with your team about their failures, so they'll know what they have to improve. Don't make your criticism personal after a loss. Don't single out any player. Usually no one feels worse than the players who made a mistake in a loss. They'll be tougher on themselves than you can be."

"After a loss, I think you must focus immediately on the next opponent. The best teams in the world have bad matches and lose. Learn from your mistakes and put the loss behind you. I know of coaches who make their team practice late at night after a bad loss. They get off the bus; and before they leave to go home they have to practice. Worse yet, they may get sent back out to practice on their home court after a loss. What sort of a message is this sending to the team? Not only the message about the game and the program, but about life. Is the game really that important in the scope of life?"

Perhaps the worse thing about this practice that Paul is condemning is that the coach may be punishing the wrong people. If there is parity in the talent as Paul said earlier, then most losses might likely be the coach's fault. Possibly something was wrong in the way he prepared his team or made adjustments during the match.

Paul equates communications about post-game assessments to communications about assessments in life: "If a coach focuses on long-term goals, and puts setbacks behind, he's making a positive communication to his team about the game and about life. Learn from losses and move on. He asks his players, 'Do you want to have a team that plays great just now and then, or do you want to have great program?' Tom Osborne had a great program."

And finally, on communications: "When you and the other coaches have disagreements about strategy or techniques—or whatever—make sure they are settled in the office—never in front of the players. The staff should always be united and put up a front that reflects the truth and your unity."

◆ ◆ ◆ ◆ ◆

CAREN
HORSTMEYER

University of California-Berkeley

- - - - - - - - - - - - - - - -

Position
Head Women's Basketball Coach

Career Record
233-140 (13 seasons)

Education
B.A.   Santa Clara University

┌───┐

Team and Personal Highlights

- ➤ Winningest coach in West Coast Conference women's basketball history.
- ➤ District Coach of the Year.
- ➤ Two-time West Coast Conference Coach of the Year.
- ➤ Six WCC regular-season titles and 2 WCC tournament championships.
- ➤ 33 All-West Coast Conference players and 4 WCC Freshmen of the Year players.
- ➤ Holds seven school records as a player at Santa Clara University.
- ➤ Enshrined in Santa Clara University Sports Hall of Fame and Marin County Athletic Hall of Fame.
- ➤ Named Redwood (CA) High School Best Female Athlete after earning 14 varsity letters in four sports.

└───┘

CAREN HORSTMEYER

Introduction . . .

Caren Horstmeyer is highly regarded as one of the bright, young head coaches in women's basketball nationwide. She took the helm of the University of California-Berkeley's struggling women's basketball program in April, 2000, after spending 12 seasons at Santa Clara University, where she compiled a 221-124 overall record. Her 64.1 winning percentage stands as the top figure in school history.

While at Santa Clara, she guided the Broncos to six post-season appearances, including four NCAA tournament selections and the 1991 WNIT championship, along with six West Coast Conference regular-season titles and two WCC tournament crowns Her Broncos teams won four consecutive regular-season titles from 1991-1994.

While at her alma mater, she coached 33 All-West Coast Conference selections, four WCC Players of the Year, one Kodak All-American, one WCC Defender of the Year, and one WCC Freshman of the Year. Her team led the nation in field goal percentage defense in 1997-98.

Caren is most proud of the achievements of her student-athletes. Santa Clara was recognized in 2000 by the **Chronicle of Higher Education** as being one of 12 schools nationwide with a 100 percent graduation rate.

Caren's playing career at Santa Clara was record-breaking. At the time of her graduation, she held seven school records. She also lettered in softball and was named SCU's Best Female Athlete. She was inducted into the school's Sports Hall of Fame in 1998.

After graduation, she played professional basketball in Greece, earning MVP honors two consecutive years. A standout at Redwood (CA) High School, she compiled 14 varsity letters in four sports, and was inducted in 2000 into the Marin County Athletic Hall of Fame. She and her husband, Bill, have one young child.

Always articulate in her conversations, Caren was eager to share her championship ideas . . .

. . . on Motivation

Caren Horstmeyer makes an interesting observation when she discusses motivation: "Early in my career, I believed you had to find a way to motivate your players every game. But over the years my philosophy has changed. Now I believe that each player must motivate herself in her own way. I noticed that some players would get too high and could not sustain their motivation throughout a game. I believe that, through most of a game, a player must play at the same emotional level, without getting too high or too low. Of course, some short periods during games are exceptionally exciting, but you can't let them wander with their emotions for the entire game."

Caren says that setting goals is an integral part of motivation. Once the goals are well defined, she likes to repeat quotations from outstanding coaches and leaders. "I like to focus on one quotation per week. I post the quotations in the locker room and have the players put them in their player notebooks, so that they get lots of exposure to the quotations."

The quotations usually relate to motivation, leadership, and hard work," says Caren. "And I'm not above posting a newspaper article about the other team in the locker room, if their players are quoted as saying something about us that I think will really get our players fired up."

Caren says she recently adopted what she refers to as incentives —consequences of not meeting specific goals for a game. "The consequence is running 15 sideline-to-sideline sprints in 65 seconds. That includes starting, running the width of the court, stopping and returning. We consider the 15 sideline sprints as sort of a currency that you bank when you accomplish goals, so that they are positive incentives, not just punishment for areas where we fail."

"For example, if we failed to meet our goal of out-rebounding our opponent and lost, that would require 15 sideline-to-sideline sprints. But if we accomplished another goal in the same game, such as holding the team under their scoring average, that would off-set the failure to meet a goal. Other goals that fit into this incentive program include performance against the opposing team's best performers. This is just a specific example of how we use incentives to motivate. And if we win a big game on the road, I'll give the team an extra day off from practice."

Another motivating consideration, according to Caren, is demonstrating to each player that you care about her as a person—not just as a basketball player. "This goes all the way back to recruiting players who show they not only have a commitment to basketball, but also to improving their lives as well," she says.

Although Caren believes that each player must be self-motivated, there are some aids to motivation that help stimulate that self-motivation. She says, "For example, we'll show a highlight video before a big game. And if a coach or a player from our next opponent has made a public statement that is likely to tweak the emotions of individual team members, we'll use this to 'jump-start' their self-motivation."

In summary, Caren's philosophy on motivation embodies focusing on self-motivation by whatever works for each individual, setting well-defined goals, providing incentives that can be positive, and judicious use of motivating quotations.

. . . on Team Cohesion

Three phrases define team chemistry and cohesion for Caren: working together, making the extra pass, and all team members acting unselfishly.

She uses several techniques in accomplishing these objectives. "We have several team social activities that help us get to know each other better off the court. We have team dinners or Bar-B-Ques. At our get-togethers, we play games like charades. And at Halloween, we had a pumpkin carving contest."

"On the road we try to take advantage of the location we're traveling to, both from an entertainment and an educational standpoint. For example, when we were in Los Angeles, we toured the movie star homes, and we met with Dustin Hoffman, who signed autographs. We also visited the Kenon Ivory Wayans television show as members of the audience. These activities help us relax and take our minds off the game. When we were in New York City, we visited Wall Street and Rockefeller Center, and in Washington D.C., we toured the FBI building."

Caren takes advantage of the services of a "sports performance trainer," who combines several aspects of mental and physical preparation. Caren: "One of the things our sports performance trainer emphasized was body language. She instructs our team to keep their heads high, without slumping shoulders, when things are not going well. 'Show confidence, and put your arms around each other when you meet at breaks in the action during a game.' This demonstration of togetherness helps build cohesiveness."

To build trust and confidence in teammates, Caren has her team go through a ropes course. Not only is the course physically challenging, but it forces the participants to fall backward with only their teammates to catch them, enhancing trust in teammates. Sail-boating is another diversional activity that requires teamwork and interdependence.

"We like to go as a group, whenever we can, to watch other Cal-Berkeley teams compete, lending our support and enjoying ourselves at the same time," according to Caren. "And I insist that all of our returning players watch the telecast of the NCAA tournament selection show. We want to be one of those teams with a television camera in our meeting room to telecast our reaction when they announce that we've made it to the NCAA tournament. Seeing the excitement of the selected teams and feeling the pain of not being among them is something I want us to experience together. It bonds us and enhances our determination to make the tournament next year."

◆   ◆   ◆   ◆   ◆

. . . on Discipline

Caren says that discipline is critical not only in basketball and school, but in life. "Anything you do well involves discipline. One of the best forms of discipline is placing emphasis on doing things on time - everything. Getting to every class, every meeting, every practice on time forces you to organize your time and to stay aware of what's happening around you. It's also a measure of being considerate. Being on time is the first step toward giving yourself to others, being unselfish and putting the team first."

"I really emphasize being on time for everything. And if a player is late for anything—practice, travel, meetings—she runs two miles at 6:00 AM in the morning. If the individual is late, she runs. If the whole team is late, the whole team runs. Worse than being late, of course, is missing a meeting or other activity. For the player who totally fails to show up, we do the "Lance Armstrong Workout," a 45-60 minute sprint on a stationary bike. All of these 'consequences' help build endurance or strength, but the stationary bike is particularly effective in building leg strength."

There are four essential characteristics to the coach's behavior in promoting good discipline: she must make sure that the players know what is expected of them, they must know the consequences of unacceptable behavior, the coach must treat each individual as an adult - with respect - and she must be absolutely impartial and consistent.

"I've found that, in addition to running, benching a player for a specified period—could be a few minutes, a game—makes her appreciate the opportunity to play. But benching is effective only if the player is totally aware of why she was benched."

"And discipline doesn't just involve punitive actions for unacceptable performance. It involves rewards for meeting goals. I've found that rewarding the team for an individual's good performance is an effective team-building practice."

Caren doesn't believe that coaches should yell at their players. "The two biggest impediments to discipline are yelling at players and failure to be consistent. Both of these activities reflect poor self discipline on the coach's part, and no coach can develop discipline among her players if she isn't disciplined herself."

◆　◆　◆　◆　◆

. . . on Mental Preparation

Caren links mental preparation to developing a consistent, repetitive routine. She says, "Perform the same routines every practice, every game, every day. Part of that routine must entail the physical preparation that is indistinguishable from mental preparation: get enough sleep, eat properly, and always exercise good posture. While these things are physical, they also prepare the mind for doing things the right way—everything you do."

Bringing in specialists is something Caren believes in strongly: "Our sports performance trainer includes both physical and mental exercises to improve performance. She recommends adding more water, vegetables, and fruit to diets, and to eat fruit at halftime, like you see professional tennis players doing at breaks in their matches. She emphasizes the importance of proper stretching in dynamic warm-ups. She was particularly emphatic about developing repetitive routines for preparation for practice and for refocusing after a distraction. The repetitive routine is just as essential in basketball as it is in a baseball pitcher's windup."

"As you might expect, the trainer is most helpful in mental preparation for shooting free throws. She studies each player's routine—some had no consistent routine—and helped them develop their own, individual routines. Most of all, she stressed the importance of going through that routine the same way, every shot. The process just almost automatically brings the mind to a focus when the critical movements are made just before the release of the ball."

Caren employs three practices for game preparation, whether at home or on the road: (1) She always prepares detailed scouting reports and actually gives written tests to the team after they've had time to digest the reports. This practice reinforces the importance of knowing your opposition. (2) The team watches videotapes of opponents to the point that they feel like they've played them before. (3) She conducts all sorts of situational practice regimes—such as, "There are five seconds left in the game, the score is tied, and the opponents have the ball under their defensive basket."

In summary, Caren integrates physical and mental preparation and emphasizes developing routines to the point that every response on the court in a game is close to second nature.

◆ ◆ ◆ ◆ ◆

. . . on Mental Toughness

Caren's treatment of mental toughness is concise, but impressive: "When the going gets tough, the mentally tough player increases her output. She has the ability to go above and beyond what you would normally consider her maximum performance, when the chips are down. She either loves pressure or is oblivious to it. She loves to be the one with the ball when there are 4 seconds on the clock and we're down one point. She thinks accepting responsibility makes her a stronger player and a stronger person."

And what is the one most consistent characteristic of players who are mentally tough? Caren sums this up in two words: "Doesn't complain." Based on her description of the mentally tough player's attitude, Nike would probably love to put their "swoosh" on Cal's mentally tough players. Caren says their attitude is "Just do it!"

◆ ◆ ◆ ◆ ◆

. . . on Communication

What does Caren want to communicate to her players before each game? Caren says that not only is what you say important, but how you say it is equally important. And she says, with passion and confidence, "You're gonna win this game!" She believes that every team member must believe this, and one of the things that makes each player believe this is that each one believes in herself. Each one knows that she is well prepared. She knows her role and she knows her teammates know their roles. And she knows that if she executes her role, and each teammate executes her role, the team's chances of winning are as good as they can get. That's what Caren makes sure everyone understands before the game starts.

But there are some technical aspects to the game Caren feels strongly enough about that she reiterates them prior to the game. Fulfilling her own admonition to follow routine, she reviews what she calls "four components" of the game. "These four components are: (1) We want to out-rebound our opponents. We quickly review the fundamentals of rebounding; (2) provide help-side defense for the post player on the other team; (3)

pressure the ball and force more turnovers; and (4) on offense, set good screens, wait for the screen, and make the extra pass."

Caren says that each opponent presents its own set of problems, so she reviews one or two special factors that apply only to the team they are about to play. "For example, I may tell them to focus on the opponent's best player, if that player's performance seems to set the standard for the whole team. Or if the team is particularly effective in transition offense, I'll remind our team to be especially alert to defend the fast break."

"After the game, I review how well we performed for each of the four components I presented before the game. If we won, then invariably our performance in at least some of these areas was good. So I link our performance in the four components to our winning. This reinforces the team's belief in these principles and in the premise that if they do these things well, they'll win. Conversely, I can always link our losing to poor performance in one or more of the four components. There is no better time to communicate than when the consequences of what you're trying to communicate are staring you right in the face."

DON KLOSTERMAN

University of Nebraska-Omaha

Position
Head Women's Soccer Coach

Career Record
96-67-3 (8 seasons)

Education
B.S.   Benedictine (KS) College
M.S.   University of Nebraska-Omaha

Team and Personal Highlights

➤ North Central College tournament champion.
➤ Coached All-Region player, two Conference Players of the Year, two NCC Freshmen of the Year players, two All-NCC players, eight NCC Honorable Mention athletes, and three Academic All-NCC athletes.
➤ Director of Olympic Development Program in Kansas.
➤ Director of Soccer for Nebraska Special Olympics.
➤ Holds United States Soccer Federation "A" License and National Soccer Coaches Association of America Advanced National License.

DON KLOSTERMAN

Introduction . . .

Don Klosterman has established excellence in his soccer programs throughout his career on the collegiate and high school levels. An experienced coach and educator, Don was hired in May, 1998, to coach the first women's soccer program at the University of Nebraska-Omaha.

In just their second competitive season, the Mavericks claimed their first conference tournament championship with a 16-5 overall record. In his first season, playing mainly with freshmen, Don led the team to a 14-5 record and a third-place finish in the North Central Conference. He has coached All-Region, All-Conference, and Players of the Year during his career.

Klosterman began his coaching career at Omaha Creighton Prep High School in 1977. He then took his first college coaching position at his alma mater, coaching the men's soccer team at Benedictine (KS) College from 1979-83. He then moved to Creighton University as the head men's soccer coach, and was the Director of Soccer for the Nebraska Special Olympics. For 10 years, he was the head boy's soccer coach at Millard South High School in Omaha, leading his teams to seven state tournament appearances. He is also active in coaching youth soccer select teams.

Don's players are strong academically, many of them making the conference honor rolls. His players also take pride in being active in community programs. He holds the highest soccer licenses from the United States Soccer Federation and the National Soccer Coaches Association of America. Don and his wife, Suzie, recently celebrated their 25th wedding anniversary. The couple has two children and lives in Omaha.

Don enjoys discussing his ideas on building excellence in one's life and career. Let's examine his thoughts...

. . . on Motivation

If you're looking for a testimonial for motivation, Don Klosterman can give it to you: "Motivation is a most critical ingredient to success in sports or out of sports. It's the one element that will allow you to get back up after repeated failure and still achieve your goals. Motivation is what drives an athlete to strive to be the best. Motivation is a stimulus that causes a person to act—that pushes the person to pursue excellence." Don goes on to say that all athletes have some spark of motivation. However, the coach cannot always be the impetus; the athlete must want to achieve.

Don equates the job of the coach to that of a salesman. The product that he and his coaches try to sell their players is the achievement of their goals, and the price is "hard work, sacrifices, and sweat in the pursuit of excellence ." He says, "Two essentials of motivation are challenging our players to go all out to reach the next level and making sure that they know we believe that they can do it."

"We meet with each athlete several times a year—not only during the season, but also during the off-season—to examine their past goals and their progress toward achieving them and to set new and more challenging goals."

Don points out some other essentials of player motivation: "Motivation is not a 'one size fits all' deal. Each individual player is different, and we must find out what approaches motivate each of them—what is their 'trigger'? Does it stimulate a player or upset her to be yelled at during the heat of the game? Or should we wait until half-time and pull her aside? What works best before a game—getting hyped, with lots of yelling or quietly discussing game plans and giving them time to think?"

"Another factor is emphasizing that there are many small steps to reaching your goal. The exercises we go through in practice are part of these necessary steps. And physical conditioning is another.

"Finally, we recognize that taking these small steps, going through some drills over and over, can be drudgery and monotonous. Monotony can destroy motivation. So we work to create an atmosphere of fun, injecting humor into practices, to counteract that monotony."

Don is just as concerned with avoiding the wrong motivational techniques. They can counteract almost all of the positive steps you take in motivation. "Motivation must be a continuous thing that becomes a part of each individual. Trying to motivate just before big competitions is counterproductive. Gimmicks and pep talks are not enough to pull off the big win. Motivation must start at the beginning of the first practice of the season and continue through every practice and every competition until the final horn of the last game of the season.

"I never try to motivate by comparing one athlete to another. This practice just creates the wrong type of rivalry, and it kills motivation. And nothing good ever comes from being negative. Being negative is a 'demotivator.' We emphasize the importance of a positive attitude and the pitfalls of negative attitudes. And the coaches, more than anyone else, must always be upbeat and positive."

◆   ◆   ◆   ◆   ◆

. . . on Team Cohesion

Don emphasizes equality in defining team chemistry: "Developing team chemistry means developing team community -a community of people of equal value."

Don says, "At UNO, we try to create an environment in which each player is respected for more than just her performance on the playing field. We emphasize that we are concerned with our players first as people and second as competitors. We develop a personal relationship with each player and get to know her outside soccer. And, as I said before, we emphasize equality of human value—every player is of equal value and deserves equal treatment, whether she's a starter or a reserve. Everyone on this team is valuable to the team—in different ways. And we measure their contribution as people more than we do by any other standard."

Friendships among team members are essential in team chemistry. According to Don, "These friendships can be developed in various ways—bonding together in facing team adversity, sharing common team goals, and, perhaps more important, interacting socially, away from soccer."

"Among our more popular social activities are team dinners. Some players who live off campus will prepare a dinner for the whole team at their house or apartment. Each coach will have the team to his or her house for a dinner. These are really fun dinners, and the focus is on almost anything but soccer.

"You may not think of community service as a team-bonding activity, but it has proven to be one of the best practices in building team chemistry. Our players work together in conducting soccer clinics for youth teams, serving dinner to Girls Inc., and taking groups from Girls Inc. to UNO hockey games. Many of our players participate in D.A.R.E. graduation programs at local elementary schools. Benefits from these cooperative activities are multiple; they perform a service to the community that the college women athletes are uniquely qualified to do, they broaden the educational experiences of the student athletes, and they strengthen the bonds of chemistry."

The UNO soccer team engages in one activity at the beginning of the season that sets the tone for the entire season. They work together to create their own team motto for the year. "Working together," says Don, "not only results in a better and universally accepted motto, but it begins our team chemistry building right at the beginning of the year. This past season, the team had the motto put on the back of sweatshirts that they had designed themselves, and they put it on name tags to attach to each player's travel bag. This activity embodies ownership, pride, and responsibility—in a nutshell: team chemistry."

◆ ◆ ◆ ◆ ◆

. . . on Discipline

Don has a profound philosophy about discipline: "Team discipline is the product of the total environment developed within a team program. It is not just a set of rules and regulations. Team discipline is an ongoing process, at the core of every aspect of the team concept. Development of discipline involves everything we do, beginning with pre-season and carrying right through summer workouts. To emphasize the importance of individual responsibilities in team discipline, we quote John Wooden: 'Discipline yourself, and others won't need to.' We challenge our players to develop and maintain self-discipline, holding out the promise that the discipline of the athlete who adheres to sound principles and practices enhances performance and enables her team to win."

On the UNO soccer team, much of the responsibility for establishing the guidelines of behavior—in the context of all activities, on and off the field of play—is placed on the team members themselves. Don says, "The team members not only develop the guidelines, they place the responsibility on the individual athletes to follow those guidelines and then encourage them and monitor to see that their teammates follow them as well. Each player signs a copy of the guidelines and keeps it to remind herself of her commitment. We also post a large copy of the guidelines in the locker room to help make them an integral part of our environment.

"Team discipline also carries over into fitness, practice intensity, and competitive attitude. The players know that not only their peers, but also the coaches are continually evaluating them as they demonstrate the results of their self discipline, and they know that their performance in these areas has a major impact on playing time."

Don says that a male coach for a women's team has to learn one thing early or his discipline program will be ineffective: "I just don't think you can use the same discipline methods when coaching women that some people use in coaching men. An in-your-face, knock-down confrontation is a sure road to disaster in disciplining women. You'd better not be sarcastic or ridicule a player in front of her teammates. I get upset, just like anyone else, and I know that much of what I say when I'm upset may be critical. So, even if I'm upset, I use a positive tone and supportive body language. Women work more enthusiastically, and they respond better to criticism when they are dealt with on an individual basis and in a positive manner."

◆ ◆ ◆ ◆ ◆

. . . on Mental Preparation

Don believes mental preparation is inseparable from other training. He says, "I think mental preparation is an ongoing process that is developed by creating an environment in which players are always challenged, where competition is expected, where improvement is encouraged, where practice is more intense than games, and where players are asked to be accountable. Maintaining an atmosphere that fosters these characteristics prepares our players mentally for any situation they are likely to encounter in competition or off the field."

An illustration of Don's contention that mental and physical training go hand-in-hand is the pre-season regime. "We take some of the grind out of pre-season practice and conditioning by developing a culture that emphasizes conditioning and fitness. The players, then, work at fitness year around, realizing the benefits and recognizing the importance of fitness in our system. They work independently during the off-season and come to pre-season practice in near match fitness. We rely on our team leaders to set examples and help us convince the other players what hard work can accomplish and demonstrate the positive feeling it brings. Developing team unity and fitness becomes a part of our tradition and culture, and integrating this culture into each player's psyche is simply part of our mental preparation."

"Preparation for home games and away games is similar in that we try to maintain the culture we have developed during the pre-season, regardless of where we play or whether a game is conference or non-conference. We talk to the team about the challenge of winning, always playing their best, and giving a total effort throughout the entire game. We remind them that mental preparation helps push their bodies to go beyond what their bodies may tell them they can go."

"But, by necessity, there are some differences between preparation for home games and away games. Sleeping in your own bed at home takes away one adjustment. Schedules are the same as they have been all week, and this is mentally comforting and physically relaxing. We like to have breakfast together on games days at home, just to relax together and talk about anything other than the game. Sometimes taking your mind off the game requires a little reinforcement, and getting together like this is reinforcing. Then later in the day we meet and begin to focus on the game, separating the team into groups by position. Finally, we regroup and focus on our team goals."

The pre-game warm-ups at UNO are non-traditional. Most teams go through some calisthenics and stretching exercises when they first come onto the field. Don does it differently. "As soon as the players come onto the field, we put them into game-like drills, working tactically as well as technically. This is definitely a mental thing that makes them know that the very second they walk onto the field, it's time to play and to integrate all the mental preparation we've already been through into their readiness to play."

Don says that away games present a different challenge mentally because of just being on the road, not sleeping in your own bed, playing in an unfamiliar environment, and having unfamiliar officials. Being familiar with officials doesn't mean that unfamiliar officials would be biased; it's like being familiar with other authority figures. It just makes you feel more comfortable. To minimize the impact of being on the road, Don says, "We try to defuse the external distractions by downplaying (almost ignoring) them and concentrating on the game and the business of winning—things that are familiar to us. Pulling together to counteract the odds and challenging our players to block out distractions and just play their game on the road has proved to be an effective team-building process."

In Don's system, late-game strategy is another integral part of the team's training. "Late-game strategy is something we talk about with our players all the time—especially during fitness training. We know that late in the game, we can use our superior fitness to outwork and outplay our opponents. That can be a huge psychological—as well as a physical—advantage when the opposing team senses our confidence in our physical superiority. We always feel—whether holding on to a lead or trying to get the winning goal—we can meet the challenge, because we train harder than the other team, and we can wear them down. We challenge our team to always be more aggressive at the end of a game, which sends a message to the opponent about the mental attitude of the UNO soccer team."

◆ ◆ ◆ ◆ ◆

. . . on Mental Toughness

Don cuts to the chase in defining mental toughness: "Mental toughness involves many aspects of what makes up the elite athlete, but I think the definition of mental toughness is simply an athlete's ability to do mentally whatever it takes to beat the opponent."

He says a mentally tough player has grit, tenacity, and an unwillingness to give up. "Mentally tough players are willing to undergo whatever it takes to achieve victory—to do their best under any circumstance. They have the internal fortitude to push themselves beyond the levels others push themselves to. Their willingness to suffer exceeds their need for comfort."

"Despite the obstacles, mentally tough players have prepared for the most challenging situations and they seek to overcome the odds and pull out a win. They have learned to gain control over their thoughts so that they block out negative thoughts or emotions and replace them with positive images—with success-oriented thinking."

◆ ◆ ◆ ◆ ◆

. . . on Communication

Don has a structured approach to halftime so that the players know what to expect. Knowing that a consistent format will be followed helps keep the players in their comfort zone and reinforces their confidence in their coaches. He points out, "In collegiate soccer, the halftime is 15 minutes. We break it into segments. During the first part of the halftime, the players get water, get their bumps and bruises treated by the trainer, catch their breath, and talk informally with teammates about the game. At the same time, the coaches discuss with each other our approach to the second half—personnel changes, tactical adjustments, solutions to problems, and what's working."

"In the second segment of the halftime, the players meet with position coaches in separate groups—defenders, midfielders, forwards. By grouping the team by position, the coaches can stress factors specific to players in each separate group, such as the roles they play, strategy, tactics, and what they need to correct and improve in the second half. Player input is a critical part of these discussions, because they have a more relevant perspective of what's happening on the field."

"Finally, we regroup as a team for the last segment of the halftime to allow the coaches to address one or two important points that apply to the entire team. Positive reinforcement is a major characteristic of this segment to make sure the team returns to the field with a positive attitude."

What happens when the team is behind at halftime? Does Don adjust the halftime structure? "We keep the same structure—basically three segments—but the content and emphasis is different according to the situation. If we're behind, we don't dwell on the first half. We tell the players to forget about it and move on. We focus on what we can do in the second half to perform better—positive things we can do to win the game. We review the importance of team commitment and challenge the team to live up to that commitment. We challenge each player to raise her level of performance, and point out how powerful individual commitment can be when combined into a team commitment. Finally, we emphasize that the second half is always our best half, because we work harder on fitness than any team we face, and our superior fitness allows us to wear down the opponent and win the game."

But sometimes it doesn't work. Sometimes you lose. Then what do you tell the team? According to Don, "One thing we never do is point fingers at one player, or even at a group of players, to blame them for the loss. We can't win without a contribution from every player; and when we lose, we accept it as a team loss. This includes every player and every coach. Because poor preparation is usually the major factor in a loss, we use this timely opportunity to stress the importance of preparation and reinforce our zero tolerance of poor commitment in practice and inadequate fitness maintenance. "

"We always look for the positive aspects of any experience. Even adversity can have a positive characteristic; it affords an opportunity to challenge our players to improve. So when we separate to go our different ways after a loss, we go with a positive attitude and a determination to fight back and win the next game. We leave looking forward to practice and to the next opportunity to win."

VALORIE KONDOS FIELD

University of California-Los Angeles

- - - - - - - - - - - - - - - - -

Position
Head Women's Gymnastics Coach

Career Record
225-47 (7 seasons)

Education
B.A.   UCLA

Team and Personal Highlights

- ➤ Four-time National Coach of the Year.
- ➤ Three national championships.
- ➤ Winningest coach in UCLA women's gymnastics school history.
- ➤ Nine Pacific-10 Conference championships.
- ➤ Eight Regional championships.
- ➤ 124 All-Americans.
- ➤ 47 Pacific-10 Conference event titlists.
- ➤ 20 NCAA individuals titlists.

VALORIE KONDOS FIELD

Introduction . . .

With three NCAA team titles in five years, UCLA head gymnastics coach Valorie Kondos Field has positioned her Bruins as the premiere program in collegiate women's gymnastics. Not only has she consistently recruited the top talent in the world, but she has produced the results. In the past six years alone, Kondos Field has led UCLA to three NCAA team titles, one runner-up finish, five regional titles, and four Pacific-10 championships.

The Bruins have had at least two athletes win NCAA individual crowns for four straight years. They have won nine of the last 15 Pac-10 championships, and have won eight NCAA Regional crowns in the last nine years. In 2001, all eight Bruins who competed in the NCAA meet earned All-American honors, a first in NCAA history.

Valorie's teams have set school and NCAA records for team scoring. At the 2000 NCAA Championships, the heavily-favored Bruins, with freshmen competing half of the routines, hit 48 for 48 in team competition despite starting on beam during prelims and ending on beam during the Super Six team finals. Kondos Field's gymnasts also excelled in the classroom, as each gymnast recorded a 3.0 or higher GPA and the team averaged 3.5 in the Winter 2000 quarter.

The four-time National Coach of the Year award winner has a unique background, having not been a competitive gymnast herself. Recognized as one of the top beam and floor exercise choreographers in the sport, Valorie's background is in dance. She is a former ballet dancer who danced with the Sacramento Ballet, Capital City Ballet, and Washington, D.C. Ballet.

She got her start in gymnastics by playing the piano for floor exercise music at a time when floor music could only be from one instrument. From there, she became a dance coach, and under the guidance of current University of Minnesota co-head coach Jim Stephenson, learned the fundamentals of the sport. She then moved on to UCLA as an assistant coach and choreographer in 1983, becoming head coach in 1995.

Kondos Field has been married for two years to UCLA Football Defensive Coordinator Bobby Field. Their combined coaching years at UCLA are approaching half a century, and they are the most successful coaching couple at the Westwood school.

Let's now listen as Valorie talks to us about the six psychological factors for success . . .

. . . on Motivation

Coach Valorie Kondos has no hesitancy in defining motivation: "Self-generated energy focused on achieving a desired goal." She says, "It's much easier to motivate someone to DO something when the goal is task oriented. For example, one challenge gymnasts face is fitness and weight management. Gymnasts find it easy to get on a fitness program, such as aerobic training or weight training. But they have a more difficult time managing food choices and the amount of food they eat. In the first case, they are DOING something, like riding a stationary bike. In the second case, they are trying to NOT DO something, such as not eating certain foods or not eating at all when studying or watching TV.

"Athletes, in general, have difficulty understanding that, in some cases, inactivity or rest is as vital to their training as active physical training is, especially if the athlete is injured. When a gymnast is injured, she wants to shorten the time for her rehabilitation as much as she can, so she thinks she needs to be actively working beyond the prescribed physical therapy and treatment to hasten the time she can begin actively working on the equipment again. But it is often the case that rest is what is needed most. 'True motivation,' then, involves the understanding one must accept and take ownership of inactivity, when appropriate, just as much as she does strenuous activity, when appropriate."

Before coming to college, most gymnasts at UCLA have performed at the elite level (Olympic level) and their training has been focused almost entirely on individual achievement. Contrary to what one might deduce from this, Valorie has found that, in training Bruin gymnasts, it is much easier to motivate them to pursue team-oriented goals than to pursue individual goals. "When an athlete is not competing up to her potential, I've had more success motivating her by shifting her focus from competing for herself to focusing on competing 'for her team'."

"My ultimate goal in coaching is to help each individual athlete understand that life is about 'choices'. The choices we make dictate the lives we lead. The process of making a choice, then, is, itself, a motivational activity, because there is an inherent goal associated with each choice we make, and goals are motivating. Once this concept is thoroughly understood, 'motivation' becomes an integral part of daily activity."

◆ ◆ ◆ ◆ ◆

On Team Cohesion

Valorie brings one of the other categories in this chapter into her discussion on team cohesion. She says that team cohesion is built on COMMUNICATION, and she adds to that the importance of TRUST: "Team cohesion is built on communication and trust that each individual, coach or athlete, puts forth in her/his honest and best effort to be the best coach or the best athlete she or he can be." She packs a lot of important terms into that package—communication, trust, honesty, effort. And, again, there is that implied goal to be "the best that you can be."

Valorie adds: "When the team is discombobulated, it usually results from factions coming about because of misunderstanding or issues that aren't being discussed." Valorie continues: " I encourage a lot of team meetings, with and without the coaches. I encourage our athletes to learn to observe without judging and to learn to help each other be proactive in problem solving. I encourage them, above all, to move forward from negative situations—not to wallow in negativity."

She cites the team unity in the Bruins' 2000 season. "Our 2000 season was the epitome of what can happen when a team is unified in goals and philosophies. Winning the national championship last year was not the highlight of the season for me, as head coach. Even hitting 48 of 48 routines in the two championship meets—something that had never been accomplished before—was not the most important achievement. What meant more to me was that each of our student athletes made the academic honor roll the quarter we were in competition. And when asked why they didn't 'party' to celebrate the championship, each one had the same response, 'We were tired, extremely happy, and content. We didn't want to cheapen the experience.' All of those factors combined to make a true winning season."

Valorie's "true winning season" apparently encompassed achieving all of the goals of the team: the academic goals, the behavioral goals, and the personal developmental goals—not just the athletic goals. It takes a lot of cohesiveness to have that "true winning season."

◆　◆　◆　◆　◆

. . . on Discipline

Valorie breaks team discipline into two components: "Team discipline can describe two different components of any successful team: (1) It can apply to the training regime followed by each individual team member with diligence, if not always enthusiasm; (2) It can describe the corrective action each athlete knows is consequential to specific actions." One could also describe these as active discipline, in which the athlete drives herself to go through activities that she considers drudgery, but knows are beneficial to her. Or she can be passive in accepting the prescribed activity (or denial of activity) resulting from some form of misconduct."

"Regardless of the discipline," says Valorie, "I have found that athletes respond best to discipline (whether punitive or part of team training) when the reasons for the discipline are explained and handled in a professional manner. Everyone deserves to be treated with respect, even when being disciplined. But respect should not be misconstrued with leniency or in any way minimize the offensive action."

Valorie is reinforcing the cardinal rules of dealing with student athletes: make sure everyone knows why actions are taken—no matter what they are—and never demean or be disrespectful. Sternness and respect are not mutually exclusive.

Valorie uses a process that builds a sense of responsibility and accomplishes both full communication and a sense of fairness. The process: "The best forms of discipline are usually those that the team determines themselves. Whenever I have made the team responsible for determining the discipline for specific negative actions, they inevitably choose much harsher repercussions than I would have chosen. And they take the responsibility for holding each other accountable for seeing the 'punishment' carried out. This process has a tremendous effect of making team members think twice before breaking team rules again."

◆ ◆ ◆ ◆ ◆

. . . on Mental Preparation

Valorie asserts, "Mental preparation is as vital to success as physical preparation. Mental preparation is having a clear mental picture of one's goal and the daily steps necessary to achieve that goal. It focuses on creating the perfect mental environment for training and competition, and knowing how to get back into the mental zone when obstacles get in the way. When one is prepared mentally as well as physically to accomplish a task, a 'calm confidence' permeates her body."

How does she prepare her team mentally for competition? Valorie says that she uses a lot of mental training and visualization techniques with her team. "Our team sports psychologist works with the gymnasts every year to teach them relaxation and visualization techniques." says Valorie. "It's interesting to me how many of our high-level athletes have poor mental imagery abilities. One our best competitors can't visualize (go through her routine mentally while not on the apparatus) her uneven bars routine without the bars turning to ice halfway through her visualization." That's an indication of the intensity of visualization and why gymnasts sometime need help in practicing visualization techniques.

"Another can't visualize a balance beam routine because the beam rotates in her mind," Valorie relates. If not corrected, that "rotating beam" would result in a fall every routine. "That's why it's vital to help each athlete find what works best for her as an individual. Some gymnasts respond well to the entire routine of 'relax, get yourself to a positive mental place, feel your slow breathing, and see what you're about to perform executed perfectly.' Others need to stand up and go through a mental routine while moving just their arms or upper body to help them feel the rhythm of the routine." It seem that Valerie subscribes to the "different strokes for different folks" philosophy when it comes to mental preparation.

Valerie points out that gymnastics is one of the few sports that doesn't involve strategy against another team or player. She says, "For the most part, a gymnast's daily training and preparation in the practice gym, both mental and physical, shouldn't change when she's in intercollegiate competition. A well trained gymnast can feel unusually calm during competition, because she has 'prepared'. The confidence that comes from full mental and physical preparation allows the athlete to keep her focus on herself and not be concerned with anything else—such as another team or the judges."

◆ ◆ ◆ ◆ ◆

. . . on Mental Toughness

Valorie pointed out again the features that are unusual, if not unique, in gymnastics. "Gymnastics is unique in that it takes focused aggressiveness. A gymnast's energy needs to be honed to a precise point. Too much aggression and you'll bound right off the balance beam. Too little and you'll crumble off the beam. On uneven bars, anxiety can make the gymnast tense up and 'muscle' her swing instead of swinging freely and rhythmically."

She then defined mental toughness as "the ability to stay focused, aggressive, confident, and positive, regardless of the situation." Valorie says, "A common characteristic of a mentally tough athlete is that she takes ownership of all she does and all that happens. She never places blame on the equipment, the order of competition, or the judges—things she can't control.

"A mentally tough athlete trains the way she competes in meets and vice versa. You can see the internal focus on a mentally tough competitor, whether she's in the gym training or in competition. She doesn't hear, feel, or see anything out of her mental focus. I love to observe our most mentally tough athletes. They have an uncanny ability to relax and joke on the floor at the competition arena one minute and then zoom into their mental focus and personal mental tunnel the next. You can actually see them in their own little tunnel—blocking everything else out. Mentally tough athletes also crave and cherish honesty. Idle praise and mundane corrections bore them and deflate their energy."

Valorie points out another characteristic of gymnastics that distinguishes it from the traditional team sports. Although gymnasts interact mentally, they are also quite independent of each other and can suffer the consequences of being alone from a physical standpoint.

She says, "A male basketball player once told me, 'Gymnastics has to be the toughest sport.' When I asked him why, he said, 'There's no one to pass the ball to.' On analyzing his comment, I understood it was directed to the mental toughness needed to compete gymnastics successfully. When you're up on that beam and something goes wrong, it's up to you and you alone to regroup and refocus in order to finish the routine with as few deductions as possible—There really is no one to 'pass the ball to'."

◆ ◆ ◆ ◆ ◆

. . . on Communication

If there is a single word that characterizes Valorie's position on effective communication, it's "honesty." She believes that every human being rises to her highest potential when treated with honesty and respect. "It's usually the coach's own frustration that leads to negative communication and coaching," Valorie points out. "That's not to say that communication needs to be 'warm and fuzzy.' I insist on honest and respectful communication, no matter how difficult it may be to speak calmly or how painful it may be to hear the truth when the truth brings disappointment. I'm included in both sides of this equation. I wholeheartedly believe that if the truth is communicated compassionately, it is better than masking the truth and misleading someone to spare her feelings. And it can be equally counterproductive to let anger confuse the ultimate message."

To Valorie, it is important to understand that athletes want the truth deep down, because they know that in the end it, will help them solve problems. You can't solve problems that you don't know about. Valorie: "I've never coached an athlete who wanted to be praised when she didn't perform to her capabilities. Nor have I ever coached an athlete who didn't respond positively to honesty. I absolutely don't believe in negative coaching or yelling."

Valorie is joining an increasingly large number of coaches who share her views on negativism and yelling at athletes. She continues, "I understand that there are many ways to convey messages, and some coaches believe that negative coaching techniques do achieve desired goals. I'm not among them."

"Every coach is first a teacher. As a teacher I take tremendous responsibility to practice the Golden Rule in treating our athletes and staff the way I'd like to be treated. I don't subscribe to the 'do as I say - not as I do' philosophy. I tell our student athletes I will not challenge them in public, and I expect the same in return. I will always take the time to talk through issues directly with the person involved instead of grumbling to a fellow coach or another team member. I expect the team and the staff to pay me the same respect."

Valorie shares with us what is considered by many coaches the greatest reward in this profession: "I have often been told that the fact I took the time to explain myself, to speak to our gymnasts honestly, and to give them the avenue to speak honestly and candidly with me was one of the most valuable lessons they learned in their four years with me."

Effective communications is key to leadership—in a setting sometimes not unlike the battlefield. Valorie puts it this way: "Once effective communication is established, it leads to something vital to every relationship—Trust. It is a tremendous asset when our athletes trust that I have a sane reason for giving them an 'order'—when there isn't time to explain why I gave the instruction. Spending the greater part of the season building that 'trust' results in their confidence in me, regardless of how absurd an instruction may seem at the time. If they doubted me, those doubts could get into their minds, cause them to perform tentatively, and negatively impact our score. They know that eventually, when things calm down—out of the 'heat of battle'—I'll explain the why's of my actions. That's what effective communication and trust are about."

THOMAS LEE
University of Nebraska-Omaha

- - - - - - - - - - - - - - -

Position
Assistant Women's Basketball Coach

Career Record
119-35 (7 seasons)

Education
ssB.A. Hastings (NE) College
M.Ed. Doane (NE) College

Team and Personal Highlights

➢ Five Nebraska State Tournament appearances.

➢ Nebraska Class A girl's state championship.

➢ Three state tournament finals appearances.

➢ Five District championships.

➢ Omaha Metropolitan Conference Coach of the Year.

➢ Nebraska Coaches Association Coach of the Year.

➢ Heartland Conference Coach of the Year.

THOMAS LEE

Introduction . . .

During his seven-year stint as head girls' basketball coach at Omaha (NE) North High School, Tom Lee established himself as a teacher of the game who instilled a strong work ethic and fiery competitive spirit in his teams. Soft-spoken off the court, Lee developed an intense game demeanor that made his teams one of the most difficult to play. Stressing team play over individual honors, his players still were recognized for many post-season awards.

A three-time Coach of the Year award winner, Tom's teams were district champions five of his seven years at Omaha North. His five district championship teams became state tournament finalists three times, winning the large-school Class A title in 1998. A 1987 graduate of Hastings (NE) College, he earned his master's degree in educational leadership from Doane (NE) College in May, 2001.

He left Omaha North in 2000 to become Dean of Students and Assistant Activities Director at Bellevue (NE) West High School. Wanting to return to coaching, the Grand Island, Nebraska, native accepted the head boy's basketball coaching position at rival Bellevue (NE) East High School in February, 2001. Contacted by University of Nebraska-Omaha head women's basketball coach, Lisa Carlsen, for a recommendation for an assistant coaching position on her staff, Lee eventually recommended himself. He assumed his new position on July 1, 2001. Coach Lisa Carlsen: "I am very excited to have Tom join our staff. He brings a wealth of knowledge, credibility, and experience with him. He is very well respected in the local basketball community and will be instantly beneficial in our local metro recruiting efforts."

Tom was meticulous when explaining his success strategies . . .

. . . on Motivation

Coach Tom Lee says that he believes motivation is "inspiring our athletes to be the best that they can be." He says, "We teach our players to never settle for second best, but to be THE best. We teach in our program that success comes only through hard work, on and off the court, as a team and as individuals. Our motto is this: 'To be the best, you must work harder than the rest.' Our players will hear me repeat that several times throughout practice, and we also tell our players, "If you are not sweating, then you aren't working hard enough—you're not digging deep enough."

An obvious characteristic of Tom's attitude, then, is that hard work and persistence will pay off. "What we try to get across to our players in practice is to give it their all the entire game." He obviously believes and wants his players to believe that they can win. "We are always encouraging and inspiring our athletes throughout those hard practices to believe that they can and will prevail. We want our players to learn that and always remember it. When it's game time, I want our players to play with heart and determination. When the game is on the line, if they have their heart in it, they will naturally dig deeper and deeper each time down the floor."

Tom says that he totally subscribes to the philosophy Pat Riley presented in his book, [**_The Winner Within_**] "If you make the team work hard in practice, the game will be easy." Tom says, "When I first started coaching, I coached women's basketball, and I was extremely hard on our players—to the point that some of them would be in tears. I was giving what I thought was constructive criticism, but I was doing it in a destructive manner. As I continued to coach, I continue to be hard on the players. But now there's a difference; I always come back with a positive comment or compliment."

"It's important to let players know when they have done something right, and I reinforce it by telling them that I have confidence in them and believe in them." This obviously accomplishes a double purpose: It is instructional in that it's important to know when you're doing it right, so that you will continue to do it that way, and it's motivational as well.

Tom points out another caution in coaching: "I do not ask players to do something I think they are incapable of. I assure them that I will not put them in a situation where they are likely to fail. If I feel that a desirable achievement is beyond their abilities, I won't force the issue." He also looks for the strengths in each player so that he can make her role on the team the one where she can be most helpful to the team—and, as a consequence, to herself. "If I approach team assignments in a positive manner, players usually accept their roles and take pride in doing whatever it is they do best."

Tom doesn't leave his relationships with the players on the court. "I pull players aside, individually, at the end of practice to talk to them. I might apologize if I think a player is feeling down, because she didn't accept my coaching as being positive—I always mean it to be. I'll reinforce what they need to do to correct mistakes I've pointed out." Sometimes when a player is giving it all she has on the court, she may be too tired for corrections to sink in and remain with her. So it's good to review them when she is resting and much more receptive to instructions. Tom emphasizes: "I want to be sure the player and I have reached an agreement. And if I sense that there may be a feeling among other team members that a player and I were in conflict, I will open practice the next day by apologizing to her in front of the whole team. When I do this, I think it helps me gain the whole team's respect. Everyone gets angry at times. I get angry with my children. But I always try to explain why I get angry. And I say to both my children and to my players, 'I scold you because I love you—because I want to see you be the best that you can be.'"

Tom summarizes: "We are always trying to motivate and inspire our players to be the best that they can be both on and off the court."

. . . on Team Cohesion

Tom believes that team chemistry is something that should be "coached," just like player's skills and game plans. "Team chemistry is the most important factor of a successful team. Coaching is often bridge building; it's teaching the players, families, coaches, and staff to come together, work together, and use each other's individual talents to create one team."

"I believe one rotten apple can spoil team chemistry. So I demand that our players work together and get along together. And I demand it from coaches and parents as well. Negative behavior is just not acceptable in our program."

Obviously, if family is involved, Tom's philosophy extends beyond the gym. He puts it this way: "I believe the only way the UNO Mavericks can win is if we have good team chemistry on and off the court. Good team chemistry does not just magically appear when the women put on their uniforms. These bonds need to be made off the court in order to be true and strong enough to withstand any mishaps that occur during a game situation. I ask the following of my players:

1. Be best friends ALWAYS—not just during the season, but in the off-season, also.
2. Spend quality time together—attend school activities together as a group. Go out together as a group and don't leave out anyone on the team.
3. Build a trusting relationship—don't keep secrets from teammates or talk about them in a negative way behind their backs.
4. NEVER come to practice angry with a teammate—whenever there is a dispute among players, we will not start or continue practice until the dispute is settled. We must all get along with each other."

By stressing the importance of these four factors, Tom demonstrates that he cares about his players as individuals, not just as athletes. He says,

"I want them to have a support system—one that is genuine. I believe that our players can make even the physically hardest practices fun, because they have each other to count on. I encourage them to be encouraging themselves and compliment each other when they perform well. When a coach is 'chewing out a player,' that player knows that she still has her teammates with her 100%. This camaraderie keeps our players working together and makes us successful."

"In tough games and other challenging situations, the results of team building really come through. When it comes down to it, our players are really all heart, and they believe in each other. If one of our players is not having a good game, she knows her 'support system' will step up and make up for her shortcomings. All of the players expect hard work to pay off in the end, demonstrating that they are the best."

How does Tom involve the parents? "We held parent meetings, and lay the ground work for camaraderie among them. All parents want their daughters to excel. Sometimes I have to explain to parents what role their daughter plays for the team. They cannot all be the highest scorer on the team. Helping parents understand this should help them avoid becoming frustrated and angry about my coaching decisions. It should also help them respect the role of other members of the team."

"I ask parents to cheer for the team, not just their daughters, although there are times when a player deserves—and should receive—special recognition from the fans during a game. The supportive attitude toward the team as a whole is really enhanced when the parents sit together at games. When parents sit together, one parent will see in the other parents' feelings toward their daughters the same feelings that they feel for their own daughter. Parent support is particularly important at away games where few of our students attend."

"Team cohesiveness and chemistry are complex. We don't always know what makes them happen. But when parents, players, and coaches bond together, that bonding brings team chemistry, and it doesn't matter whether we understand it or not."

"In building these bonds the coaches must know the players as individuals. We must instill in the team as a whole a sense of where the team is headed and the confidence that the players, coaches, and parents—working together—can get there. This feeling has made us a tough team to beat. The results demonstrate that we must be doing something right."

◆ ◆ ◆ ◆ ◆

. . . on Discipline

Tom says emphatically that he's a disciplinarian: "I believe that without discipline or accountability, there is not team. It's difficult for us, as coaches, to gain the respect of our players if we allow them to make mistakes on and off the court and fail to discipline them. But it's important to be consistent and equitable with all our players. Although occasionally a parent will think I've been unfair to his daughter, I've been able to demonstrate to most parents that by working at it hard, I am fair to each member of the team."

Interestingly, Tom has found that making all players pay for the mistakes of one is effective in discipline. After all, this is what happens in a game; if one player turns the ball over, the score at the other end of the court goes against the whole team—not just the player who made the mistake. So Tom says, "When one player makes a mistake in practice or off the court, the entire team has to pay for it. This creates accountability among players. It increases their tendency to watch out for their teammates. The players encourage and help each other to stay focused on their objectives and avoid mistakes."

"A specific drill in applying "whole-team" discipline is putting a player at the center of the court in practice, after a mistake, and having her watch her teammates run laps because she made a mistake. But I have to use discretion in applying this exercise. It will backfire if I haven't built team unity first. But if team unity is established first, then the player recognizes that she must accept more responsibility for the way she plays, because it affects the whole team."

Discipline doesn't always have to be associated with punishment. "We use 90-second drills after practice—to teach discipline, but not as punishment. It's part of conditioning and improving shooting skills."

"Another effective disciplinary action is holding a player out of a game or part of a game because of mistakes or improper behavior. No one wants to practice, practice, practice and then not be allowed to compete. How many girls would come out for the team if she never played a game? When we know in advance that a player will have to sit-out a game, we might even use her more actively in practice the week before. This accomplishes the purpose of keeping her conditioned while at the same time intensifying her concern for not playing in the game."

Tom says he has learned that some forms of discipline don't work— or at least they don't often work. "All coaches, at one time or another, have had an individual run extra lines or laps for discipline. But often a player will run the laps thinking, 'Hey, this isn't so tough.' So she isn't convinced that she absolutely can't make that same mistake again. And, in fact, she is likely to make it again, so the punishment wasn't effective."

In reinforcing his philosophy on discipline, Tom reflects on observations he's made of other teams: "Over the course of years, I've seen several teams that obviously lack discipline. You can see a lack of team unity, and they don't appear to be motivated. The players often show their disapproval of each others play. Those teams never seem to play up to their potential, and they often lose to less talented teams who are well-disciplined. There is a time for discipline, and for our team it's easy to figure out when that time is: EVERY DAY."

◆ ◆ ◆ ◆ ◆

. . . on Mental Preparation

Tom makes about as strong a statement on the importance of mental preparation as can be made: "I tell our players that the game of basketball is 90% mental and 10% physical. We want them to believe that they can do anything they put their minds to. During the pre-season conditioning we tell our players, 'It's not the will to win, but the will to prepare to win.' If we can get that across, then when they set their own goals for the season, those goals will include plenty of mental preparation."

"We separate those who want to prepare to win from those who don't have the necessary determination, in the first week of practice. We start with a one-hour session of running hard and lifting weights. Those who really want to play the game will tough it out. Those who don't have the heart to win, will drop out. Next, we do full court drills to see who can push to get up and down the floor, even when they are tired from the previous exercise. And in other drills, we try to find the players who make good decisions, especially without the ball."

In every sport, staying focused is paramount. In basketball, it's no less important. Tom puts it this way: "During the instructional periods some players lose concentration because they can't block out their tiredness from the physical drills. We are trying to identify those players who can stay focused and who can execute plays at the end of the game when they are physically tired." How many basketball games are decided in the last minute? It seems like the vast majority are.

In thinking of basketball, most fans consider free throws the most intensely mental part of the game, with the shooter going through the same rituals before each shot, to block out every thing except the free throw. Tom puts drills for shooting from the floor and free-throws at the end of practice, when the players are most tired. "When it comes to crunch time, our players need to execute under pressure, even when they're exhausted. So we train them to shoot when they are exhausted."

When most statisticians analyze basketball teams' performances, they separate home games from away games, because winning on the road is much more difficult. Although the court is the same size and the goal is the same height above the floor and the same diameter, the backgrounds are different. This may cause a little difference in depth perception, but it may cause even a greater difference in mental perception. "We had two gyms and actually changed gyms, after the players had adjusted to one gym. This helped the players develop a flexibility in dealing with backgrounds and other perceptions, so that when we played on the road, the effect of the different gym is minimized," says Tom. "We reminded our players that to win the ultimate prize, the state championship, we would have to win it on a 'neutral court' and the team that has better mental focus is likely to win."

And then there's that thing about the difference in the opponents' abilities. "You bet," Tom agrees, "You have to stay just as focused and play just as hard against a team with a poor record as you do against a team that nearly always wins. This is important for two reasons. (1) If you ever let down, you may not be able to turn it back on, so you never let down. (2) Any team can be beaten if they let down.

"Finally, there's the problem of playing a team for the second or third time in the same season. If we beat them in the last competition, they will have extra incentive to beat us and will have prepared very hard. So we can't lose our incentive and focus. We must treat the game like they beat us the last competition, so that we gain that incentive. We must never be intimidated, we must stand tall, visualize clear mental pictures of our goals, and work to make those visions a reality."

◆ ◆ ◆ ◆ ◆

. . . on Mental Toughness

In Tom's eyes, "Mental toughness and mental preparation go hand-in-hand. All of those drills we do at the beginning of the season for mental preparation also help make our players become mentally tough." He defines mental toughness as "the ability to handle any circumstance that comes about—good or bad, hard or easy."

"A mentally tough player is a strong leader. Her charisma and confidence will cause other players to take on challenges. Mentally tough players can get chewed out by the coach and turn that negative into a positive, by resolving to correct whatever it was that provoked the coach to chew her out. Mentally tough players thrive on competing at the other team's gyms before tough crowds that might intimidate a less mentally tough player. They love challenges, because challenges test their abilities, and help them grow toward reaching their maximum potential. Some of our players actually performed better on the road before a rowdy crowd. This definitely helped take away the home court advantage and minimized the difference between our home score average and our road score average.

"Without question, the mentally tough players we have had over the years have brought great strength to our team and contributed measurably to our success."

◆   ◆   ◆   ◆   ◆

. . . on Communication

Tom says, "The key to good communication is to know when to be hard on our players and when to lighten up. In my earlier years as a coach, I didn't realize the importance of communication. I've learned that when the game is on the line, you must remain calm and positive. No one can communicate effectively when her emotions are controlling her. Through both your words and actions you must make players understand that you have confidence in them. If the ability to do this is not inherent in a coach, he will do well to spend whatever time it takes to become an effective communicator."

"An excellent example of how I've learned to communicate calmly is the way we conducted our half-time sessions. If we are trailing at the half, I take the time to go back and stress strategy. We act like the score is 0-0, at the beginning of the game. We can't dwell too much on the first half because it's over and we can't replay it. Even if we are ahead, we approach the second half as if the game were just starting and we need to get out on top early. Most basketball analysts will say that the first few minutes of the second half is the most important period of the game. That's when the momentum of the second half is set, and the second half is the last half.

"When I remain calm and relaxed, it's contagious. The players become calm and relaxed. Conversely, if I appeared to be up tight or stressed, then our players would be uptight and unable to perform well in the second half. And I can't say it enough: 'Show confidence in your players.' Let them know you believe in them, and they will believe in themselves. During the early part of the season, we may become a little negative in our instruction to emphasize the importance of certain principles. But at game time, it's important to be 100% positive. We all must believe that we can win. And as important as the mental aspect of the game is, if we believe we can win, we probably will win."

But what happens when you lose. Everyone loses occasionally. Tom: "When we lose, I always take the blame, because 'if the player hasn't played well, the coach hasn't coached well.' Right after a loss is one of the best times to get the team's attention, so I take advantage of it. I let them know why we lost. They are looking for assurance that, even if they didn't win, they could have won. That's positive, and it helps ease the pain of losing. At the same time I let them know that we can't let losing become a habit. After a loss is a good time to try to communicate this to them, because they are feeling the pain of defeat at that very moment, and they don't like it."

"And when we get back to the practice gym, we go right to work correcting those mistakes we identified during the game and focus on becoming champions. Coming back and performing well after a disappointing loss (all loses are disappointing) shows character and team pride. 'To be the best, we must work harder than the rest.'"

RICK MOODY

University of Alabama-Tuscaloosa

- - - - - - - - - - - - - - - -

Position
Head Women's Basketball Coach

Career Record
253-118 (12 seasons)

Education
B.S.   Troy State (AL) University
M.A.   University of Alabama-Tuscaloosa

Team and Personal Highlights

- ➤ National Coach of the Year.
- ➤ Eight NCAA Tournament appearances.
- ➤ Final Four and five Sweet 16 appearances.
- ➤ Three Kodak All-Americans.
- ➤ 12 First-team All-SEC players.
- ➤ 34 Academic All-SEC players.
- ➤ Gold Medal winner as East Head Coach in U.S. Sports Festival.
- ➤ Exchange Club Outstanding Alabamians' Court of Honor award.
- ➤ Winningest women's basketball coach in University of Alabama history.

RICK MOODY

Introduction . . .

On March 20, 1989, Rick Moody became the sixth head basketball coach in the 27-year history of University of Alabama women's basketball. Fulfilling a life-long dream, Moody has the longest tenure (12 years) and has been the most successful (253 victories). Heading into the 2001-2002 season, he needs just 15 victories to become the University of Alabama's winningest basketball coach ever (men's or women's).

Following a highly successful prep coaching career in Florida and Alabama, the Grove Hill, Alabama, native quickly established the Tide program as one of the nation's best. His first two teams won 33 games, and then the Tide exploded onto the national scene. Beginning in the 1991-92 season, Moody's teams would begin an eight-year run that produced eight 20 win seasons, eight NCAA tournament appearances, five Sweet 16 appearances, and the only Final Four appearance for an Alabama women's basketball team in school history in 1994.

Moody espouses the same philosophy as the master showman P.T. Barnum: He never met a promotion or motivation method he didn't like. That was evident in 1990 when he ate a live worm after his team won a Southeastern Conference tournament game.

And then there is Moody Time. This is the official time (whether it's 10 minutes early or 10 minutes late from Greenwich Mean Time) that all players synchronize with Coach Moody when the team is traveling to a game. One minute late to the bus or practice will result in Moody Running Time.

Rick's legacy may be the number of former players now joining the coaching ranks because of his influence in their lives. No less than 17 of his former players are now coaching in the prep ranks, at junior colleges, or at Division I schools. Because of his notable contributions to the State of Alabama, he was also awarded the Exchange Club Outstanding Alabamian's Court of Honor citation in 1994.

A committed Christian, Moody is active with the Fellowship of Christian Athletes and is a deacon in his church. He is also a popular speaker for church and civic groups. Away from the game of basketball, Rick enjoys spending time with his wife, Sandra, and being outdoors hunting and fishing. He can also be found on the golf course challenging son, Ben, for family bragging rights.

The highly-energetic Tide coach absolutely loved having the opportunity to talk about his thoughts . . .

◆ ◆ ◆ ◆ ◆

. . . on Motivation

Coach Moody brings into play all of the building blocks that combine to motivate athletes. He defines motivation as "that inner determination that drives one to excel in any of life's endeavors—that sparks an athlete to do her best." He goes on: "Total motivation encompasses the heart, mind, body, and soul—working together as a single entity to achieve a specific goal." You notice that one of the factors that is probably key in Rick's definition is "goal." Motivation without a goal is like a wild horse without a harness. All of that energy and effort going no place—without a goal.

Rick recognizes the difference between men and women and the present-day challenges coaches have that are different from some of those of the past. "Motivating today's female student-athlete poses a unique challenge," he says. "You must always tell them the good things they are doing before telling them the mistakes they are making. Be positive and encouraging. Never be negative. Never be authoritative. Concentrate on the individual first and then the team." And Rick says that a coach cannot stop to rest when motivation is involved, and you can't deviate from your course. "Make sure you keep athletes motivated consistently by giving positive encouragement."

Rick lists three elements of effective motivation:

1. "Always be enthusiastic and positive.
2. Teach athletes to believe in themselves.
3. Organize your individual goals and team goals and then work to achieve them."

Notice how the things Rick lists that a coach should do are the same things he wants his athletes to do. They must be positive. He has to show them he believes in them to make them believe in themselves. And when he organizes his goals and reviews them with the team, his goals become the team's goals.

As you might expect, when asked about the impediments to motivation, Rick doesn't hesitate in turning around his first element of effective motivation:

"A coach must NEVER exhibit negative behavior."

. . . on Team Cohesion

Rick says that in order to build team cohesion (or chemistry) you have to identify the strengths and weaknesses of the team, from the standpoint of team chemistry. Look for common interests that tend to bond them and for minor differences in attitudes that could fester into divisiveness. He defines team chemistry as "the ability of a diverse group of individuals to work together to realize a common goal." He mentions "goal" again, stressing the importance of staying focused on that goal. Rick says that one measure of team chemistry is "the combined individual sacrifices that team members make to achieve the team goals. Team unity," Rick says, "is built on respect for other team members and self esteem."

Rick mentions goals again in elaborating on team cohesion: "Team cohesion stems from that same desire—the desire of team members to work together to achieve a common goal. The more cohesive a group is, the more effective it is in achieving its goals." He expands the scope of people who impact team chemistry: "Communications and trust among all the staff as well as the team are key elements in the development of team cohesion. Open communication paves the way to trust."

He believes that team chemistry or cohesion cannot be maintained unless it extends beyond the court. Off-the-court activities are involved, too. "Doing things together, as a group—things you would do whether you're an athlete or not—is essential in building team cohesiveness. Eat meals together. Work together in community service. Go to church together."

Rick likes to bring in motivational speakers and have devotionals together. Here are the four elements he lists as effective in building team cohesion and chemistry:

1. "Treat the team as a family.
2. Encourage older players to mentor the younger ones.
3. Have invited speakers—or even team-member discussions— frequently to focus on the importance of playing individual roles and how each person's role is absolutely critical to team success.
4. Make sure that the coaching staff is on the same page. Cohesiveness starts at the top."

Things Rick warns against as potentially destroying team cohesiveness are:

1. "Being inconsistent in the enforcement of team rules and showing partiality.
2. Failing to recognize the necessity for the coaching staff's involvement with the team off the court. We're all involved—all the time."

. . . on Discipline

Rick seems to envision an orderly world as the mark of good discipline. "Discipline means expectations are in order," he says. And he puts a high premium on making sure those "expectations are well understood by every member of the team. Always let players know what's expected of them."

He recognizes that players are different. What works for one may prove to be a big mistake with another. So Rick thinks that interactions with players, one-on-one, must be tailored to the individual. Again, he stresses the necessity for a coach's having a positive attitude. "Criticism must always be constructive." Make sure you put the results you want to achieve above the need to release your frustration."

"All forms of discipline must put the team first, relative to the individuals, even though the action must be tailored to the individual." The established goals must be factored into discipline, just as they are into motivation.

"Consistency is paramount," says Rick. Nothing can destroy team discipline faster than treatment of individual players that the team perceives to be partial. "Perceives" is a key word. The team must understand that factors other than the immediate action must be considered in deciding on the most effective discipline. When you tailor discipline to the individual, you may prescribe different corrective actions for what appears to be the same mistake made by different team members. You must communicate to the team that fair treatment of people is not necessarily identical treatment.

Rick has a four-point prescription for effective team discipline:

"Taking away playing time is an effective means of discipline." Athletes work hard and practice hard in order to compete against other teams. They consider competing a reward. And taking playing time away is a positive step in that it gives another team member a chance that she might not have otherwise to prove herself.

"Involve the players in making team rules." In the discussions with the team leading up to formulating rules make sure that the rules are perceived to be fair and that everyone understands the reasons behind them."

"Meet with team members individually." Individual attention demonstrates a coach's caring for a person and enhances the "tailored treatment" Rick mentioned.

"Be firm, fair, and consistent." There's a difference between firmness and harshness. You can be soft spoken and firm. Do you think John Wooden wasn't firm? But he was quiet and gentlemanly.

With that prescription for effective discipline, it's pretty easy to predict Rick's warning concerning ineffective discipline:

"Enforcing rules unfairly and yelling and screaming at players."

. . . on Mental Preparation

Rick brings an interesting factor into mental preparation: time management. He says that individual and team priorities enter into mental preparation. Rick defines mental preparation as "the ability to focus on what's important and to be aware of what's happening around you." The time management element enters into the ability to stay focused because college athletes are involved in so many activities other than athletics—as they should be. But Rick feels that he needs to help his team members organize the time devoted to those activities so that when they are trying to focus on one activity, they can completely block out the others. This can be done only if the athlete feels free from concern about her other obligations. Good organization and time management can help establish this freedom.

Rick counsels his players not to spread themselves too thin. He says, "My minister once told me to be careful what you commit to, because if you commit to too many things, you wind up not being committed to anything." That's where working with players as individuals to organize the things they want to commit to in the order of what's most important. Academics, personal conduct, health, and the team must be among the top priorities. Other priorities will vary from one individual to another. Once organized, the athlete can start at the bottom of the list and eliminate or reduce time assigned to those things that can wait until another time.

At that point, the time management practice has, indeed, become a critical and positive element in mental preparation.

. . . on Mental Toughness

Having an "even keel" demeanor is a characteristic Rick assigns to mentally tough athletes. And he says that a mentally tough athlete will maintain that demeanor under the most adverse conditions. More specifically, Rick defines mental toughness as "the ability to stay focused on your goals during difficult situations."

Rick believes that mental toughness, while somewhat inherent, can be developed through the practice of putting athletes through adverse circumstances in practices. He believes that by creating game-type stressful conditions in practice, his Crimson Tide women will be prepared to handle similar situations in real games. This will give them the upper hand over a team that hasn't been prepared for the tense moments of the game. And how many basketball games are decided during the last minute—quite a few, even with buzzer beaters?

Again Rick enumerates the importance of training for mental toughness:

"Put your athletes in tough situations on the court in practice. Make the situations as 'game-like' as possible, so that they will be prepared for real situations in games."

"One way of creating these tough situations is to organize practice in a way that makes the practices competitive and challenging. Try to make the practices tougher than anything anticipated in a game."

"The coach must demonstrate mental toughness. Like leadership in any other aspect of coaching, the coach has to set the right examples."

The opportunity that comes up most often is the opportunity to exhibit the "even keel" demeanor in both winning and losing. While it's only human and appropriate for a coach to show pleasure, even exuberance, in winning, he must not let the exuberance convey to the team that he only appreciates winning performance. At the same time, he must let his team know that he believes in them and will help them correct mistakes after a loss.

Rick also enumerates what to avoid in developing mental toughness:

"Don't come to practice without a plan." It doesn't take players long to discern that the coach has shirked his responsibilities when the practice is disorganized. And the team will feel let down, because their efforts will not gain them as much when organization is lacking.

"When confronted with a player who is giving less than her all, be consistent. Try to find out what her problem is before you try to correct it." In developing a plan to deal with any problem, you must "get the facts first." Sometimes you can make a fool of yourself if you don't.

"Don't make excuses or listen to excuses," says Rick. There are reasons for every action. But some reasons don't excuse the action. A mentally tough athlete who makes mistakes will take responsibility for the mistake and leave it up to the coach to determine why the mistake was made and to what degree it's "excusable." In setting a good example, a good coach will explain what went wrong, take responsibility, and work to remedy the problem. In his weekly television show the Crimson Tide's legendary football coach, Bear Bryant, frequently pointed out, "That's my fault," when a play went wrong. Not many did. And nobody ever accused Bear Bryant of not being mentally tough.

◆   ◆   ◆   ◆   ◆

. . . on Communication

"Don't expect any good relationship to last long if the two people in the relationship don't communicate." That's what Rick Moody thinks of the importance of good communication. He equates his communications with his players to communications within a family. After all, he considers his team a family. Rick says, "Family relationships sustain themselves through openness, honesty, and effective communications."

How many problems are created just because one person doesn't know what another person is thinking? How often have you read a novel or watched a movie where the entire plot was based on misunderstandings? You sit and say to yourself, "Why don't they just tell each other what's going on or how they feel?" Rick equates the player-coach relationship to that of the characters in a book or movie. "Players want to know where they stand and what's expected." Coaches need to know what his players are thinking and what is troubling them. Sometimes a player is doing a good job and is discouraged because the coach doesn't tell her how she's doing. And if she needs instruction and doesn't get it, she'll continue to perform poorly—just because of a lack of communication.

Rick extends his communications beyond just his players. Often players confide in parents, grandparents, or close friends, before they confide in their coach. Rick considers these good sources of information and also good resources in reinforcing the coach's expectations and concerns. "Often, I've been able to reach a player with help from someone other than myself whom they are accountable to. And sometimes this has avoided problems and disciplinary action."

Rick has a two-pronged formula for maintaining effective communications with his players:

"Have an 'open-door' policy so that players feel free to just drop by the office and talk. Frequently, they just need reinforcement that you believe in them. And other times, they have problems that you don't know about."

"In addition to the "drop by" meetings, schedule periodic one-on-one appointments with the players to share feelings on the status of playing time, roles on the team, academic performance etc." Often players look forward to these "performance discussions" as an opportunity to discuss things that they couldn't find an appropriate time or place to discuss otherwise. They don't want to initiate the discussion, but they want to have it. These meetings almost always end with both the coach and the player feeling better. That's communication.

BILL MUSE
Connors State College

- - - - - - - - - - - - - - - - - -

Position
Head Men's Basketball Coach

Career Record
236-66 (7 seasons)

Education
B.A.   University of Mississippi
M.A.   University of South Alabama

Team and Personal Highlights

➤ Six Bi-State East Conference titles.

➤ Four Region II crowns.

➤ Four consecutive trips to the NJCAA national tournament.

➤ Two Final Four appearances at the NJCAA national tournament.

➤ Six Bi-State Conference Coach of the Year awards.

➤ Four Region II Coach of the Year honors.

➤ Four District II Coach of the Year awards.

BILL MUSE

Introduction . . .

The national publication **Basketball Times** identified Bill Muse as a leading candidate for a Division I head men's basketball coaching position. The New Jersey native possesses all the skills that a Division I school covets: Outstanding teacher and coach, savvy and intelligent recruiter, strong administrative skills, wry sense of humor, exciting brand of basketball, out-going personality, and loyalty to his school.

Bill has won 77 percent of his games since arriving at Connors State nine years ago. His teams have won six conference crowns, they make annual trips to the National Junior College Athletic Association national tournament, and they have finished in the Top Five three times, with two appearances in the Final Four. He has garnered 14 Coach of the Year awards since 1993.

Muse has a strong Division I coaching background. He had a four-year stay at the University of South Alabama in the early 1980's. He then was Associate Head Coach at Georgia State for two seasons. Bill then took the head coaching and general manager positions with the Georgia Peaches professional women's basketball team for one year. He returned to college coaching at Morehead State for three seasons before heading to Clemson for two years. When Connors State came calling, it didn't take long for Muse to jump on the offer. Bill and his wife, Connie, have one son and live in Warner, Oklahoma.

Let's listen to Coach Bill Muse discuss his winning thoughts . . .

. . . on Motivation

Bill Muse says, "The key to motivation is enthusiasm, and enthusiasm is contagious." Sounds like he has something here that may make it easier to motivate the whole team, if he can introduce motivation to key team members and start an epidemic. Bill defines motivation as, "the ability to get a person to perform a particular task with maximum effort at a higher level than normal."

Then defining that "particular task" may be critical. This is the way Bill approaches this critical area. "Through individual conversations with our players, we establish both personal and team goals that will help them be more successful. And those goals must be more challenging than what they have been challenged to do before."

There must be rewards for achieving goals and for 100 percent effort. Bill says, "We don't wait 'till the end of the season to recognize good performance. The journey through a long season is too long to wait for recognition. So we give out awards after each game. Then, at the end of the season, we give additional awards for the total season's performance."

Motivation comes from knowledge. If you know your opponent, then you know how to match your offensive skills against his defensive skills and tendencies, and you know what his favorite offensive moves are. Bill Muse says, "We give in-depth scouting reports to each of our players." Bill Russell, the former Boston Celtic, says knowledge is the key to defense. Remember his TV commercial: "I got most of my rebounds before the shooter ever took the shot." The more a player knows about his opponent, the more confidence he has in his ability to beat him, and confidence is a great motivator.

Bill says that tangential factors enter into motivation. "Clean locker rooms, good practice gear, well-organized practice sessions, and classy uniforms set the stage for motivation. When the stage is set, we hand out motivational literature to augment what we try to get across in our conversations." Just as in any other communication, the first presentation needs reinforcement to increase confidence in the points being made and to help athletes remember the points.

One recurring theme among coaches is that a positive attitude is essential. They express this theme in different ways. Here's what Bill has to say about it: "It's absolutely necessary to maintain a positive practice environment. Players respond much better to positive reinforcement of the things you teach and to your observations of the things they do well."

Conversely, the biggest impediment to motivation is a negative environment. "Fear can destroy motivation. It makes players tentative, and tentativeness takes the edge off performance. Players have to feel confident that their coach is supportive of them and will not embarrass them if they make mistakes while putting forth their best effort. Players do not react well to threats of punishment if they make mistakes. Coaches simply must maintain a positive attitude in motivating their teams."

. . . on Team Cohesion

Bill recognizes two types of goals, individual goals and goals for the team. He says, "A coach must combine the individual goals so that they become integral parts of team goals." Then, when you address either type of goal, you are enhancing the achievement of both types. Bill defines team chemistry: "Team chemistry is working together, both on and off the court, to achieve a common vision. We begin trying to build team chemistry the day players arrive on campus. We emphasize team, as opposed to individual players, at our very first meeting."

Off-the-court activities are as important in Bill's program as on-the-court practice. This is especially true in building team chemistry. "I believe that a person develops an interest in another person through his knowledge of the person's background and interests. We encourage players to talk to each other about their families and backgrounds. What do their parents do? How many siblings do they have? Where do they live? What do they like to do other than play basketball. What are their career goals?" Knowledge of these things identifies more areas for finding common interests and for expanding interests toward those of your teammates."

"We try to have lots of group functions where the players interact with each other," Bill says. "I take the team to church at least once a month. We have personal growth seminars once a week, at night, where outside speakers address things like social and cultural awareness, study skills, alcohol and drug abuse, goal setting, personal finance, motivation—even nutrition. I believe that helping each other develops team chemistry." Many college athletes have not been subjected to a highly regimented regime prior to coming to college, so they need some help in just getting into the swing of college activities. "I encourage the entire team to help make sure that everyone is up for breakfast, gets to class and meetings on time, and—of course—gets to practice on time."

The team really gets together in a different environment when they travel to away games. "We assign roommates at the motels and try to make sure that team members room with roommates other than their roommate back home." A lot of conversation usually takes place between the time players go to their rooms for the night and the time they actually go to sleep.

So far we've talked about developing team chemistry off-the-court. What about on-the-court? "Development of team cohesiveness begins with the conditioning drills. The upperclassmen encourage—push is more like it—our younger players to exert themselves and make their running times. The encouragement from the running drills carries over to the locker room, to the practice floor, and finally to the games, where teammates are pulling for individuals in a sense, but only in the context of pulling for the team as a whole." Bill believes in giving game time to as many players as possible. One of the things he says really bonds the team together is to see and hear the starters pulling for the reserves. The starters could never develop their skills if it were not for the reserves, pushing them in scrimmage. They recognize this and appreciate it, and they show their appreciation by yelling for the reserves when they are in the game.

"Good team chemistry scores points," Bill says. "In practice, we stress finding the open man and making the extra pass to him." The statisticians are beginning to recognize assists in games, and recruiters look at a player's assists record in evaluating not only his technical skills in seeing open players and passing the ball, but also his attitude and how he will fit into the chemistry of the team. "In practice, both the passer and the one who takes a successful shot as a result of the pass recognize and appreciate each other." You'll see the high fives between them as they take their defensive positions after a successful collaboration for a goal. Bill summarizes: "All of the things we do to enhance team chemistry and cohesion fit into our philosophy that 'a team that plays together wins together.'"

◆ ◆ ◆ ◆ ◆

. . . on Discipline

There is discipline and then there is discipline. Bill says there are two types: "Off the court, a player has to manage his activity-packed college life—classes, study, basketball, and social life etc. That type of discipline taxes the ability to organize and stick with a schedule, no matter how tiresome it gets, mentally, sometimes. Then, on the court, the player has to 'suck it up' and put forth all of his effort in stamina conditioning, weight training, and skill development. That discipline taxes his determination to endure physically demanding activities." Bill thinks that most players actually want to be pushed; it reinforces their self-discipline. Sometimes when you'd really rather be doing something else, it helps if you know you have to answer to the coach if you don't complete all the activities, both on and off the court, that being a college student-athlete demands.

"Discipline has to be perceived to be consistent, but it has to be tailored to each athlete as the situation calls for," says Bill. "Different strokes for different folks" is as important in making sure each athlete gets the guidance he needs as it is in any area of human relations. You will recall that Bill said giving team members playing time (particularly non-starters) helps bond the team together. He believes playing time can be a tool for getting players attention when corrective action must be taken. "Games are the most fun for players. If you seem to be having trouble getting a player to respond to constructive criticism, try benching him—if he's accustomed to playing a lot. He'll get serious in a hurry." And, as said earlier, the benefits of developing more players who feel comfortable in game situations and building team chemistry are extra bonuses to this type of discipline.

But what if the player doesn't get enough playing time to notice that he's benched? That's his normal position. Bill says going to the next level of denying participation comes into play then. "You can leave him off the traveling squad for a game or so. Or you can not allow him to dress out for a home game or so." And Bill says that the more traditional forms of discipline are still options. "Running early in the morning is still effective." Bill reminds us that a coach is not by himself in dealing with athletes. "They have other authority figures—parents, for example. Consulting them never hurts." College athletes are still young men—not adults. Most are away from home for the first time. So seeking parents' advice lets them know you care about their son, and often they have some good ideas about what forms of corrective action are more effective. "Assigning extra study hall and tighter curfew hours not only helps athletes understand that they must answer to authority, it also enhances their academic performance, which almost always needs enhancing."

But Bill draws the line at verbal abuse. He says, "Yelling, being sarcastic, and using language you don't want the players to use aren't discipline. They're just ways some coaches get off their frustrations, and they NEVER have positive results."

◆ ◆ ◆ ◆ ◆

. . . on Mental Preparation

You don't have to sell Bill Muse on the importance of mental preparation. Bill considers it the single most important aspect of basketball: "It's been said that today's game of basketball is 80% mental and 20% physical. I'm not trying to downplay the importance of physical talent, but we've all seen, time and time again, games in which teams with more physical ability are out performed by a less physically talented team, because the less physically talented team was better prepared mentally."

Bill says that basketball players need to use imagery (or visualization—different coaches use different terms) in preparing for a game. But they need to do it at least several days before the game. "A player must visualize his opponent guarding him and picture himself executing different moves against him. Or he may visualize the opponent's moves and how he's going to react to stop them. The clearer picture he can form in his mind, the more comfortable he will feel facing that opponent, and he'll feel just like he had actually practiced against the same guy during the week. I can't stress enough the importance of beginning your mental preparation at least several days before the game. You can't wait until game day. When you wait too late, there's not time to really let your mental preparation sink in and become second nature."

What Bill says about mental preparation being 80% of the game begins to sink in when he talks about some of the drills he has his team go through. He doesn't just practice executing certain plays—sort of in a vacuum. He actually paints a situation, like a play or movie director sets a scene. He'll say, "OK, we're up by 10 points with eight minutes to go." The situation influences the strategy the players use. Do they run clock before going into their half-court offense? Or he may say, "OK, we're down by 10 points with eight minutes to go." Will the mental strategy be different from that when they're ahead by ten? Or he may paint this picture: "The ball's out of bounds under the opponents' basket with just two seconds to go. We're behind by—it could be one, two or even three points—and the game is still within reach mathematically. We've got to get that ball down court and score or get fouled. We do different 'time and score' situations for every score differential and from every part of the court. You can bet your boots that the team who hasn't prepared mentally is going to lose to the team who has."

Bill points out that the season is long, and with all the pre-season conditioning—running, weight lifting, and skill training—players get physically tired. He trains his team hard enough that the physical exertion during a game will be relatively easy compared to pre-season work. But he says, "Players get tired mentally, too. So we give them a day or two off every week. Actually the NCAA wisely requires one day off a week, but we've found that two helps more than one many times. When the players return to practice after a couple of days off, they're fresher and sharper, both physically and mentally."

◆　◆　◆　◆　◆

. . . on Mental Toughness

"Most mentally tough athletes are born mentally tough. It's inherent. It's difficult to teach," says Bill. "Mental toughness is the ability to block from your mind everything except the task facing you. It's a refusal to lose, deeply imbedded in a player's mind." As specific examples demonstrating mental toughness, Bill cites the player who goes up "in a crowd" and gets a crucial rebound as the clock is running down. It may be the player who prevents his opponent from taking the last shot—without fouling. And, of course, the classic example is the free throw shooter, blocking out the noise of a screaming crowd in the other team's gym, and the sight of all those tubular-shaped balloons waving in the background of the basket.

Although Bill says that mental toughness is largely inherent, he still believes that certain physical practices help develop mental toughness. It comes forward when a player is physically spent, and you can help develop it by asking players to perform certain feats when they are physically exhausted. "For example," he says, "we will put them through a physically tough and long practice and then put them on the free throw line. They have nothing left physically, but that mental toughness kicks in and makes those muscles execute the throw, while they are totally concentrating on all of the elements of shooting learned over the months (or years) in practice. That's mental toughness, and success comes to the mentally tough."

. . . on Communication

"You can throw out all your offensive schemes, your defensive set ups, and your special situation maneuvers unless you can communicate, because they are all dependent on the team and the coach communicating effectively during the game." That's how important Bill Muse says effective communication is. And he says it's just as important off the court. And communicating off the court is a two-way street. "Listening is part of communicating, and listening is of the essence in communicating with players off the court. But you also have to be able to put your thoughts into words that accurately convey those thoughts." That's not particularly easy when you consider the diverse backgrounds of the players that typically make up a college basketball team. You have to speak their language. What you intend to say is not the most important thing in communicating with your players. It's what they heard that counts.

Halftime messages fill two important functions. According to Bill, "You have to make corrections during the halftime, and you have to be able to communicate these instructive comments clearly and concisely. You don't have much time, and if any one of the players doesn't understand, he could make the wrong correction for the second half." The other function of the halftime message is to motivate the team. Bill says that he changes his halftime approach frequently, adjusting to different situations and also to keep the team alert. He says he changes the tone of voice to get their attention. One thing he never changes, though, is his positive attitude. "Even if you aren't particularly pleased with the way things went in the first half and don't have a lot of confidence they'll get much better in the second half, you absolutely must not let the players see your pessimism. You have to convey a positive message to them." Build their confidence in themselves, by assuring them the changes you suggest will work, and in you, because you exude confidence.

"When a team loses, they feel dejected. Right after the game they are looking to their coach to provide encouragement. The thing that usually helps them most is for you to be able to tell them why they lost." If they believe that the coach knows why they lost, then they believe that he will know how to correct it. The players see in that correction a way of winning the next game against the team who just beat them, and that sometimes displaces the thoughts of losing with thoughts of winning. You hear the almost sarcastic "Wait 'til next year." from the fans of the losing team after a football loss. But while it may be sarcastic and said with bitterness, sometimes it eases the pain of defeat by replacing it with at least some other thought.

"You can be more stern in your corrective instruction after a game sometimes than you can at halftime, because you don't have to be as concerned about an immediate negative response. But in your harsh criticism you still have to remain positive. Otherwise you could lose the team's respect for the rest of the season," says Bill. "And whether it's in practice, during play in the game, at halftime, or in the locker room after the game, your communications must be well thought out, unambiguous, and always positive. Effective communication is an integral part of coaching."

LUTE OLSON

University of Arizona

- - - - - - - - - - - - - - - - -

Position
Head Men's Basketball Coach

Career Record
639-225 (28 seasons)

Education
B.A.   Augsburg (MN) College
M.A.   University of Minnesota-Duluth

Team and Personal Highlights

- ➢ 1997 NCAA National Champion.
- ➢ Three-time National Coach of the Year.
- ➢ Six-time Pacific-10 Conference Coach of the Year.
- ➢ Two-time Big 10 Conference Coach of the Year.
- ➢ Two-time Pacific Coast Athletic Conference Coach of the Year.
- ➢ Seven-time District Coach of the Year.
- ➢ Nine Pacific-10 Conference championships.
- ➢ 17 straight NCAA tournament appearances at Arizona.
- ➢ Taken two different teams to the Final Four.
- ➢ 18 All-American players

LUTE OLSON

Introduction . . .

Lute Olson is one of the most loved and respected college basketball coaches in the nation. With his perfectly-coifed silver mane, Arizona tan, and impeccably-tailored clothes, he has truly taken on the role and look of an ambassador for college basketball. And with the tragic passing of his adoring wife, Bobbi, in January 2001, Lute looked for strength from his basketball "family."

His Arizona Wildcats have rarely let the coach down. Three teams have advanced to the Final Four, with the 1996-97 Cats squad winning the national championship.   With 17 consecutive NCAA tournament appearances, Olson's teams have the longest current streak in college basketball.

Lute is one of 14 coaches in collegiate history to coach in four or more Final Fours. He is one of 11 coaches who have taken two different teams to the Final Four (Arizona and Iowa).   His 22 tournament appearances are second-most among active coaches, and his 33 NCAA tournament wins are third-most among active coaches.

His Arizona teams have won nine Pac-10 championships, and eight teams have appeared in the Sweet 16 of the NCAA tournament. He has averaged nearly 25 victories per year during his tenure in Tucson, plus his teams have won 94 percent of their home games since 1987. He has coached 18 All-Americans, and 37 All Pac-10 players. He has also won three National Coach of the Year honors.

Born on a farm just outside of Maryville, North Dakota, he attended high school in Grand Forks, North Dakota, and led his team to the 1952 state championship. An Augsburg (MN) College graduate, he coached in the prep ranks for five years in Minnesota and seven years in California before taking a job at Long Beach City College in 1971. He then moved on to Long Beach State for two years and to the University of Iowa for nine years before heading to Tucson in 1983. Lute has five grown children and 13 grandchildren.

Listen, now, to the wisdom of a true champion with Lute Olson's philosophies . . .

. . . on Motivation

Success breeds success, and Olson is quick to address the fact he feels fortunate that his teams have always been highly motivated.

"The players in our programs have always been highly motivated," he begins. "The credit must go to the players themselves and to my coaching staff. You recruit highly motivated young men, so you can see that my assistants have done a great job in that area over the years."

Lute defines motivation in terms of an inner drive that sparks a person to do his best.

"Motivation," he states, "involves a stimulus that is needed to obtain a maximum effort."

Coach Olson mentions that each player has his own reasons for being highly motivated.

"Some have high self-esteem and they love a challenge," he says. "Another's stimulus may be pride or ego or rising to the level of competitive spirit of their teammates.

"We have a good reputation with the players we recruit. Another stimulus may be a desire to be a part of our program. You just can't pinpoint one reason that blankets everyone."

Olson agrees with the other coaches in this book when he mentions the most effective method of motivating players.

"The only way you're going to keep athletes motivated consistently is by giving positive encouragement," he states with conviction. "We make sure that the environment around the program is open, comfortable, and very positive."

Least effective motivation techniques surround negative behavior, he says.

"A negative approach will get you negative results," Lute asserts. "Studies concerning motivation have consistently proven that a positive approach to a situation will get you positive results and a negative approach brings negative results.

"I believe that all successful organizations have a philosophy of being positive with the members of their group, so that has been my philosophy since I started coaching," he concludes.

In summary, Coach Olson states that motivation is a prime ingredient for success in every organization, and he feels fortunate that his athletes have always been highly motivated.

He defines motivation as a stimulus needed to obtain a maximum effort. That stimulus can vary, he believes, because athletes are different and they have their own reasons for self-motivation.

Finally, Olson mentions positive encouragement as the most effective method of motivation, and lists a negative approach as the least effective motivation method.

◆ ◆ ◆ ◆ ◆

. . . on Team Cohesion

One comment that follows Lute Olson teams wherever he has coached concerns team cohesion. The comments may vary, but the idea is universal. You hear the statement, "You know, Lute's teams are like a family." That type of statement is at the heart of the success of the Olson-coached teams.

"Yes, I've heard those kinds of comments over the years, and they're very flattering," he admits. "But you have to make sure that the people around you in your program feel the same way."

Olson quickly mentions the fact that he has surrounded himself with personable, sincere and competent assistant coaches and excellent support staff.

"You're only as good as the people around you," he says. "And we've had the kind of people who fit in perfectly for the kind of atmosphere we want to establish in our program."

Coach Olson defines team cohesion as the ability of a diverse group of individuals to work together to realize a common goal.

"If everyone believes in the same goals, then reaching those goals will be easier," he says. "If some individuals aren't sold on those goals, then problems arise."

Olson mentions that there are several effective methods of building team chemistry. Those methods include both team and individual meetings, but he says there's another element that brings the team together.

"We try to involve the players in the decision-making process," he states. "We want their input in a number of areas, but one area in particular."

That one particular area is recruiting.

"Even though the coaching staff is responsible for the recruiting process, we want each player to take an active part in helping select the players that will ultimately be in our program," he concludes.

A recruit on campus for his official visit will be scheduled for numerous activities and will be under observation by team members for much of that time. At the conclusion of the visit and after the recruit has departed, Arizona players are asked for feedback and recommendations as to the impression the recruit made upon them and if the players would want that person in the program.

"Again, the coaches make the ultimate decision," Olson states. "But the recommendations of the players are highly valued. Plus, they very rarely are incorrect in their impressions about the recruit. The thinking of the coaches and players are remarkably similar in most cases."

Coach Olson goes on to explain the importance of team and individual meetings with players.

"Our team meetings focus on team policy and many decisions are made during those meetings," he says.

Individual player meetings are a little different.

"During these sessions, we evaluate them and get them to understand their roles on the team. We discuss their strengths and also areas that need improvement" he states.

In summary, team cohesion is a trademark of Lute Olson teams. Coming to the University of Arizona to obtain a college degree and play basketball for Olson is like joining an extended family. The environment is energetic, comfortable, and conducive to the player's home atmosphere.

He defines team cohesion as the ability of a group to work together to realize a common goal. How closely the group meshes concerning meeting those goals dictates how cohesive the team will be, he says.

Effective methods of building team chemistry include team and individual meetings plus an active part in the decision-making process.

Team policy is made during team meetings and player evaluation is discussed during individual meetings, Lute states. Player involvement in decision-making also includes recommendations concerning the continued recruitment of an athlete into the Arizona basketball program.

Player impressions are sought after a campus visit, and the coaching staff utilizes this feedback to come to a consensus to either continue recruiting the athlete or stop the process at that point. Coach Olson comments that very rarely do the coaches and players differ on their evaluation of the recruit.

◆ ◆ ◆ ◆ ◆

. . . on Discipline

Discipline is a trait of the championship team and individual. Olson believes that discipline and decision-making are closely related.

"Involving the players in making team rules makes the entire process so much more effective and easy to enforce," he says.

Coach Olson's philosophy concerning team discipline involves a working arrangement with the upperclassmen in the program.

"I meet with the upperclassmen, especially seniors, and we discuss things that I believe are important for our success," he begins. "The upperclassmen then will meet with the team to set team rules."

Olson proudly discusses rules set by the team.

"The players will set tougher standards than the coaches," he asserts. "And the players will be more inclined to follow the rules if they are their rules."

Coach Olson mentions individual meetings and peer pressure as the most effective methods when handling discipline.

"Sitting down with the individual and discussing the problem is always best," he says. "Team pressure is also very effective in preventing discipline problems."

Lute lists any form of negative behavior on the part of the coaching staff as least effective in handling discipline cases within the team.

"Screaming, yelling or threatening a player just won't work, at least for us," he states.

In summary, Coach Olson once again believes that giving players an active role in decision-making improves team discipline.

He mentions meetings with upperclassmen to discuss team needs as the first step in setting team rules. The upperclassmen then take those ideas to the team, ideas are gathered from all the players, and team rules are established through this democratic process.

Olson is happy with this policy because the players set tougher standards than coaches, and players are more inclined to follow rules which they have established.

Finally, he lists individual meetings with players and peer pressure as the two most effective methods of handling discipline. He also mentions negative coaching behavior (screaming, yelling, threatening) as least effective methods of disciplining athletes.

◆ ◆ ◆ ◆ ◆

. . . on Mental Preparation

All successful coaches mention mental preparation as essential to team and individual success. Coach Olson has long been a proponent of the mental aspect of the game, and has actively incorporated mental training into his program.

"In order to keep an edge on our opponents, the only edge is really the mental edge," he states. "Division I athletes are very similar physically and athletically. We believe that if they are mentally more alert than the opponent, then we have a better chance of winning."

He has utilized outside sport psychology consultants in addition to university professors versed in sport psychology techniques.

"We've had people come in to teach the players relaxation and visualization skills," he says. "We also have the players learn concentration techniques to help them during free throw situations."

Olson defines mental preparation as "being prepared to give your best effort." He says there are different ways to prepare for a long season.

"During pre-season, we want the players to have fun, so we will change our practice routines and also change drills, just to keep the players mentally fresh," he states. "It's also good to keep teams evenly balanced talent-wise during practice so that the competition stays healthy."

Non-conference games are utilized as a means to an end.

"We understand the importance of all non-conference games, especially with our competitive schedule," he says. "But we also are striving for later goals . . . to win our league and advance to the NCAA tournament."

Mental preparation for conference games is not a problem, Olson asserts.

"Conference games need no big push from the coaches," he says. "The players understand that this is the most important time of the season for us."

Late-game strategy, he says, is a matter of practice organization and execution.

"We work on late-game situations in practice on a regular basis," he contends. "We want the players to gain confidence from the repetition and fully understand what they are going to do when that pressure situation arises late in a game."

In summary, Coach Olson strongly believes in the benefits surrounding mental preparation, and has incorporated mental training on a consistent basis within his programs.

He utilizes outside sport psychology consultants or university professors to teach mental training techniques. The skills taught include relaxation, visualization and concentration.

Lute defines mental preparation as being prepared to give your best effort. He uses various methods to mentally prepare his teams for the season, he says.

Pre-season practices are meant to be fun for the players. He often changes practice routines and drills so that the players do not become bored. He also stresses the importance of keeping teams balanced talent-wise during practice so that maximum effort and healthy competition exists.

Non-conference games are viewed as important stepping stones to league and NCAA tournament play. This is a time to learn and improve, both mentally and physically, he says.

The focal point of the season remains on conference games, Lute asserts. He also mentions that mental preparation for conference games becomes easier to implement because of the importance of league games.

Finally, he states that late-game strategy is simply a matter of practice organization and execution. Late-game situations are practiced regularly so that the players understand what they are supposed to do and establish the confidence needed to successfully execute the strategy during games.

◆ ◆ ◆ ◆ ◆

. . . on Mental Toughness

Olson agrees with the theory that mental toughness is not an inherent human characteristic, but rather a personality trait that can be acquired. He is also in agreement with the theory that all great competitors possess mental toughness to some degree.

"To me, mental toughness means having the ability to stay focused on your goals during difficult situations," he states.

Those difficult situations can be off the court as well as on the court, he says.

"You need to be mentally tough to prepare for semester finals or go through a job search," Olson contends. "So being mentally tough can help you in all aspects of your life."

Coach Olson lists four characteristics of mental toughness.

"There are probably a lot more than four," he states. "But these four seem to stick out with me."

"First, a mentally tough person is dedicated. It takes a tremendous amount of time to be a successful Division I athlete. I'm very pleased to see the NCAA taking action to shorten the basketball season.

"As a matter of fact, I've been pushing the idea of making basketball a strictly second semester sport. Begin practice on December 1 and begin play on January 1. That would give athletes the complete first semester to attend to their academics and not worry about athletics.

"There are not very many people who agree with me right now on that. But that is the way the NCAA President's Commission seems to be going, and I'm all for it," he says.

Determination is the next characteristic of a mentally tough person, Lute asserts.

"The mentally tough person is very determined. The-nose-to-the-grindstone kind of thing. The person who keeps bouncing back from adversity."

Self-confidence and a good work ethic are the final two characteristics of a mentally tough person, he says.

"The mentally tough person is very self-confident. I don't mean cocky or a braggart. But a person who quietly goes along trying to do the right things.

"Finally, the mentally tough individual has a great work ethic," he states. "You know that he will be doing everything that's asked of him, plus a little bit more.

"Many of my teams have been called 'overachiever,'" Olson recalls. "I think that's one of the nicest compliments anyone can receive."

In summary, Olson believes that mental toughness is a trait that can be developed by the athlete. He defines mental toughness as the ability to stay focused on goals in difficult situations.

He alludes to the fact that mental toughness is a life skill, one that will help any person in any career in life.

Finally, Coach Olson considers dedication, determination, self-confidence and a great work ethic to be the traits of the mentally tough person.

. . . on Communication

Olson seems to be blessed with the complete package: good health, excellent physical condition, good looks, sharp mind, great family and winning tradition. The key element in keeping it all together, he says, is the ability to communicate your thoughts clearly to those around you.

Critical situations demand appropriate communication and two critical parts of a game occur at halftime and again at the end of the game.

"At halftime, we don't get into pep talks," he notes. "Halftime is a time to reflect on the successes and weaknesses of the first half and make the needed technical adjustments.

"We also give the players much positive reinforcement. If we're behind, we want to make sure they understand that we can still win the game. If the players keep hustling, we tell them that things will turn our way," he relates.

A tough loss calls for just the right words," he relates.

"Try never to criticize after a loss," he says. "Following a loss, the players' confidence level is down. Encouragement is needed at that time. The exception would be if there has been a lack of effort."

In summary, Coach Olson believes that communication skills are very important in building and maintaining successful teams.

At halftime, his talks focus on positive encouragement and technical adjustments. Post-game talks following a difficult loss are handled very gently. He makes it a point to keep comments positive and criticism mute during this delicate time period.

◆ ◆ ◆ ◆ ◆

PAT PECORA
University of Pittsburgh-Johnstown

Position
Head Wrestling Coach

Career Record
317-92-3 (25 seasons)

Education
B.A.   West Liberty State College

Team and Personal Highlights

- ➤ Two-time NCAA Division II national champions.
- ➤ 15 NCAA Regional championships.
- ➤ Three-time National Coach of the Year.
- ➤ 10-time NCAA Regional Coach of the Year.
- ➤ President, National Wrestling Coaches Association.
- ➤ 83 All-Americans.
- ➤ Five individual NCAA national champions.
- ➤ 45 All-Academic Wrestling Team members.
- ➤ Enshrined in four different Halls of Fame

PAT PECORA

Introduction . . .

Pat Pecora is a coaching legend in the state of Pennsylvania and nationally. In the 25 years since taking the helm of the University of Pittsburgh-Johnstown wrestling program, his teams have captured 15 NCAA Regional Championships, including four straight from 1987 through 1990, and ten in a row from 1992 through 2001.

Pecora has been selected 10 times as the NCAA Regional Coach of the Year. His Mountain Cat squads have finished in the Top 20 in the nation 18 times, and have combined to win 45 team tournaments and 317 dual meets. Pat has tutored 83 All-Americans and five individual national champions. Academically, his teams led the nation in the National Wrestling Coaches Association All-Academic Wrestling Team selections from 1997 through 2000. Since its inception in 1990, Pecora has coached 45 NWCA All-Academic Wrestling Team members.

In 1996 and 1999, his teams captured the NCAA Division II National Championship, the first and second in school history. Pat is a two-time National Coach of the Year award winner, and in 1999, he received the NWCA Coaching Excellence Award, given to the best coach in all divisions. He earned his 300th career dual-meet victory in January 2000.

Pat served two terms as president of the National Wrestling Coaches Association. He has also been inducted into four Halls of Fame: Pennsylvania Sports Hall of Fame-East Boro Chapter, Cambria County Hall of Fame, West Liberty College Hall of Fame, and the Pennsylvania Wrestling Coaches Hall of Fame. Pat and his wife, Tracy, have four children.

Pat was honored to have the opportunity to present his championship view . . .

. . . on Motivation

Pat Pecora adds a different twist to the definition of motivation, "discovery." If an athlete doesn't recognize that he is motivated, he probably isn't. So awareness of motivation is essential. According to Pat, "Motivation is the ability to discover power in all areas of performance: mental, physical, and emotional."

He lists, as one of the most effective means of motivating his wrestlers, one-on-one talks about achieving success, "on the mats, in the classroom, and in your personal life. You must convince them that they are capable of achieving success," Pat says. Confidence is a big part of the battle. You must believe you can succeed before you can succeed. In his one-on-one talks, Pat tells his athletes, "Success comes from hard work, strong character, and sound moral principles." He believes that defining goals is essential in order to reach your ultimate potential.

Another essential to motivation of athletes is recognition of achievement. Pat displays prominently in the wrestling room the names of All-Americans, Academic All-Americans, and National Champions from Pittsburgh-Johnstown. Seeing these displays lets current wrestlers know that they will not only achieve success for the present but their success will be there to motivate wrestlers who come behind them. Pat promotes his team in the media, first on campus and then within the community, as a means of recognizing achievement. He puts his team before their fellow students and the public by prominently displaying team posters and effectively distributing media guides. Finally, at the end of the season, the team has a recognition banquet for the team, fans, and parents.

"The head coach must be a leader in displaying his own motivation in order to motivate others," Pat says. "You must live the life you preach. Put your effort into running a first class program on and off the mat. Stay in shape physically and keep abreast of the continually changing attitudes on the mental aspects of team motivation by reading and interacting with others who are motivating and positive You must lead by example. No team will become motivated and remain motivated until their leader is motivated first. And coaches and team leaders must always stay positive."

And what impedes motivation? Pat cites two problem areas: "You must convince athletes that there is no secret to success that is kept from them—make sure a wrestler doesn't feel that success is only for those who are blessed at birth with physical attributes, not attainable through hard work. And you must never let a negative environment develop around your team. Avoiding a negative environment starts with the head coach and continues through the assistants and the team leaders."

Pat emphasizes the importance of starting out right and continuing to the end. "Create an overall motivating positive environment in your program the moment a student-athlete meets you 'till the day he graduates— one that will stay with him the rest of his life"

. . . on Team Cohesion

Pat defines team chemistry as "growing from a team to a family— when each member (regardless of his ability, background, or role on the team) binds together with all of the other team members to pursue a common goal."

He says, "Team chemistry is built one block at a time. It starts with the coach, demonstrating his philosophy that the individual is not more important than the team and showing how that makes the team stronger. But a coach must treat each athlete the way he would want his son treated. It's important to get across to each individual wrestler that the surest way to become a champion is to help someone else become one." If you're all on the same team, no one can become a team champion unless the whole team becomes one—they're bound together. "So," says Pat, "helping and pushing each other to accomplish their goals is the most effective way to achieve your own goals."

Pat recounts a moving and meaningful story told by one of his athletes at a recognition banquet: "He said that if he was hanging off a cliff by a rope and had to pick one person to hold the other end of the rope, he'd pick me. Why me? He told the audience, 'He'd let the rope burn through his fingers before he'd let go.' Of course I was deeply moved by his confidence and admiration. Ever since then, I tell that story to the team and I ask them, 'Who do you want holding your rope?' I encourage each team member to try to be the one picked as the 'rope holder' by each other team member. If they can work to be that person, they're working to build that feeling of family and team chemistry, and it will surely develop."

Pat finishes his ideas about chemistry with a statement from his grandmother: "She always said that your hand is like a family. She would hold up her hand with the fingers spread and say, 'Each finger is different, but it belongs to the same hand as the others.' And then she'd bring all the fingers together to make a fist and give you a loving punch."

◆　◆　◆　◆　◆

. . . on Discipline

Pat talks more about how you attain good discipline than he does about defining it. He says you have to lay out your expectations and boundaries early. "In the very first meeting with the team each year, tell them what you expect from them and how you expect them to act. Talk about the type of students you expect them to be, the type of athletes you expect, and the type of person you want representing the University of Pittsburgh at Johnstown. We want every wrestler to set as his goal being an All-American or winning a national title. But we want to achieve our goals with class and dignity. And we get across right away, if they don't already know it, that these lofty goals can be attained only through hard work." Pat says that developing the proper characteristics in the younger wrestlers pays off in that when they become upperclassmen, they are role models for the next group of freshmen.

He cites some typical quotations to illustrate how he thinks a coach can encourage and reward his athletes, always looking for something good to acknowledge, even if he has to correct mistakes. The examples: "I love when you run back to the middle of the circle." "I saw you getting in an extra workout. That'll pay off for you someday." "You never quit. That's why you won the match." "Great GPA last quarter." "That was really thoughtful of you to help out that fellow. Believe me, people will notice those things." He says, "I truly believe that clearly establishing the person you want your athletes to be and recognizing them for being that person leads to positive results. You must always remember to be fair and consistent.

"In taking corrective action, never embarrass an athlete in front of peers or fans." No matter how frustrated you may get with an athlete, never let your frustration overcome your good judgment in dealing with people. "And if a coach administers extra physical activity as punishment, that only confuses an athlete. Physical training should be a positive thing, not punishment. Use of physical activity as punishment is the least effective discipline a coach can administer."

◆　◆　◆　◆　◆

. . . on Mental Preparation

Wrestling demands continuous physical concentration, so Pat says that physical and mental preparedness go hand-in-hand in wrestling. According to Pat, "A mentally prepared athlete believes he has done everything possible to prepare himself for the competition. He's ready to challenge himself to see how good he can be.

"Build your own machine. I believe that you must be the best that you can be by concentrating on your system and philosophy." Organization is implicit in this statement. Pat says. "In getting across to your team that they are better prepared physically, they automatically become better prepared mentally." This builds confidence, which can actually strengthen an athlete physically. He can dig down and get that extra strength because he believes he has it.

Goals are paramount in mental preparation. You must know what you're preparing for, whether it's physical preparation or mental preparation. Pat: "Be determined to be a little better when you leave the practice room each day. Define your immediate goals—even in practice. For example, be in the top five in the run today; have a goal of a specific number of take-downs; have a goal of not giving up a take-down."

The coach must make practice as interesting as possible. Do this by adding variety when appropriate. "My suggestions for varying practice: Change conditioning and running drills without losing any benefit from them. Change the length of periods you wrestle." But he says that athletes must recognize that sometimes getting the job done most effectively won't always be fun. It can be downright boring. And team members must always keep the purpose of the repetitive parts of practice in mind. That's where the mental and physical meet.

Ideally, Pat likes to prepare his team for the season and the goal of winning the national championship by scheduling difficult matches and scheduling matches at the site of the national championships. This takes the mystery out of the championship. "But," he says, "you can't always arrange to meet the teams you'd like to meet or arrange for meets at the national championship venue. It's great to meet the teams you'll meet at nationals during the season, so you'll know what to expect from them. But, when we can't, I tell my team that there's an advantage there, too; they won't know what to expect from us, if they haven't met us."

Pat says that a coach must believe in himself in order to get his team to believe in him. "They have to believe in you; and more important, they have to believe in themselves. Confidence in each other and in the system you have taught them to trust is essential. Believing can bring a team back from overwhelming odds." And believing is a part of mental preparation.

◆ ◆ ◆ ◆ ◆

. . . on Mental Toughness

Pat's definition of mental toughness is concise, but it conveys a strong message: "Mental toughness is the ability not to break or quit in the most difficult situation." There is no need to elaborate on his definition. It says it all.

He cites several characteristics of mentally tough wrestlers: "Mentally tough wrestlers have a never-give-up attitude. I love a wrestler—or any athlete for that matter—who never quits, who never gives up on himself, his coach, or his team. A mentally tough wrestler is always a hustler—always runs back to the middle of the circle.

"He's 'in-your-face'. You don't have to look for the mentally tough wrestler. He'll let you know he's there. He's in-your-face." Pat goes on to ascribe other attributes to the mentally tough athlete. "He competes through minor injuries. I wouldn't risk an athlete's health by having him compete with an injury where aggravation could cause serious or permanent disability, but it's safe to compete with some injuries (even painful ones), and our trainers know the difference. The mentally tough wrestler gets tougher under tougher circumstances." This is a variation of Richard Nixon's admonition to his staff: "When the going gets tough, the tough get going." He attributed that to his athletic training in college.

Pat wants his athletes to be just as tough mentally off the mat—in their everyday lives—as they are on the mat: "A mentally tough person does not sacrifice his integrity for an easy way out. He trains by a code and he lives by a code."

Just as Pat began with a concise definition of mental toughness, he concludes with an assessment of mental toughness in wrestling: "The sport of wrestling is loaded with mentally tough athletes."

. . . on Communication

This book is about the psychology of team building and competitive excellence. In elaborating on these subjects, we sometimes tend to separate them, although we know the concept of the book is that they are inseparable. Pat doesn't have the problem of tending to separate them. Just as he said that physical and mental preparedness go hand-in-hand, he extends the concept even to communications: "In communicating, I have to go by what I feel. And most of the time I combine my belief in the team—and their belief in me—with something physical, technical, or strategic. I try to relate something they do physically to their spirit. It takes both to assure victory."

What does he say to his team after a tough loss? "Most of the time," Pat says, "I don't address the team immediately after a tough loss or a poor performance." What a coach says to his team after a loss is extremely important. It can impact the way they view the loss until the next practice or even longer. Saying the right thing can do much to ease the pain of defeat, but saying the wrong thing can do serious damage to the team's morale and chemistry. Pat thinks the potential for harm on the downside can be greater than the potential for good on the up side. So he wants to make sure he handles it right. "I usually wait till the next day so I can put things into proper perspective and also set up the next game plan—to provide a look to the future in helping to minimize bad thoughts about the past. After all, I'm emotional too, and you are more likely to make good decisions when you can set aside emotions. And team emotions are running high after a loss. Sometimes it's best to let each wrestler sort things out for himself. They are different human beings, and a talk that may be helpful to one could be detrimental to another's attempt to deal with the emotional pain."

But when it's an individual loss, Pat looks at it differently: "I talk to athletes individually immediately after an individual loss, because they may feel alone. I assure them that I believe in them and try to help them put the loss in the proper perspective. We don't like to lose, but one loss is just that—one loss. It isn't the end of the world, or even the end of the season." Pat doesn't let the physical and mental aspects of communications get separated, and it's obvious why he doesn't. They shouldn't be.

RON POLK
Mississippi State University

- - - - - - - - - - - - - - - -

Position
Head Baseball Coach

Career Record
1,122-534 (28 seasons)

Education
B.S.   Grand Canyon (AZ) College
M.A.   University of Arizona

Team and Personal Highlights

- ➤ Five Southeastern Conference championships.

- ➤ 18 NCAA tournament appearances.

- ➤ Seven College World Series berths.

- ➤ 28 All-Americans.

- ➤ 65 All-SEC players.

- ➤ Two-time National Coach of the Year.

- ➤ 122 players have signed professional baseball contracts.

- ➤ Enshrined in four Halls of Fame.

RON POLK

Introduction . . .

People say you can't come home again once you leave. But don't tell that to Ron Polk. Just four years ago, he retired as head baseball coach at Mississippi State, became the main fundraiser to revitalize Dudy Noble Field in Starkville, got the coaching bug again and went to the University of Georgia for two years, then realized that what he really wanted to do was just come back home. So on June 19, 2001, Ron was again named head baseball coach for the Bulldogs.

Perhaps no figure in all of college baseball is more respected than Polk, who became the winningest coach in Southeastern Conference history during a remarkable 22-year run as Mississippi State head baseball coach from 1976 to 1997. During that time span, he led the Bulldogs to SEC regular season or tournament championships five times, and secured MSU's baseball place on the national map with 15 NCAA regional tournament berths and five appearances in the prestigious College World Series.

In 28 years as a collegiate coach, Polk is one of only two head coaches in the history of college baseball to guide three different teams to the College World Series. His 1973 Georgia Southern team advanced to Omaha after winning the District 3 championship at Dudy Noble Field. After being named the head coach at Mississippi State in the fall of 1975, he proceeded to take three Bulldog teams to the CWS. Finally, in his second and final year at Georgia, he once again led the team to college baseball's hallowed ground in 2001.

A two-time National Coach of the Year award winner, Ron has also been inducted into the American Baseball Coaches Hall of Fame, the Mississippi and the Mississippi State University Sports Halls of Fame, and the Georgia Southern Hall of Fame. He also spearheaded a conference-wide drive that has seen new stadiums built and significant other improvements made to the baseball complexes at every SEC school.

Still a confirmed bachelor, the Boston, Massachusetts, native is the author of **The Baseball Playbook**, the nation's leading college textbook for baseball. Dudy Noble Field was officially renamed Dudy Noble Field, Polk-DeMent Stadium in April, 1998, in honor of Polk and long-time baseball booster, Gordon DeMent.

Let's listen to Ron Polk's intriguing thoughts . . .

. . . on Motivation

Coach Polk believes that outside influences have an effect on the motivation of today's athletes, but he also thinks that each person is responsible for self-motivation.

"Motivation to me is the will to do the very best one can do within the restrictions of one's mental and physical capabilities," he says.

"Motivation should also be a self-made trait," he continues. "But at the same time, outside influences like the crowd, aspirations to play pro baseball and peer influence, can play a big part in a young man's motivation to succeed both on and off the athletic field."

Through his coaching experience, Polk has found what works and what doesn't work in the motivation techniques he has observed over the years.

"The least effective techniques are embarrassing a player in front of his peers or in the press or on radio or television," he says. "Another is establishing unrealistic goals by the coach."

Coach Polk lists several techniques that he has found to be highly effective in motivating his student-athletes.

"First, you have to treat each player with love and kindness," he states, "But you must also set rules for discipline.

"You need to provide a positive program for him to develop his skills, and you need to organize his practice plan so that he sees progress within each practice session.

"It's also motivating to surround him with quality people, both in the coaching staff and teammates," he says.

Fan support, bringing in outside speakers, and personal evaluation periods are additional motivational techniques.

"Build a program around fan support, the radio network, and television," he says.

"I also like bringing in former players to speak with him and the team about what athletics has done for them both on and off the athletic field.

"I enjoy visiting with each player two times a year for 45-60 minutes, evaluating his performance both in the classroom and on the baseball field," he says. "We also have his teammates as well as the coaching staff evaluate his performance."

Finally, Coach Polk motivates his players by discussing the player's future in baseball.

"We try to establish the fact that outstanding skill development might lead to a pro baseball future," he states.

In summary, Polk defines motivation as the ability of a person to utilize his mental and physical capabilities to the utmost degree. He also believes that outside influences can have a motivating effect on a person.

Polk lists two methods as being ineffective when motivating athletes. Those methods include public embarrassment of the player in front of his peers or the media, and establishing unrealistic goals for the player.

Effective motivation techniques include treating each player with love and kindness, providing a positive program in which the athlete can develop his skills, and organizing practices so that the player can see consistent improvement.

He lists additional effective motivation techniques, such as bringing in former players to discuss the positive effects of athletics and academics at Mississippi State, utilizing personal evaluation meetings with each player twice a year, providing each athlete with evaluation data from other coaches and teammates, and surrounding each player with quality teammates and coaches.

Finally, Coach Polk believes that building a program through fan support and media coverage can be highly motivating for his players, as can be discussing with each player the possibility of a future professional baseball career.

◆   ◆   ◆   ◆   ◆

. . . on Team Cohesion

Team cohesion is a vital ingredient for ultimate team success, but Coach Polk believes that team chemistry is most beneficial when a team is having problems on the field.

"Good cohesion and good chemistry plays a significant role when a team is struggling on the field," he says. "But talent is still the primary ingredient in team success."

Ron defines team cohesion as the ability of each player to accept each team member as an important part of the team.

"I define team cohesion and team chemistry as the degree of acceptance each team member has for the entire team, regardless of personality differences," he says. "Cohesion and chemistry might also assist a team to reach certain positive goals."

Polk mentions that his techniques for building team cohesion are similar to those he uses to motivate his players.

"I believe that team meetings where positive comments are the rule helps build team chemistry," he says. "I also think that most players living together in a dormitory setting can build team cohesion."

The most important element, however, is the understanding each player has concerning his role on the team.

"Making sure each player understands his role on the baseball team at every opportunity has been very helpful in building team chemistry on our clubs," Polk says.

In summary, Coach Polk defines team cohesion as the degree of acceptance each team member has for the entire team, regardless of personality conflicts. He also believes that team cohesion is most effective when teams are struggling on the field.

Effective methods for building team cohesion include activities in which all players are participants, he says. He lists team meetings, living together in a dormitory, and each player understanding his role on the team as the best methods of building team chemistry in the Bulldog program.

. . . on Discipline

Coach Polk has established himself as a no-nonsense type of person, and his philosophy concerning discipline reflects that attitude.

"Team discipline is very important on any team," he says. "Rules and regulations must not only be talked about, but each player needs to receive a copy of the rules at the first team meeting of the year."

Ron reinforces the discussion of his discipline philosophy with illustrations of some Bulldog baseball rules.

"We follow a strict time schedule for both practices and games," he states. "We have a dress code on the road.

"We believe class attendance reflects individual and team discipline. We also believe that maintaining a clean locker room both at home and on the road reflects team discipline.

"We have a strict curfew on road trips. We think the manner in which the players come on the field at both practices and games is discipline-related.

"Finally, the manner in which the players handle themselves with the press and fans says a lot about self-discipline," he concludes.

Coach Polk believes that effective discipline is a result of team participation in the rules-making process.

"Most effective for us has been discipline that is fair due to the fact that team rules have been set," he say. "We encourage each player to discuss any team rules that might not be in the best interest of the entire team."

Least effective discipline methods would include arbitrary and vindictive kinds of rules enforcement.

"Any discipline that is spotty and only reinforced when a team is struggling just won't work," he says.

Showing favoritism in the enforcement of team rules can also cause problems.

"Violation of any team rule will be dealt with immediately and without any concern in regard to the value of the player to team success," Polk says.

In summary, team discipline is very important in Coach Polk's program. He believes that team rules should be set by team members and that each player should receive a written copy of the rules at the first team meeting of the year.

He illustrates his philosophy on team discipline by listing several rules of the Bulldog baseball program.

Finally, he believes that effective discipline methods include fair treatment and immediate enforcement of team rules, while ineffective discipline methods include arbitrary rules enforcement and showing favoritism in the enforcement process.

. . . on Mental Preparation

All successful coaches say that mental preparation is an important element for team and individual success. Coach Polk agrees with that statement, but states that mental preparation holds many definitions.

Mental preparation means different things to different people," he says. "At Mississippi State, we want each player to be relaxed at all times, but also play aggressively."

Polk believes that practice and repetition assist the athlete in more ways than one.

"Skill development and repetitive training in practices help the player develop a baseball instinct," he states, "The better a player's skill level, the more positive he feels about himself as a player. Good results breed confidence and poor results breed lack of self-esteem and confidence."

Mental preparation also means keeping a balanced mental approach to each game.

"We do not want our players to get too high when things are going good for him or the team," he points out. "We also do not want him too low when things are going bad for him or the team."

Polk claims that mental preparation is an individual responsibility, but that the atmosphere surrounding the Bulldog program makes it easier for the players to prepare.

"Each player must find his own manner to prepare for each game or series," he says. "Here at M.S.U., we have led the nation in average daily attendance the last couple of years. We do not have a difficult time getting our players to play hard since they have many people rooting for them. This is also the case for non-conference games."

Late-game strategy is practiced daily, but it still is important for the players to be relaxed when a crucial situation arises during a game.

"We never build up one game or one series that we must play harder," he states. "Baseball is a sport that one must be relaxed playing. When one presses, the skill level generally drops."

In summary, mental preparation is important for team and individual success. Coach Polk defines mental preparation as being relaxed, but playing aggressively at all times.

He believes that skill development and repetition training in practices assist the player in gaining confidence and self-esteem. This confidence and self-esteem is essential for mental preparation and correct execution, he says.

Finally, Polk wants his players to keep a balanced mental attitude for each game, not getting too high nor too low depending upon the situation. He stresses the importance of playing relaxed and not pressing when crucial situations arise during games.

. . . on Mental Toughness

Mental toughness is a trait found in the highly-successful athlete. Coach Polk believes that mental toughness is an ongoing test for a player.

"Mental toughness to me means that a player must be able to withstand prosperity and despair each time his skill level is tested," he says. "That might be pitch by pitch, game by game, or season by season."

Polk thinks that there are several characteristics of a mentally tough individual.

"Mentally tough players get after it at all times," he states. "They always play with enthusiasm and aggressiveness."

Coach Polk also believes that mentally tough players avoid any kind of slumps.

"They are not generally slump-prone due to the fact that they understand their limitations," he says.

Consistency and being a positive role model are the final two characteristics of mental toughness.

"The mentally tough players are consistent in the way they handle themselves at all times, on and off the field," he says. "They also pick up other members of the team by the way they go about their business on a daily basis."

In summary, Coach Polk believes that mental toughness is the ability of a player to react in a positive way when his skill level is tested. This test can occur pitch by pitch, game by game, or season by season.

Finally, he lists several characteristics of a mentally tough person. These traits include being enthusiastic and aggressive, not being slump-prone, being a good role model for other teammates, and being consistent in their behavior at all times, on and off the field.

◆   ◆   ◆   ◆   ◆

. . . on Communication

Coach Polk will never be accused of a lack of communication. He prides himself in the fact that he keeps the lines of communication open at all times, with his players, with his correspondence, and even with opposing players.

"I have a policy that before I leave each night, every letter is answered and every phone call returned," he says. "If somebody says I didn't return a phone call, then I never got the message."

His open-door policy with players is very important in keeping communication lines open.

"My players know that I hate wasted time during the day," he says. "But they also know they can come in at any time and discuss anything with me. That's important to me and always will be."

He also keeps in touch not only with former players, but some opposing players. He personally types each letter.

"I'll write Dale Murphy, because I've known him for years. And I'll write Roger Clemens, who we played against when he was at Texas. Sure, those guys get thousands of letters, but it's important to let them know that you care how they're doing.

"And I think it's especially important to keep in touch with kids in the minor leagues. It might be one of my former players or a guy who used to play at Alabama. I get *Baseball America* and *The Sporting News*. If I see where a kid went 3-for-4, I'll drop him a note and tell him 'Congratulations. Hang in there.' Why not? It only takes a minute. I know what they're going through."

Polk believes that once a game begins, the motivation of the players must be the primary source of inspiration, and not a speech from the coach.

"Baseball is not a 'locker talk' type of sport," he says. "Football, basketball, wrestling or those sports where one must maintain physical strength and endurance are dealt with by motivation techniques."

Post-game comments are always positive in nature, he asserts, unless the effort level of the players was not very good.

"We always find good things to say about a loss unless one player or others might not have played hard to achieve team success," he states. "We try to give them confidence in themselves and in the team by asking them not to do anything they are not capable of doing. Performance is reflected by practice preparation and instincts."

In summary, communication skills are very important in Coach Polk's program at Mississippi State University. He enjoys communicating with his players, former players, and opposing players.

He strictly adheres to a personal policy of answering every letter and returning every phone call on a daily basis. He personally types each letter that leaves his office.

He believes that motivational speeches are not appropriate or effective once a game has begun. He says it is the responsibility of the players to keep self-motivated during games.

Finally, Coach Polk keeps all post-game comments positive in nature. The exception to that rule would be evidence of a lack of effort on the part of one or more players. His post-game comments are meant to build confidence in the players, and he believes that player performance is reflected by practice preparation and instincts.

RHONDA REVELLE
University of Nebraska-Lincoln

- - - - - - - - - - - - - - - -

Position
Head Softball Coach

Career Record
343-192 (9 seasons)

Education
B.A.   University of Nebraska-Lincoln
M.A.   San Jose State University

Team and Personal Highlights

- ➤ Three Big-12 Conference regular season and tournament championships.
- ➤ 12 NCAA tournament appearances.
- ➤ Four consecutive NCAA "Sweet 16" appearances.
- ➤ 12 All-Americans.
- ➤ 41 All-Conference players.
- ➤ Two College World Series berths.
- ➤ Four Academic All-Americans.
- ➤ 27 Academic All-Conference performers.
- ➤ Three-time Coach of the Year.
- ➤ Hall of Fame inductee.

RHONDA REVELLE

Introduction . . .

Rhonda Revelle is the consummate scholar-coach. She is comfortable teaching in a classroom setting or on the softball diamond. She enjoys talking about philosophies and how to implement them for optimal effectiveness. This kind of solid preparation has made her Husker softball teams one of the best in the nation.

A former Husker pitcher from 1981 to 1983, she has led her teams to three conference championships, advanced to the NCAA Tournament every year, including four consecutive "Sweet 16" appearances, and broken nearly every school record along the way, including most wins over any five-year period.

A three-time Coach of the Year award winner, Rhonda's student-athletes have consistently earned national and conference awards for athletic and academic excellence. During the past eight years, 12 Huskers have won All-America awards, including nine first- or second-team members and 41 All-Conference players, including 25 first-teamers. Revelle also placed a school-record four Huskers on the 2000 Academic All-Big 12 first team and a school-record six student-athletes on the 1999 Academic All-Big 12 first team. In the past eight years, 27 of her players have earned first-team academic all-conference awards for their dedication in the classroom. In addition, Revelle has seen four of her student-athletes earn GTE Academic All-American honors.

The Eugene, Oregon, native has had coaching stops at San Jose State and California State University-Hayward. She was also the head coach at Nebraska Wesleyan University, guiding the Plainswomen to back-to-back conference championships. For her efforts in coaching, playing and promoting softball in the state of Nebraska, she was inducted into the Nebraska Softball Hall of Fame in 1997.

The highly articulate and charismatic coach meticulously outlined her success strategies . . .

. . . on Motivation

According to Rhonda Revelle, "Motivation is a trait that everyone possesses. For some, the motivation in life (or a sport) is like a high performing engine at full throttle. Others have the same engine, but it's idling or not running. The challenge in coaching is to get each player's motivational engine revved up and rolling."

"The first step in motivating a team is two-fold: bringing in recruits who have a strong desire to excel, and personally caring for the individuals who form the TEAM. If I expect a group to come together, work toward a common goal, accept and embrace roles, and sacrifice a great deal of individuality, then I'd better be committed to those individuals. I need to care about each of them sincerely and show it. And I need to take the time to get to know them personally—not just as athletes. I need to know their dreams for the future, their experiences from the past, and as much in between as they are willing to divulge."

Rhonda points out the importance of trust in motivation. "I have found that people are more motivated by something/someone they trust. They are more apt to pursue a goal actively, if they believe in the system or in the people leading them. One of the best ways I've found to build mutual trust between team members and me is by holding bi-monthly, one-on-one meetings. Once academics has been addressed in the 30-minute meetings, the remaining time is an open forum. Over the years, my softballers have discussed many personal, sensitive, and vulnerable topics. Cleansing tears abound as well as those wrapped in painful memories. Among freshmen, I see apprehensive faces, similar to those on schoolgirls being summoned to the principal's office. As seniors most players have come to enjoy those chats—as do I—so much that they miss them when they graduate."

"Some of the things I believe have made these meetings meaningful in building trust and motivation are very simple practices. First, I turn the ringer off the phone and close the door, because I want the individual to KNOW that she is the priority for this time. Second, I ask thoughtful questions that require thoughtful answers—not just small talk. Third, I listen with my entire being. I look them in the eye, sometimes I lean forward in my chair, and when appropriate, I make some sort of physical contact with the person—as you would with anyone you feel close to. Finally, I concentrate on observing their body language and 'unspoken words,' not only with my eyes, but with my heart as well. Without question, these meetings are essential to our team building process."

How does Rhonda move from individual motivation to team motivation? Rhonda: "The philosophy of an organization is embodied in the organization's deep rooted traditions. Our most-echoed team philosophy is, 'There is no individual more important than the TEAM, when we are on team time.' The team stands firmly on that philosophy, and when it's challenged, they defend it and restore team equilibrium. How do we reach that pinnacle? We do it by empowering our team members—by involving them in establishing TEAM goals, policies, and procedures. We want them to feel as much a sense of ownership as possible, because the more they are invested, the stronger is their motivation to serve and improve the group. When they have direct input into setting standards, they usually set higher standards than the coaching staff, alone, might set. They have fewer complaints, and morale is better. And they see, first hand, the importance of team cohesion. As participants in setting standards, they immediately understand that to reach team goals, they have to find a way to make sure 'all the people in the boat are rowing' and 'all the oars in the water are moving in the same direction'."

But if the team members are allowed to be major decision makers, what happens when they make a decision that runs countercurrent to the coaches' ideas? "Obviously the coaches' wisdom, experience and authority determine the areas where team members can make decisions maturely. We are involved from the time of our first team meeting. But even at that meeting, I ask for input, such as the team's feeling about alcohol and tobacco use, class attendance, and tardiness at team events. On some of these things they must eventually come to the coach's way of thinking—such as underage drinking: it's not an option; it's against the law—but if they can come to the coach's way of thinking without having it rammed down their throats, then those ideas will stick with them more solidly."

Rhonda says, "Success is a magical motivator. Success builds confidence. Success and confidence are synergistic. A coach can motivate by creating an environment that allows failure. Making mistakes provides a great learning opportunity, if players aren't afraid to make mistakes. Correcting mistakes is how players perfect their skills. Coaches can also organize practice to make use of the powerful tool of repetition. Knowing that the coach works to perfect the practice organization tells the players that the coach cares for them. She wants them to make the best use of their time so that they will reach their potential.

"There are two primary forms of motivation: motivation by fear and motivation by love. Fear-based motivation comes from external stimuli (punishment and rewards). Love-based motivation comes from within (pride and caring). Fear-based motivation should be used sparingly and timely. It can be effective, but its results are temporary. If a coach attempts to motivate constantly by fear, respect for the coach's intent is lost. Conversely, love-based motivation is real and lasting. Internally-motivated athletes train because they want to, not because they have to. 'There is nothing more powerful than a human soul on fire.' Motivation is the internal drive that keeps your heart saying, 'yes,' when your body is saying, 'no'."

◆ ◆ ◆ ◆ ◆

. . . on Team Cohesion

Rhonda likes to think back to her playing days when she thinks of team chemistry. "When I was an athlete, the things I enjoyed most were the feelings of working together as a team, committing to a team mission—rising above adversity together and celebrating achievement of team goals together. I loved the sport, my teammates, and competition. This experience gave me a deep appreciation for life and the awesome fullness in spirit. These experiences were what made me select coaching as my profession. I wanted to help others witness the beauty of true TEAM experiences. I believed that, as a coach, I could establish an environment for harboring positive team chemistry."

Rhonda asks the question, "How does a team achieve good chemistry. Does it happen by chance, or do team members make it happen? The answers are elusive. But I believe that there are some definable skills in team building, even though every team has a different dynamic and personality. Building respect is the most critical element in achieving good team chemistry. And there is no better way to build respect than practicing 'The Golden Rule: Do unto others as you would have them do unto you.' It's all about love and respect. Pat Summitt, University of Tennessee basketball coach says, 'You don't have to like each other, but you do need to respect your colleagues' opinions and decisions, because your personal success depends on commitment to the overall plan and doing your part to make it work."

"Last year we had many new players, a new assistant coach, and a new manager. Many returning players were asked to take on new roles. The team was struggling to find its identity. Internal conflicts were showing up everywhere. I called a team meeting to try to open lines of communication and help them to know each other better. At the time, the team simply hadn't been together long enough to start the process of growing respect for each other. I let them know that THEY were responsible for building team chemistry and that they needed to express opinions in the meeting and ask questions of each other and of me. To start the dialog, I asked a simple question: 'Do you believe respect should be earned or given to a person automatically?' The discussion started the team building process—planting the seeds of compassion, understanding, and respect. Later, a follow-up discussion took place to list the ingredients for and deterrents to good team chemistry. This process gave us a path to follow in building team unity. And it enhanced our awareness of the necessity for team cohesion. It also made each of us more accountable in increasing the strength of our team's fabric."

"Effective team building is a constant work in progress. We encourage a steady stream of respectful thoughts. For instance, we believe in the magic of 'please' and 'thank you.' Mutual respect is a natural side effect of consistent use of please and thank you. I also strongly recommend complimenting others. One day, while I was visiting with several members of the team, they were praising some teammates who were not there. I said to them, 'Your remarks are so nice. Have you ever told them what you're telling me?' They had not, so I decided to make this a 'teachable moment' and asked them, 'How would you feel if someone said to you what you have just said about your teammates?' Of course, they would feel deeply touched. Those remarks, coming from teammates, would have much more impact than they would coming from me. Great things are created from little things. As Mother Teresa said, 'Kind words are short and easy to speak, but their echoes are truly endless'."

"Our team participates in a semi-annual team building event that has reaped numerous benefits. We sit down and talk about the individuals on our team. People take turns listing the positive traits about a selected person. We also talk about their contributions to the team and how their presence makes the team special. The coaches record and make copies of the discussions and distribute them to each team member so she has a copy of her valuable traits as defined by her peers. These traditional meetings are pleasantly anticipated. They provide a cornerstone for developing deeply-rooted trust and concern for one another."

Rhonda says that gossip can destroy team chemistry. "We confront the evils of gossip head on by encouraging the parties involved to engage in face-to-face dialogue to discuss the topic of gossip openly and honestly."

"Our coaching staff constantly relays to our team that it is not wins and losses they will remember 10 years from now. It's the friendships and relationships that will stay with them. The more cohesive the unit, the greater the motivation to work hard for each other and the greater the enjoyment of the experiences and bonding shared together. Taking charge of their own destinies creates success and fond memories."

◆ ◆ ◆ ◆ ◆

. . . on Discipline

"Discipline is motivation turned inside out." What a great definition! That's Rhonda's definition of discipline. She explains: "Team discipline is self discipline magnified and multiplied by the number of people involved in the program (including coaches). Discipline has to be a priority in any successful pursuit by a group or by an individual."

"As a head coach, I have learned that if we focus on what we SHOULD DO and not on what we SHOULD NOT DO, our team discipline is much more effective. For example, we have a team rule to 'leave the practice environment (field, locker rooms, hotel rooms, etc.) in as good as or better shape than it was when we arrived.' We take pride in this, and our administrators and hotel managers have praised us for being good custodians. But if we simply told our team not to litter, we'd be focusing on what NOT to do, and there would be no sense of responsibility, no initiative, no authority—no SELF discipline." This rule may be considered petty or small, but it teaches the underlying principles of discipline."

Rhonda explains, "Just the knowledge that we have a CODE OF CONDUCT and knowledge of its contents are enough to guide most players to act appropriately. But there are times when we must take action to see that people comply with our code. Establishing the rules is something we think about carefully. They have to be clear, concise, and few in numbers. Sometimes, however, being too detailed can lead to non-uniform interpretation and, hence, dispute. To avoid this, we leave interpretation of some rules up to the team members. For example, our dress code for travel reads, 'something about which your mother would say, "That looks nice, dear".' In my seven years as coach, I've only had one person ask for an interpretation. (I guess her mother was pretty liberal.) Having too many rules dilutes them, and lessens their effectiveness."

Rhonda has found that involving the team in establishing rules can be highly effective. She points out, "We have a 'Unity Council' composed of five team members. I asked them to recommend a set of team rules and the consequences for rule violations. The coaches reviewed and assisted in writing the rules, and submitted them to the entire team to vote on them. Of course, the team accepted the rules, because they knew that the Unity Council approved them, and they felt they would be fair. The rules turned out to be even more stringent than the coaches would have devised without team input. It has been a refreshing and successful experience. The one violation we had turned out to be a major team building moment, because everyone knew the rules were fair, and the consequences were well known."

Sports psychologists can be helpful in making judgments about team conduct and in helping team members overcome mental blocks etc. For example, in basketball, they often can help improve free throw shooting. But a coach must be the final judge in seeking the advice of sports psychologists. Sometimes they are off the wall. Always weigh their advice against your own judgment and common sense. Rhonda recounts an excellent example of accepting advice from a sports psychologist without thinking it through:

"A friend who became the new coach at another university accepted the sports psychologist's suggestion that the team have no rules for a year. His reasoning was that it was a senior-laden team, with the experience of going to the NCAA play-offs nearly every year. He thought that having no rules would be an excellent way of telling the team, 'I trust you. I respect your past success, and I believe that you will conduct yourself accordingly.' She followed his advice. The team thought it was a great idea. Morale and motivation seemed to soar—FOR A SHORT WHILE. Then it became disastrous. When something went wrong, the coach had to either ignore it or renege on her promise to have no rules. The 'tail was wagging the dog.'

The team was divisive. Different people had different motives and agendas, and there were no consequences to keep everyone on the same path. Needless to say, she has never employed that mode of discipline again."

Rhonda follows some common practices in administering discipline. (1) Discipline should be carried out immediately after an infraction. (2) The disciplinarian must have her emotions under control at the time she discloses the consequences. (3) The discussion should not come across as a personal attack on the player, rather as a positive corrective action, much like instructions on how to execute in practice. (4) Although you must make certain the player understands what she has done wrong and why it was wrong, you must also make sure she understands that you care for her. (5) When the disciplinary action is completed, the player must know that there is no continued animosity on the part of the coach.

"But to avoid having to exercise disciplinary action, one of the biggest deterrents to misconduct is the coach's taking the time to listen to, to show she cares for, and to exhibit respect for her players."

◆ ◆ ◆ ◆ ◆

. . . on Mental Preparation

Rhonda says, "One of my biggest responsibilities is to have the athletes understand the correlation between mental preparation and consistency of play. Freshmen enter college either taking mental preparation for granted or not even considering it at all. They have to learn that they may have different inherent physical skills and to some degree different inherent abilities to focus on the game, but they can all improve their mental preparation through proper training."

"Softball is a slow-moving sport in between pitches, physically, but a lot is going on among every member of the team, whether you're playing defense, hitting, or on base. The athlete is headed for trouble if the brain stops working even for a second or so." Anticipation is mental, and anticipation is as big a part of softball as response to an action is, which is also mental. Rhonda points out a more subtle aspect of mental preparation: "A person has to have command over her emotions before she can have command over her physical performance."

Rhonda says the ability to prepare oneself mentally can be an acquired talent. How? "During the first semester we put all of our new athletes, freshmen and transfer students, through a 'mental training and orientation' conducted by our sports psychologist, Dr. Wes Sime, and me. We meet weekly for four to six weeks and cover topics such as Positive Self Talk, Staying and Playing in the Moment, Elimination of Muscular Tension Through Proper Breathing, Relaxation Techniques, Imagery and

Visualization, and Establishing Routines. Many of the ideas we use are adapted from '*Heads up Baseball: Playing the Game One Pitch at a Time*' by Dr. Ken Ravizza and Tom Hanson."

"At the beginning of the second semester, when the season in only six weeks away, the entire team joins the mental training sessions. The topics in the second session vary, depending on the personality and maturity of the group." Notice that Rhonda assigns these characteristics to the group, as opposed to individuals. This tells you something about her thoughts on team unity. She continues. "We always revisit some of the topics for taking responsibility for your own mental preparedness through Proper Breathing, Muscular Relaxation Techniques, and Positive Self-Talk. I call these the staples of our mental training program."

While you may consider some of the mental preparedness training the lecture room, Rhonda makes the practice field the "laboratory" part of the mental training program. "We believe that the players must actually act out their mental training. For example, if a player makes an error in scrimmage, we get them to go through the things we taught in the mental training program, such as taking a deep breath, having three seconds to be upset, release the error and focus on the moment, and 'show me confidence.' Baseball Hall of Famer, Al Kaline said, 'I tried to practice the way I played, You can't practice one way and then expect to do it differently in a game'."

"And you can't expect to do it one way at home and another on the road, or one way early in the game and another late in the game. The key to mental preparation is to follow your season-long routines, stay in the moment, keep your focus on the task at hand. This will keep distractions at bay. Practicing what you know about mental preparedness consistently will help athletes trust their preparation and consequently become more confident in their game."

Rhonda stresses that mental and physical preparation can't be separated. "We get input from the team about what mental preparation they feel they need. The coaches reinforce the players' trust in their mental preparation by simulating game situations in practice. For example, if we are working on hitting the outside pitch to the opposite field and the athlete is having some success, we point out the factors that made them successful so that they can reproduce the situation more readily in games. Through daily rehearsals, at both slowed-down and game-speed versions, the athletes become more confident and better equipped to handle all types of situations."

"Keeping it simple is a matter of working on something—regardless of what it is—long enough that it becomes simple," Says Rhonda. " I refer to this process as 'mastery through repetition.' Just as you can master the physical aspects of the game, you can also master mental preparation, once you accept the fact that it is a skill you can control. Once you control your mental preparedness, you increase your self confidence; and this ultimately leads to reaching the goal of consistently performing at your potential."

◆ ◆ ◆ ◆ ◆

. . . on Mental Toughness

"Adversity is guaranteed in athletics. The most consistently successful athletes are those who learn skills to handle adversity through compensating and adjusting to ever-changing circumstances during competition. 'It's 20% what happens to us and 80% how we react,' according to an old adage." And that's according to Rhonda Revelle. She continues: "Some people claim that mental toughness is a trait you're born with. Although people do begin to develop mental toughness early in life, it's a characteristic that can be developed as a result of our experiences and our responses. A mentally tough person faces adversity with courage and determination. She plays to win, rather than not to lose. She shows tremendous tenacity and locks in on her goals like a heat-seeking missile. Her mind is leading her body to one place, victory, by whatever means it takes."

Although Rhonda believes that life's experiences help us develop mental toughness, the athlete has to take advantage of the learning opportunities afforded by those experiences. She cites a passage by Hank Aaron from "**Heads Up Baseball**": "For me, my ability to fully focus on what I had to do on a daily basis made me the successful player that I was. I think I learned how to focus. It wasn't something that I was necessarily born with. I realized early on that if I was going to be one of the best players ever to play the game, I had to do things other players weren't doing. I've seen players with as much or more ability than I had, but somewhere along the way they lost sight of what they were doing; they just couldn't keep in tune. Having great concentration and being in control of yourself are not things you decide to do one day; they're skills you have to develop over time. It's kind of like learning your ABCs as a child; you learn through repetitions. It's not going to come to you overnight."

Rhonda reiterates the necessity of dealing successfully with adversity: "Adversity breeds the necessity for mental toughness. It's part of the ebb and flow of competition. So it's imperative that successful athletes be prepared with a strong mental game."

"The most valuable by-product of mental toughness is being able to play the game with confidence. And confidence can instill a reverie that is often referred to as 'being in a zone.' When you're in a zone, you block out distractions, and you move precisely and under control. Teammates can see and feel a player's focus and confidence, and it's contagious. The whole team is lifted by a player's mental toughness. Mentally tough players are any team's greatest assets. They are leaders, the team's heart and soul, and the reason any team experiences consistent success."

. . . on Communication

Rhonda offers this story as an example when effective communications resulted in the desired objective:

"We were playing in the semi-finals of our conference tournament. A sound showing in the tournament would assure us a berth in the NCAA regionals. Up until this game we had been playing excellent defense. But in this game, it was like the wheels fell off. In the first two innings, every one of our infielders made and error, and we found ourselves down 5-0. The team was so hyped before the game that they couldn't focus. During this fitful time for the defense, I took my one allotted trip to the mound. I mustered up all the calm I could and reminded the team to get back to concentrating on basics—taking care of the ball and getting one out at a time. When the top half of the inning ended, we huddled together to re-plot our course. We believed that if the team set their minds to scoring just one run each inning, then we would win this all-important game."

"Guess what? We won the game in the bottom half of the seventh with a solo home run with two outs. I believe the way the coaching staff handled that second-inning situation was critical. First, we needed to get the team on an even keel emotionally—not too high, not too low. We kept them focused on the task as hand, without dwelling on what had occurred earlier. Our demeanor in communicating with them was the key. We talked calmly and assuredly, and our body language and mannerisms were consistent with the message and our feelings."

Rhonda also stresses the necessity of knowing your players. She says that the best coaches are masters of both verbal and non-verbal communication. But she cautions that effective communications requires that you know your players and how they like to be communicated with. Here's an example of how she learned she was communicating in the wrong manner: "Last year, I thought I was on the right track with my on-the-field communication style with a transfer student (first time on our team). Although I had never asked her about communications, I thought I knew that she would want me to demonstrate that I believed in her."

"During the second half of the season, she surprised me in telling me that when I said 'Come on clutch hitter, you're right where you want to be,' it really distracted her, and she felt additional pressure. All the time, I thought I was letting her know that I believed in her—that I thought she was a clutch hitter. I learned to ask each player what communication style suited her best when she was at bat."

There is nothing wrong with feeling pain when you lose, according to Rhonda. "I openly acknowledge my pain when we lose. I think we gain strength by acknowledging and facing adversity. How we deal with misfortune defines who we are as athletes and as people. If we played our hearts out, but yet came up short on the scoreboard, I tell the team to be proud of their tears and of the wrenching in their guts. Feeling that way is a testament to what went into their preparation and the game itself. It's really the only way to play the game—to care so much that success is sweet and defeat is agonizing."

"But the agony of defeat should be short lived and within the confines of proper perspective. We need to make the negative of losing into a positive. And we can do this by analyzing our play and determining what we can do better both physically and mentally. We can use the experience to catapult us to future success. We want our athletes to have no doubt that failure is temporary, not terminal."

When the team plays poorly, Rhonda likes to take notes as she asks the team to assess what they did—on offense, defense, level of hustle, adjustments made, etc. And she says that she is not always calm after a loss. "Sometimes I really come unglued in a post game speech, when we played poorly. I'm not systematic in my comments. I just unleash the passion in my heart, and sometimes I don't remember exactly what I said. But even when I come unglued, I am still accountable for my actions and instinctively I don't go beyond the boundaries of proper language or restraining anger toward an individual."

"Inadequate communication is root to most player/coach or team problems. Honesty, good eye contact, and listening are essential ingredients of effective communication. If you take time to know your team as individuals, it will pay big dividends in communicating."

◆ ◆ ◆ ◆ ◆

RUSS ROSE
Pennsylvania State University

- - - - - - - - - - - - - - - -

Position
Head Volleyball Coach

Career Record
721-127 (22 seasons)

Education
B.A.   George Williams College
M.A.   University of Nebraska-Lincoln

Team and Personal Highlights

- ➤ 1999 NCAA national champions.
- ➤ Four-time NCAA tournament finalists.
- ➤ Six Big Ten titles.
- ➤ 20 consecutive NCAA tournament appearances.
- ➤ Eight straight Atlantic-10 Conference titles.
- ➤ 36 All-Americans.
- ➤ 62 Academic All-Big Ten selections.
- ➤ 25-time Coach of the Year honors.
- ➤ Number one all-time winning percentage
- ➤ Winningest coach in Penn State school history.

RUSS ROSE

Introduction . . .

If you didn't already know that Russ Rose was a highly-respected, national-award-winning Division I volleyball coach, a quick glance at his media guide picture would peg him as an easy-going, fun-loving guy that doesn't have a care in the world. You would only be partly correct. Because under that jovial exterior lies the heart of a disciplined warrior who loves to compete.

Upon arriving at the State College campus in 1979, Russ discovered that his program consisted of three in-state scholarships and some hand-me-down basketball jerseys. Things have gotten considerably better since then. Prior to beginning the 2001 season, the Penn State volleyball juggernaut was rolling steadily along: six Big Ten titles, eight Atlantic-10 conference championships, 20 consecutive trips to the NCAA tournament, and a national championship.

The Russ Rose file is incredibly impressive: the 2000 Olympic Committee Coach of the Year, two-time American Volleyball Coaches Association Coach of the Year, three-time *Volleyball Monthly* Coach of the Year, four-time Mideast Region Coach of the Year, four-time Big Ten Conference Coach of the Year, District II Coach of the Year, six-time Atlantic-10 Conference Coach of the Year, and four-time Northeast Region Coach of the Year. He holds the number one all-time winning percentage of .850.

Another legacy may be his influence on future coaches. No less than 20 individuals within the college coaching fraternity have gained instruction from Rose. A former instructor in the USVBA coaches certification program, Rose has served as a national referee and evaluator and state director of volleyball for the Special Olympics. He also has international coaching experience, being a member of the United States delegations to the Soviet Union and Canada.

A graduate of George Williams College, Russ was a member of the school's men's volleyball team that won the 1974 National Association of Intercollegiate Athletics national championship. He played professionally in Puerto Rico for a year before returning to George Williams as an assistant coach. Russ married Lori Barberich, a former three-time All-American at Penn State, in 1986. They have four sons.

Russ was most pleasant and focused while relating his championship thoughts . . .

. . . on Motivation

Coach Russ Rose says that motivation is not just a word coaches use in talks to their players; it's action and effort, and, "determination to succeed. I challenge my players to always be accountable. They need to come to practice prepared to understand where they can make a contribution. The most complete players are the ones smart enough to build a niche for themselves and to follow through on the practice arena." Building that "niche" is goal setting, and following through is what results from motivation to achieve that goal.

Russ says, "The most effective methods of motivation are communicating to players what is expected of them and then helping them live up to, or exceed expectations, by working with them in their personal skill development, as well as developing team cohesion and a fighting spirit." That "fighting spirit" comes close to being another definition of motivation. Russ also feels that "ownership" can motivate: "I want the players to understand that it is their team and that they are responsible for performance. It is my job to keep them on task and provide positive feedback." Again, he's stressing those goals and stimulating the players to go after them.

Does any coach think that embarrassing players is motivating? If there is one, it's certainly not Russ. He says, "The least effective way to motivate is to yell at players and embarrass them in front of their peers or their fans. Few people improve performance from embarrassment. If our team has performed poorly, it's my fault, and in addressing the media, I emphasize this. I leave the correction of mistakes to the times we can work in practice. The public doesn't need to focus on our team's individual mistakes."

"Coaching is a teaching process. But it's also a learning process—much of the learning is from making mistakes. And in twenty-five years of coaching women, I've learned that a coach has to embrace the opportunity to improve as a coach and as a leader, or he won't serve his team as well as they deserve being served. In the end, it's all about effort, not results." It's about motivation, not about winning.

. . . on Team Cohesion

"Team cohesion deals with the commitment the players make to develop a 'team attitude'," according to Russ. Normally you think of an attitude as being a personal attribute—not a team characteristic. But in analyzing Russ' statement, binding individual attitudes so tightly that they become a singular "team attitude" puts forth another unique and provocative definition of team cohesion. He specifically mentions the team's response, as a group, to challenging situations. Russ brings into play "team accountability" as a further expansion on the idea of team cohesiveness. He takes what we normally consider personal characteristics and makes them TEAM characteristics—team chemistry.

"In my opinion," says Russ, "volleyball is the ultimate team sport. My approach to coaching is to select the best combination of players who will play together and, at the same time, seek to fulfill their own roles and goals."

Russ believes that a coach must deal with a variety of issues that affect team chemistry. He says that good chemistry involves happiness, and pursuit of excellence. And Russ believes in ownership: "I want the players to recognize that our team is their team. The team results will correlate directly with their commitment and dedication to team cohesiveness. Even our team drills must integrate challenging the team physically, mentally, and even socially—to challenge our team's togetherness."

A question of balance always comes into play when coaches work to apportion emphasis between team harmony and physical and technical attributes normally associated with winning. Russ ponders this, too. "Do I emphasize performance on the court or harmony in the locker room?" He says he's seen coaches who focused almost exclusively on winning and overlooked team cohesiveness—who didn't "clear the air" when confrontations arose among team members or staff and team members. And he's seen some of those coaches fired for not winning. So the distributions of coaches' efforts are sometimes influenced by the environment the coaches work in. Russ says, "Chemistry in and of itself is great, but many players and coaches look at the end results of competition." Are these two concerns mutually exclusive, or are they intimately bound together? A coach who was fired for not winning may have lost because he didn't put sufficient emphasis on team chemistry. It's an inseparable part of team performance. Whether athletic administrators recognize this or not, the coaches have to."

And Russ does: "The chemistry that exists among the team members is what has kept us competitive, and the energy that exists between our team and the town of State College is what has kept the juices flowing."

◆ ◆ ◆ ◆ ◆

. . . on Discipline

"Discipline entails an individual's commitment to do everything within her grasp to enhance both her chances and the team's chances for success." He says he prefers goals and guidelines to too many specific rules. He doesn't want to deal with hearsay—only factual information. And he doesn't believe in punishing the entire team because a single athlete has made a bad decision.

To the extent of being practical, Russ likes to let the team decide what values are important. "I want to give them a small taste of democracy in college athletics. I have found this to be the most effective way of keeping the players on task."

However, the team does have some "specific behaviors," as Russ calls them, that he does monitor, "because I feel they contribute to success and they deal with team preparation. For example, I want each team member to be both physically and mentally 'there,' to go for every ball, and to communicate with the other players."

Russ looks at other teams' disciplinary methods, trying to determine which appear to be successful for the other team and which ones do not. Then he tries to decide which of those methods might work for his team. In answering the question, "Which disciplinary methods are least successful?" Russ quips, "the ones you just experienced failure with." That's his way of saying, "learn from experience." He has a good point, and he reiterates his position that what works for one team may not work for his, and what works for one athlete does not necessarily work for another.

Russ does have three hard and fast rules concerning his own behavior:

1. "Never yell at a player.
2. Never embarrass a player.
3. Always be honest, even if your honesty may be considered 'brutally honest' in hindsight"

. . . on Mental Preparation

"Mental preparation can make the difference between winning and losing. Most teams practice the same physical skills, so the team that prepares better mentally has the advantage," says Russ. In volleyball, focus is often the key to success. If a coach prepares his team in practice by concentrating on the strategic and technical aspects, then these aspects become second nature in the match. That's when mental preparation kicks in.

According to Russ, "Preseason is tough. It's the time when coaches determine the physical level of the players and when they work to refine technical skills. Also, the coaches try to define the dynamics of the group—

how they work together. We always emphasize the skills that may separate us from our opponent. We try to make pursuing every ball second nature. And we work on communications among team members—both verbal and non-verbal." Because teamwork is paramount in volleyball, every team member has to know what every other team member is going to do before she does it. If she waits, the timing is all off, and the play won't work. But it's not like football, where on most plays there is little innovation. Volleyball is almost all innovation—in the sense that "plays" are set up almost instantaneously on the basis of verbal communication, eye contact, or body language.

"Preseason isn't supposed to be fun," Russ says. Players have to understand the importance of what is done in preseason—that it will mean the difference between success and failure. Russ continues, "While players need to understand what it takes to be successful, they also need to have fun. The games can be and should be fun."

"We prepare for all opponents—highly ranked and unranked—the same way. The outcome of most games depends on how well prepared you are." You see in Russ' statement one of the reasons for upsets and what he does to guard against them. How many times do you hear or read, after an upset, that the losing team was "looking beyond" the opponent who upset them?

Russ continues: "The only game condition you can't duplicate in practice is emotion and flow of adrenaline that accompanies big matches. Good mental preparation can enable a team to look forward to the emotion of the match and not crash because of poor preparation, or burn out because of too much emphasis on the mental aspects of the match during practice."

Russ doesn't have any magic formula for late game strategy. He says that while late-game strategy is sport-specific, he depends largely on mental preparation, before the match, to guide his players through critical times late in the game. "I want my players to push to the end and not worry about who is winning and who is losing. Let the crowd and the emotion bring you to the 'finish line,' not the fear of 'losing at the buzzer'."

"The more chances you give yourself to win and finish, the better are your chances of finishing the job on top."

◆　◆　◆　◆　◆

. . . on Mental Toughness

Russ says that both college and professional coaches continually look for players who possess the critical component of mental toughness. "You won't develop mental toughness in a classroom—a class on sports psychology. It is athlete-specific. Some players have already developed it before they get here. Some learn it in our program, from experiences, from coaches' drills, or from other players. And, unfortunately, some players just never develop it. Hopefully, a coach can blend those players who are not so mentally tough in with the ones who are—hide them so to speak—and depend on the mentally tough to carry the team," says Russ.

Russ defines mental toughness as "a trait that emerges when players and teams prevail and keep pursuing their goals in the face of various obstacles." He says, "We all fail at times. Coaches aren't exempt from failure. I feel that one of our biggest challenges is to develop every player, not just the team performance. I think this is where most of us feel we fail." But coaches, I'm sure, develop mental toughness, too. Recognizing that they failed a team member by not developing her to her full potential may be one of the most difficult things for a coach to accept. But good coaches recognize failure and increase their determination to work that much harder to develop the next player who isn't performing up to what the coach thinks is her potential. And that's where mental toughness in coaching pays off. Development of each athlete is like the challenge of a competitive match. And the rewards of success are what keep a lot of coaches in the field.

But what are some of the obstacles that teams and players face? "They face adversity in tough opponents who may have more raw physical ability than they have, and both teams know it. Hostile crowds present challenges. An official's unfair call is really tough to deal with. Sometimes you just aren't performing up to snuff and don't know why. That is frustrating, big time. You set a teammate up for a terrific spike, and she blows it. The mentally tough athletes will accept these as challenges, keep on digging deep, and just build more determination."

How do those players who learn mental toughness in Russ' program learn it? "I like to make practices hard and challenging so the players can have experiences dealing with some of the factors that might cause a player or team to crack in competition. I'd prefer to have a player lose her composure in practice than in a competitive event. In our drills, we can monitor the players and look for signs that may indicate a tendency toward mental weakness. You can evaluate mental toughness by observing how players handle various setbacks during their career. Things such as injuries and wrong personal decisions that may affect eligibility force players to learn from these tough experiences."

Tough experiences and mental toughness. The first can help build the second. Or it could bring a person down, unless she is mentally tough.

◆ ◆ ◆ ◆ ◆

. . . on Communication

Russ says that his coaches and he have found that each team is different and each individual on the team is different in terms of what type of communication works best with them. "We have to find out how best to communicate with each player. One size doesn't fit all personalities. Some players are quite independent and don't want too much instruction. Others are highly dependent on the coaches and staff to provide guidance, even during matches."

He discusses addressing the team at mid-match break when the team is behind: "If we're trailing at the break or late in the match, I try to reinforce the patterns we need to exhibit to compete. Whether we're playing below par or the opponent is playing at the top of their game, the key to dealing with the situation is patience. Teams cannot perform their best when they have lost their composure. And it never helps a team for the coach to lose his composure." So composure is paramount in communications. Anyone communicating must be composed and anyone receiving communications must be in a receptive state of mind.

Russ believes that post-match talks are important because they determine the direction the team takes immediately and may take for an extended period. "I try to touch on the areas that need improvement," he says. "This is usually one time when achieving that receptive state of mind is almost automatic, so I try to capitalize on the players' awareness." And he knows that effective communication has to be exercised continually. But there are times when it's more effective than others.

KELVIN SAMPSON
University of Oklahoma

- - - - - - - - - - - - - - - -

Position
Head Men's Basketball Coach

Career Record
332-217 (19 seasons)

Education
B.S.   Pembroke (NC) State University
M.A.   Michigan State University

Team and Personal Highlights

- ➢ National Coach of the Year.
- ➢ District Coach of the Year.
- ➢ Three-time Conference Coach of the Year.
- ➢ National Association of Basketball Coaches Board of Directors.
- ➢ Head Coach, United States Junior National Team.
- ➢ Assistant Coach, Goodwill Games.
- ➢ Head Coach, West team, U.S. Olympic Festival.
- ➢ Eight consecutive NCAA tournament berths.
- ➢ Enshrined in two Halls of Fame.

KELVIN SAMPSON

Introduction . . .

Prior to his arrival in Norman, Oklahoma, Kelvin Sampson was dubbed "the number one new hot coach in the next wave" by **College Sports** magazine. He has certainly lived up to the early hype.

About to begin his eighth year as Oklahoma head men's basketball coach, Kelvin Sampson has guided the Sooners to over 22 victories per season and seven NCAA tournament berths, including a Sweet 16 showing in 1999. Sampson is also one of just two current Big 12 coaches (Kansas' Roy Williams is the other) to make seven straight appearances in the "Big Dance."

The 2001 season saw Sampson's Sooners finish with a 26-7 record, a second-place finish during the regular season, a Big 12 tournament championship, a Number 4 seed in the NCAA tournament, and a final Associated Press ranking of Number 13 in the country.

Kelvin won National Coach of the Year honors in 1995 after guiding the Sooners to 23-9 overall and 15-0 home marks. It was the second-best overall record posted by a first-year coach in Big Eight history. The team's regular season performance resulted in a Number four seeding in the NCAA Tournament's Southeast Regional.

Sampson began his coaching career at Montana Tech in 1981, leading the Orediggers to a 73-45 record in his final four seasons, including two NAIA District 12 championship games. He was named the league's Coach of the Year in 1983 and 1985. Washington State came calling in 1987, and Sampson guided the 1994 Cougars to their first NCAA Tournament berth since 1983.

The Laurinburg, North Carolina, native excelled in the classroom and the athletic arena during his prep career at Pembroke High School and later at Pembroke State University (now UNC-Pembroke). He captained his high school basketball team while playing for his father John W. "Ned" Sampson, played quarterback in football, and was a catcher-outfielder in baseball, earning nine varsity letters in the three sports.

At Pembroke State, Sampson earned four letters as point guard on the basketball team, being named team captain his senior season. He also earned three letters in baseball. He earned Dean's List recognition throughout his collegiate career, and was awarded the Gregory Lowe Memorial Award as the school's outstanding physical education major his senior year.

Sampson was inducted into the Montana Tech Hall of Fame in 1996 and into the Pembroke State Athletic Hall of Fame in 1998. He and his wife, Karen, have two children and live in Norman.

The highly-charismatic coach was eager to discuss his success strategies . . .

. . . on Motivation

Coach Kelvin Sampson doesn't try to pin a specific tag on motivation or on what motivates people. He says, "Motivation is anything that creates or sustains your drive to work toward your goals. Each individual is different when it comes to what motivates him."

Kelvin says that the players easiest to motivate are those with high self-esteem. They're already motivated to a large degree. "All you have to do is to make sure they stay focused on their goals by occasionally pointing them in the right direction. These players already have high expectations and an inner drive to succeed."

"The most effective motivational tool we use is instilling in our players a constant fear of not being good enough or not working hard enough," according to Kelvin. Some coaches may develop this fear through competition for recognition within the system or competition for playing time. Kelvin says that he makes sure his coaches feel the need to continue to "out work" coaches of other teams, too. "Our belief is that great effort is more important than talent. The team who works hardest will win the game. We never want to feel that another team has out-worked us or out-hustled us."

Kelvin believes that positive reinforcement is motivating. But he says, "Coaches must balance positive and negative reinforcement. Too much of either can lead to problems or set your team up for failure." A combination of the stick and the carrot. How much stick? How much carrot?

When the imbalance becomes too heavy in the negative direction, according to Kelvin, "That can be the least motivating experience. Players will respond to negative motivation, but if the positive contributions are never recognized, the players' responses can be turned in the wrong direction. Players recognize the need for discipline, and for letting them know about mistakes. They want to work hard, because they know that you win only by giving a total effort, but they also must know that you care for them and believe in them."

"Too much focus on winning can backfire on your motivational efforts. My philosophy about basketball—and about work in any area—is that if you constantly work your hardest to do things right and pay attention to details, winning will take care of itself." Winning may be an ultimate goal, but setting it as your only goal provides no instructional value and leaves too many opportunities to stray off the course to that goal. Kelvin puts it this way: "Focus on the process to success, step by step. We focus on A,B,C, etc. How else can you get to Z?"

◆ ◆ ◆ ◆ ◆

. . . on Team Cohesion

Kelvin puts team chemistry in the context of the system: "Everyone must understand and accept his role within the framework of the team. Each player must understand what the team needs from him. He must understand how his role impacts team success." Not everyone on the team has to be a prolific scorer. Assists, blocking out, rebounds, steals, drawing fouls, getting back on defense etc. are all part of the system. One weak link can hurt the entire team. Kelvin puts it this way: "The coach must clearly define each player's role. Each player must accept his role and make sacrifices—in terms of getting fan recognition—for the benefit of the team."

Kelvin brings player leadership into his discussion of team chemistry. "The most important factor in building and maintaining team chemistry," he says, "is for the best player to also be your hardest worker. The coach must place the highest expectations on the best player(s) and demand the most effort from them. To take any other route would risk causing jealousies and envy." He also recognizes the necessity for fair treatment. "Treat all players fair. What good does it do to baby your 'star' and demand total effort from your 5th, 6th, and 7th men?"

Kelvin reinforces his belief in parceling out the praise to every individual on the team who does his job. "The coach not only defines the roles on the team, he must also give feedback to each player regarding his role. He can't ask a player to accept a role of setting screens, playing defense, rebounding, etc., if he only praises the scorers. Once the roles are defined, reinforce the importance of each role by recognizing the players in relation to their roles."

"We use an analogy with our team about the hand and the fingers. If your hand is open and the fingers are spread, there's not much strength. But when the five fingers—'five players'—come together to make a fist, there is great power. Successful teams are like the fist."

. . . on Discipline

Kelvin believes that communicating what is expected of his team members is the first essential element of discipline: "At the very first team meeting, a coach must clearly express to the team what he expects in terms of behavior—the rules, the consequences of not following them. The coach must be consistent, and firm with discipline. Think about your rules carefully before you lay them out, but don't set rules unless you're going to enforce them. You can't be arbitrary. Players will respect you and adjust to your expectations, if you are consistent."

Coaches differ on the effectiveness of holding the entire team responsible for the actions of a single member. Kelvin comes down on the side of holding the whole team responsible. "The most effective disciplinary method I use is punishing the whole team when one member makes a mistake." While some coaches don't go along with this, it has certainly gotten across the fact that when a player makes a mistake in a game, the whole team suffers. He can't erase the two points an opponent makes off a turnover when he telegraphed a pass. Basketball is a team sport. There are individual statistics, but there is only one score.

So it makes sense to emphasize the importance of every player's role in a game by extending the team concept to behavior off the court. "Peer pressure is powerful," according to Kelvin. "Players will think twice before breaking rules, if they know that their teammates will be punished for their poor judgment. As a result of this practice, we have very few instances that result in adverse actions."

To reemphasize his philosophy of enforcing rules, once set, Kelvin says, "If someone breaks a rule, we don't let it slide until the infraction is repeated. We take action the first time the rule is broken. We nip the problem in the bud." If a player gets away with an infraction once, he may try it again. How many times are you allowed? The only way to be consistent is to enforce rules for each infraction. Kelvin says that limiting the number of rules he makes helps in emphasizing the importance of the ones established. It also helps players remember them. "But," he says, "the ones I establish are important to me, so I enforce them rigidly."

In the end, Kelvin goes back to common sense, which, after all, is what standards of conduct are based on: "Coaches must use good judgment and common sense in dealing with their team. This approach is easy to understand and remember, and it leads to the fewest problems."

◆ ◆ ◆ ◆ ◆

. . . on Mental Preparation

Unlike some coaches who stress physical conditioning during the early preseason and wait to focus on mental preparation later, Kelvin says his team begins work on mental preparation along with that first day of conditioning. "We start building a 'mental framework'."

"That framework comes from working hard every day from the very first day of practice. Mental preparation is being able to get your mind and body focused to produce maximum performance. Players must learn to compete and push themselves each day, to work harder, and to get through their own 'personal ceiling.' This early period is when coaches learn about players' mental preparedness and leaders start coming to the fore. It's also when players learn to find their inner strength—learn that they can do more after their bodies become tired and want to quit. The players need to take initiative in pushing themselves harder than the coaches do, because in competition, the coach has to concentrate on situation strategy. The players who learn to push themselves are the ones who go on to succeed and lead the team to victory."

Kelvin believes in preparing for all teams the same way. There are no 'gimmies' in college basketball today. Just take a look at the teams seeded from 10 to 16 who win one to three rounds in the NCAA tournament. "At Oklahoma," Kelvin says, "we always watch film of our upcoming opponent with the players and go over a detailed scouting report. But our biggest focus in preparing for the next game is on what WE need to do. What will be our keys to being successful? We stress some constants, no matter whom we are playing: defense, rebounding, playing unbelievably hard, and playing unselfishly. This philosophy is the foundation of our program. So these are the things we focus on each and every day for each and every game."

Mental preparation for late-game situation games determines the winner in a major percentage of basketball games. "Repetition, concentration, and confidence are the keys. We build confidence through repetitions when we exhibit total concentration. We practice selected situational offensive and defensive plans and repeat them until the response of the players is second nature. I believe in conducting these drills in game-like conditions, so we do them near the end of practice, when the players are tired. They must sharpen their concentration skills under the adverse condition of fatigue."

"Typically, near the end of a game, the players are tired, the crowd is noisy, and the game is hinging on a basket from the floor, a free throw, a turnover, or a foul. Players feed off the coach's confidence in his team, his calmness, and his encouragement. If your mental preparation drills have prepared them for this situation, they will find a way to 'make it happen.'"

◆ ◆ ◆ ◆ ◆

. . . on Mental Toughness

Kelvin relates mental toughness to work ethic: "I believe mental toughness is strongly related to how much work you have put into your practice and preparation. As the old saying goes, 'the harder you work, the harder it is to surrender.'"

He defines mental toughness as "the ability to fight through adversity and focus on attaining your goals, regardless of the circumstances or the environment. Mental toughness comes from within. It's the ability to find inner resolve."

"We look for players who have been through adversity and who are willing to work hard to overcome hardship and improve their skills. Mental toughness is directly related to work ethic. The mentally toughest players I've coached are the ones who had the strongest work ethic. It's hard to have mental toughness without the strong work ethic, and it's also hard to maintain a strong work ethic without mental toughness."

◆ ◆ ◆ ◆ ◆

. . . on Communication

"Be clear. Be concise." Those two statements pretty much wrap up Kelvin's philosophy on communication. "It doesn't make any difference whether it's during play, at halftime, during a late-game situation, or after the game, be clear and concise," according to Kelvin.

But there are differences within those two constants for different situations. "I generally use halftime for making adjustments on offense and defense. Sometimes at halftime, I have to get on to a player concerning his overall effort or his concentration—to play harder or to rebound, etc. But the main objective of my halftime talk is to get the players to come out in the second half and play right away. The first five minutes are so critical," says Kelvin. Catching the momentum at the beginning of the second half is so vital, because that period is the last major momentum-capturing period of the game. You don't have another chance to really help your players "get into the game." Time-outs can't be used to motivate. There's not enough time. They're for communicating strategy.

Kelvin: "If we've played really well during the first half, I compliment the team, but then I might focus on mistakes just a little more, to bring them down. Overconfidence can make you relax during that first five minutes of the second half, and that can be fatal. Conversely, if we have played poorly, I need to emphasize the positive to pick up their confidence."

"I've said earlier how much emphasis we put on late-game situations. They are really critical. And effective communication is the key in the game, as opposed to practice, because we have been through our late-game drills over and over. I must make sure they identify the right situation. I must instill confidence in them by presenting a calm demeanor, even though my stomach is churning like mad. If I haven't prepared for these situations myself, I may not communicate as calmly and as confidently as I need to in order to be clear and concise. But sometimes in these late-game situations, my reactions come down to my gut feeling and my past experiences, because no two situations are identical."

Kelvin prefers to keep his post-game remarks after a tough loss short and to the point. He'd like to see the game tapes before he gets detailed, because he knows how important it is to provide the right instructions after a game. But something has to be said at the moment. "First of all, it's important to be honest. But at the same time, you can't tear down their confidence, especially after a tough loss."

"After I analyze the game tape, I'm in a much better position to tell them what they did wrong and, just as important, to tell them what they did right. Finally, this is the best time to begin preparing them mentally for our next game, letting them know how we're going to correct our mistakes and win that next game."

◆ ◆ ◆ ◆ ◆

BRET SIMON

Stanford University

- - - - - - - - - - - - - - - - -

Position
Head Men's Soccer Coach

Career Record
180-67-23 (13 seasons)

Education
B.S.   University of Massachusetts-Amherst
M.B.A. Berry (GA) College

Team and Personal Highlights

➢ Four-time Coach of the Year.

➢ Two Missouri Valley Conference regular-season titles.

➢ Four Missouri Valley Conference tournament championships.

➢ Six NCAA tournament appearances.

➢ 2000 College Cup national championship match.

➢ Winningest soccer coach in Creighton University school history.

BRET SIMON

Introduction . . .

Bret Simon enters his first season at the helm of the Stanford men's soccer program. Simon came to The Farm in February of 2001 after serving as the head men's soccer coach at Creighton University for the past six seasons.

A member of the Creighton University men's soccer staff for eight years, Simon finished his sixth season as the program's head coach in the 2000 College Cup national championship match.

A four-time Coach of the Year honoree, his Bluejays teams won 96 matches during his tenure, including a pair of Missouri Valley Conference regular-season titles, four post-season MVC tournament championships, and six consecutive appearances in the NCAA tournament. His 96 wins mark the most soccer victories ever by a Bluejay soccer head coach.

Last season, Simon led Creighton to its most successful season in history. The Bluejays (22-4-0) earned a trip to the College Cup for the second time in five years, and ended their season with a 2-0 loss to Connecticut in the championship match. The team's appearance in the NCAA championship contests was the first by any CU athletic squad in school history. Bret's squad also set the school record for most wins in a season (22) with their 2-1 three-overtime victory over two-time defending national champion Indiana in the semifinal round of the College Cup.

The high-energy, highly-charismatic Simon took over the head coaching duties from his mentor, Bob Warming, on July 27, 1995. He quickly guided the Bluejays to a sweep of the Valley's regular-season and tournament titles. His second year produced a 17-5-2 record and the first trip to the NCAA College Cup. Also during his stay at the Omaha, Nebraska, Jesuit school, he coached five players that were named the MVC's "Player of the Year." His teams were always very active in the community and stellar students in the classroom.

After graduating with a degree in Sports Management from the University of Massachusetts-Amherst, he took his first coaching position at Berry College in Georgia. He was an assistant coach for six years and head coach for seven years. His seven-year overall record was 84-41-14. In 1993, he joined Bob Warming as an assistant at Creighton before taking the head coaching position in 1995. Bret and his wife, Pamela, have two young sons.

The classy coach with the quick smile was very happy to share his winning thoughts . . .

. . . on Motivation

Coach Bret Simon extols the assets of optimism and positiveness in discussing motivation. He also uses the term, "desire," in his definition of motivation. Then he puts the desire, optimism and positiveness together to arrive at a program to motivate his soccer players.

Bret defines motivation as "the desire to attain individual and group goals regardless of the physical and psychological sacrifices required." That's a lot of desire, but in the context of competitive athletics, it's in line with what's required to be a consistent winner.

Bret says coaches should work toward the objective of developing SELF motivation in every player. While this may be a tricky and challenging task, in the long run it reduces the necessity to work on motivating your players continually. Once they become self-motivated, a coach can concentrate on other facets of training. How does he develop self motivation? Says Bret, "Open communication between coaches and players in setting short and long term goals is essential." To stimulate self motivation, he suggests, "being optimistic and developing self confidence in players and mutual trust and respect between players and coaches."

According to Bret, "Avoid negative talk, except in unusual cases where it may be warranted, and then only briefly. Don't ever try to motivate through fear. While such approaches may work effectively for brief periods of time, they end up being major detriments to maintaining a positive attitude among players and can counteract the powerful force of self motivation."

◆　◆　◆　◆　◆

. . . on Team Cohesion

Bret has a somewhat different perspective on the importance of team cohesion. While he agrees that it is essential to achieve "ultimate team success," he says that it may not play as big a role as some others suggest in simply achieving a superior won/loss record, which he doesn't consider success, in and of itself. He puts it this way: "Team cohesion is not always necessary to achieve success in terms of wins and losses. But I would agree that it is important for 'ultimate team success', which I believe is more than just a team's won-loss record."

Aside from the different perspective, you might not notice that Bret's philosophy is different from observing his training program. His definition is compatible with other definitions, and he believes the same general principles are important. He seems so dedicated to the principle that "winning is not the only thing" that he makes sure that principle is integrated into his perspective of team cohesion. Bret's definition: "Team cohesion/team chemistry is the dynamic synergistic effect of a group of individuals with similar goals and motivation to achieve them."

Regardless of where Bret is coming from in evaluating the importance of team chemistry, it is apparent from the way he conducts his program that he emphasizes its importance. "We use many different methods to develop team chemistry: Allow all members of the team—freshmen, seniors, head coach, team manager, star player, and seldom used sub—to have input into the development of the team. A sense of team ownership is essential."

"Encourage the team to get together without the coaches in non-soccer-related activities—social activities."

"Form a democratically-elected council to help set team policy and make decisions on everything from the training schedules, to team personal conduct rules, to choosing uniform styles, even to selection of warm-up music."

"Treat all players with respect and dignity. Be consistent in applying team rules while being fully cognizant of the differences in personalities among team members and the differences in individual needs."

"Coaches must 'practice what they preach.' If a practice or rule is good for the players, it is probably good for the coaches, too. There should not be two standards of behavior. For example, the coach who stays out late and has poor personal health habits should not be surprised if his players follow that lead."

Bret leaves no question on his evaluation of team cohesion/chemistry. He puts it right at the top of his priorities, regardless of the route he took in arriving at this evaluation.

◆   ◆   ◆   ◆   ◆

. . . on Discipline

Bret doesn't attempt to define discipline. Instead he provides his philosophy on team conduct, the establishment of rules, criteria for their establishment, and enforcement of rules.

"The entire team—or player representatives—and the coaches should decide jointly on basic team disciplinary practices. If all affected people have input and representation in the development of basic team disciplinary practices, all of those affected will be more committed to implementing and adhering to policies."

"The issue of team discipline in a college setting is complicated by legal and moral dimensions. For example, is the use of alcohol condemned, condoned, or ignored? How much out-of-season training is to be expected or required? How much should a player's past history, with respect to disciplinary problems, influence his treatment when he commits another rule infraction? Can a player build a 'bank of points' for team leadership, community service, and extra effort? All of these questions need to be considered in establishing and administering disciplinary practices. It's not always a black and white issue."

And Bret has some "methods," he calls them, for applying disciplinary action. "My general rule is to always look at what's best for the individual in light of what's best for the team. Occasionally in doing this, I have to make difficult decisions that may impact the team or an individual negatively, in the short-term. But the focus is on the long term. So the temporary negative impacts should be more than off set, if the proper disciplinary action helps achieve our program's goals, which go beyond day-to-day results of games. The end result of disciplinary practices should be the creation and maintenance of an environment that enhances excellence—on the field, in the classroom, and in our players' personal conduct."

. . . on Mental Preparation

Bret puts an interesting phrase in his definition of mental preparation, "taking the time to . . ." While it may be understood in performing any activity that time is involved, by putting the phrase up front, Bret emphasizes the need for assigning a high priority for mental preparation. His definition: "Taking the time as an individual and as part of a team to digest and rehearse the tactical requirements of the upcoming game and to develop the proper psychological mindset."

Interestingly, in addressing mental preparation, Bret stresses physical preparedness. He explains how this ultimately helps his players prepare mentally: "College soccer's preseason lasts only a couple of weeks, so most of the physical conditioning must occur well in advance of the season. My approach is to teach the benefits of year-round conditioning and a stair-step approach to increasing physiological abilities (i.e. strength, power, foot speed, aerobic fitness etc.). This approach necessitates goal-setting based on specific physiological targets that are measured prior to preseason and again at specific times throughout the year. It is helpful for some players to use a diary to chart workouts, sleep cycles, and eating habits to develop a logical, consistent self-motivated approach to fitness." Organizing activities and keeping track of them yourself helps organize the important thought processes as well.

Bret believes that preparation for games should be pretty much repetitive, without much variation, regardless of the opponent. "Though ideally, we would like to be at our mental peak for every game, that may not be possible, especially for the younger and less experienced players. But approaches should not vary. Stability can help develop confidence and lower stress prior to games. Mental rehearsal (imagery) and sticking to routine activities are generally the best ways to help players prepare for important games."

Of course, the coach plays a role in mental preparedness for individual games. Bret: "The most important way a coach can help is by showing confidence in the players' abilities to 'succeed' and by helping each player find the proper level of 'looseness'—not too relaxed and not too tense."

Late-game strategy isn't quite as much different from that employed during the major part of the game in soccer. It isn't like two-minute offenses in football or full-court presses in basketball, where there are all sorts of varied situations that require as many different strategies. "But still," according to Bret, "there are times when a team must change mentally. We may need to take fewer risks (if we're up a goal) or greater risks (down a goal). The length of time we have to protect a lead or to catch up determines our strategy. 'Changing gears' according to the situation requires composure and added concentration—beyond the normal concentration on executing."

"For this reason, we practice being 'up a goal' and 'down a goal' in training, with a specific amount of time to protect the lead or catch up. This training allows players the luxury of having already been in situations they may find themselves in for games."

◆ ◆ ◆ ◆ ◆

. . . on Mental Toughness

Bret says, "Mental toughness is the resolve and psychological ability to overcome obstacles, opponents, and difficult circumstances to perform at optimum level."

He doesn't believe that mental toughness and skill level are necessarily connected. He says that some highly-skilled athletes can struggle with their resolve. "They can have self doubts and lose their composure, which affects their performance adversely." Conversely, players with less talent can perform up to their potential more frequently because they are mentally tough. Sometimes mental toughness can be a stronger influence on overall performance than raw talent.

Bret assigns four characteristics to mentally tough players:

1. They have self-confidence.
2. They have a commitment to achieve goals, both team and individual goals.
3. They have a strong work ethic, exhibiting self discipline and dedication to staying focused on their assignments.
4. They are realistic. They accept their own and the team's weaknesses, which increases their abilities to overcome them. At the same time, they have an accurate assessment so they can capitalize on their own and on the team's strengths.

. . . on Communication

Bret says, "The most important consideration about halftime discussions is that they must be conducted in a way that leaves the players confident and up-beat. How you achieve this depends on the circumstances. For example, the team may be giving it all they have, but they are not achieving their goals because I haven't provided tactical information to fit the situation they are in. The obvious approach to a halftime discussion in such a case is to focus on tactics—identifying the problems with first half tactics and explaining what is needed to fix them."

"Or the team may be following the right tactics, but the ball just hasn't bounced right or the opponents are just playing better than normal. The team needs to understand that momentum swings; and if they stay focused, it will swing back their way. And sometimes the team just isn't giving their all, and they may not even realize it. When this happens, 'scolding' may be appropriate to help them jack up their effort—a bit of a jump start. More often than not, a combination of these approaches is called for, and the coach has to make a judgment pretty fast to put his halftime discussion together to make it most effective. But regardless of the situation, the players should never leave the halftime feeling self-doubt or lacking confidence."

Sometimes it's best to leave most of the post-game remarks, after a loss or poor performance, for a later time, according to Bret. "When the team is tired and the coaches are somewhat mentally drained, they both need time to digest what has happened. By waiting until the next practice or meeting with the team, a coach has time to assess the game performance and determine the best approach to dealing with it. Then he can avoid saying or doing the wrong thing, which will be difficult to rectify. One caution a coach should remember when he puts off a post-game discussion: he must make sure the team understands that he is waiting until the proper time to address the team and that he is not making specific comments because he doesn't care. Letting the team think that you don't care is the worse thing you can do."

Bret brings up another situation. The team doesn't operate in a vacuum. He says, "There are times a team must be prepared to face the media or other non-team people—fans, family, and friends. They must be dignified and mature, even though they may be hurting inside. If they know that maturity and dignity are part of their roles as players and that they have the coaches' respect and support, they will react positively, and this will help their spirits."

PAT SUMMITT
University of Tennessee-Knoxville

Position
Head Women's Basketball Coach

Career Record
759-153 (27 Seasons)

Education
B.S.   University of Tennessee-Martin
M.S.   University of Tennessee-Knoxville

Team and Personal Highlights

- ➢ Naismith Coach of the Century.
- ➢ Coached Naismith Player of the Century.
- ➢ Enshrined in four Halls of Fame.
- ➢ Six NCAA national championships.
- ➢ 12 Final Four appearances.
- ➢ 19 Southeastern Conference tournament and regular-season titles.
- ➢ 11 Olympians.
- ➢ 16 Kodak All-Americans.
- ➢ 45 All-SEC performers.

PAT SUMMITT

Introduction . . .

They call her "Pat." Just "Pat." Every student-athlete who she meets for the first time on a recruiting visit to the day they walk across the stage in the Arena to receive their diploma from the University of Tennessee. Pat Summitt is the consummate warrior coach: tough, demanding, disciplined, loving, bigger-than-life. And she wouldn't have it any other way.

For 27 seasons, she has been walking the sidelines as head women's basketball coach for the Tennessee Volunteers. Her reputation for excellence precedes her in everything she does. Her coaching records are amazing: six national titles, 70 NCAA tournament victories, 12 Final Four appearances. She does not get compared to other female basketball coaches; she gets compared with John Wooden, the legendary UCLA men's basketball coach who has won 10 national championships.

Summitt's achievements are unparalleled in the collegiate coaching ranks. She was inducted in October, 2000, into the Basketball Hall of Fame in Springfield, Massachusetts, the first time she was eligible for the Hall's ballot. She became just the fourth women's basketball coach to earn the Hall of Fame honor. In addition to her induction into the Hall of Fame, she was named as the Naismith Coach of the Century in April, 2000. She was doubly honored when former Lady Vol Chamique Holdsclaw was selected as the Naismith Player of the Century. Prior to those announcements, ESPN selected her program as the "Team of the Decade" (1990's), tying with the Florida State Seminole football machine under Bobby Bowden, another author in this book.

Summitt's Coach of the Year awards are very diversified: *The Sporting News*, Associated Press, U.S. Basketball Writers Association, Women's Basketball Coaches Association, Frontier/State Farm, Utah Tip-off Club, and the Columbus (OH) Touchdown Club. Her name has become fused in the same sentence as coaching great Wooden, or joined to the accomplishments of the recent dynasties of sports, the Chicago Bulls and the New York Yankees.

Pat is also most proud of her players' work in the classroom. The incredible graduation rate of her players and the successes they have garnered in life long after their playing days makes her smile. Every Lady Vol who has completed her eligibility at Tennessee has received her degree or is in the process of completing her degree requirements.

Who would have thought that the daughter of Richard and Hazel Head of Henrietta, Tennessee, would be enshrined in not only the Naismith Hall of Fame, but the Women's Sports Foundation Hall of Fame (1990), the

National Association for Sport and Physical Education Hall of Fame (1996), and the Women's Basketball Hall of Fame (1999)?

Pat played basketball and volleyball at the University of Tennessee-Martin. After graduation in 1974, the University of Tennessee in Knoxville showed its confidence in her abilities to coach when the school offered her a graduate teaching assistantship and the reins to the women's intercollegiate basketball team as a 22-year-old. Combining teaching classes with coaching, and playing for the U.S. Olympic team in Montreal during the XXI Olympiad, made for a very exciting time for Pat. Upon returning from the Olympics, Pat began her full-time coaching duties in Knoxville, and hasn't looked back since.

Pat is married to R.B. Summitt and, along with son Tyler, make their home along the banks of the Tennessee River in Knoxville. Listen closely as Pat Summitt shares her championship philosophy . .

. . . on Motivation

Motivation is a prime ingredient for success within all organizations, and Coach Summitt believes that inner drive and goals play a big part in the self-motivation process.

"Motivation is harnessing an inner drive and pointing it toward the attainment of a specific goal," she says.

Motivating today's student-athletes can be a difficult assignment, but Summitt contends that bringing the right person into the program negates much of that problem.

"We look for quality people to represent Tennessee," she states. "That's staff and players included. When you get good people, you have a strong base to work from."

Summitt says that some motivation techniques are not very effective.

"The least effective techniques are gimmicks or temporary tactics, such as newspaper articles, threats or bribery," Summitt says. "Those kinds of methods just aren't productive."

Effective methods of motivation include all techniques that develop self-motivation.

"The most effective techniques are those which enhance self-motivation," she points out. "The techniques can help develop intensity in the player, they can improve work habits, and they can assist the athlete in maintaining a high level of expectations."

In summary, Coach Summitt defines motivation as harnessing an inner drive and pointing it toward the attainment of specific goals. She adds that self-motivation is enhanced when quality persons are brought into the program, both as players and staff members.

Least effective methods of motivating today's student-athletes include techniques that bring only temporary results, she says. Those tactics include newspaper articles, threats or bribery.

Finally, Summitt states that the most effective methods of motivation enhance player self-motivation. These individualized techniques help the player to develop intensity, improve work habits and maintain a high level of expectation.

◆ ◆ ◆ ◆ ◆

. . . on Team Cohesion

Team chemistry is a vital ingredient for ultimate team success. Coach Summitt believes that team cohesion can be developed through leadership and trust.

"I would say that I'm the type of coach that would rely heavily on strong leadership from players," she says. "From our strong base of quality people, we look for strong leaders and I believe that leadership has been extremely valuable to us."

A feeling of trust is also important, she states.

"With players and coaches, I think you have to have trust," she says. "You have to trust the players on the floor and you have to trust your assistant coaches."

Summitt characterizes team cohesion as a process involving several elements.

"In order to build team chemistry, you first need to identify individual strengths and weaknesses of the team," she begins. "Players must also recognize and accept their roles on the team. Finally, a plan must be developed for how each individual must respond on and off the court to help the team reach its goals."

Summitt believes that utilizing team leadership and incorporating total player involvement in the rules-making process are the best methods of building team cohesion.

"When you have strong leaders like we do, you learn to delegate responsibilities," she says. "We expect our team leaders and players to identify our team goals and then design a code of conduct to help us achieve these goals. When all players have input in determining team rules, there is a strong commitment to uphold that code."

In summary, Coach Summitt believes that team cohesion can be developed through leadership and trust. She also states that team cohesion includes identifying individual strengths and weaknesses, recognizing individual roles, and committing to a plan for team behavior on and off the court.

◆   ◆   ◆   ◆   ◆

. . . on Discipline

Discipline is a trait of the championship team and individual. Coach Summitt claims that discipline is at the heart of her coaching philosophy.

"Certainly we are a disciplined program," she says. "We are very proud of our discipline. We view it as a positive that we do have discipline. I think the expectation that we have in our student-athletes to accept responsibility for themselves and represent Tennessee is important.

"By establishing discipline, we feel like we're all working toward the same goal, that we have a plan and a guideline for getting there. We're not going to move away from it."

Summitt's approach to discipline has remained the same over the years.

"Be firm, fair and consistent," she states. "Be honest and have open communication at all times."

Inconsistency is the coach's worst nightmare when dealing with team discipline.

"Inconsistent discipline can be detrimental to the team and also ineffective individually," she states.

Effective disciplinary procedures involve peer pressure and consistent application of the rules.

"The most effective discipline happens when the teams helps to establish the policies or team rules," Pat states. "Peer pressure can be a very effective form of discipline.

"Each coach must also use their own style or philosophy and remain consistent in disciplinary actions."

In summary, Coach Summitt lists discipline as a top priority within her program. She believes that student-athletes at Tennessee accept the responsibility of representing the university and state in a positive manner.

Summitt's philosophy concerning team discipline has remained steady over the years. She says that the head coach must be firm, fair, consistent and honest during all communication with players.

Ineffective discipline methods are a result of inconsistent administration of the rules by the head coach. She adds that inconsistency can harm the individual as well as the team.

Finally, Summitt states that effective discipline methods include player participation in making team rules, peer pressure and consistent disciplinary action by the head coach.

. . . on Mental Preparation

All successful coaches say that mental preparation is essential to team and individual success. Coach Summitt believes that mental preparation begins with a basic understanding of team philosophy.

"Mental preparation is a basic understanding and knowledge of our team's system, both offensively and defensively," she says. "Knowledge and repetition are elements of good mental preparation."

Summitt states that goal setting is imperative during pre-season practice.

"The long pre-season practices can wear you down, no doubt about it," she says. "Therefore, we use goal setting to a great extent during this time. The process involves daily goal setting and long-range goal setting."

Mental preparation for non-conference and conference games is similar.

"For both non-conference and conference games, our mental preparation is the same," she begins. "We discuss and review keys for success in each game. It's then up to the individual players as to how they respond to each challenge."

Late-game strategy can lead to victory, and Summitt mentally prepares the team for all possible scenarios.

"We create various late-game situations in practice," she says. "Very rarely do we ever run a play late in a game without first having gone over it in practice."

In summary, Coach Summitt is of the belief that mental preparation is effective when each player has a basic understanding and knowledge of the team's offensive and defensive philosophy.

Mental preparation for the grind of pre-season practice includes daily goal setting sessions in addition to long-range goal setting, she says.

Repetition of key elements for success in each game enhances the mental preparation process for non-conference and conference games, she adds.

Finally, late-game strategy is practiced daily so that the players are confident when the situation occurs during a game.

. . . on Mental Toughness

Many people believe that mental toughness is a trait found in highly-skilled athletes. Coach Summitt begs to differ with that type of thinking.

"I do not totally agree that all highly-skilled athletes are mentally tough," she states. "It's not something you're born with. It's something you have to develop on your own."

She mentions that a mentally tough person reacts favorably to adverse conditions.

"I believe that the mentally tough person has the ability to concentrate and successfully perform in adverse or pressure situations," she concludes.

In summary Coach Summitt believes that some great athletes are not mentally tough. She asserts that mental toughness is not inherent in players, but must be developed like all other fundamental skills.

Finally, Summitt says that the mentally tough person is able to concentrate and perform well in all pressure situations.

. . . on Communication

Effective communication with staff and players is an important psychological factor for the success of the program. Coach Summitt has always been a strong advocate of open communication with her players and staff.

"As I've mentioned before, open, honest communication is the most important element in building trust within the program," she says. "The head coach must take the leadership role in establishing an open communication policy."

Halftime comments and comments during timeouts late in a game in which the team is losing are positive in nature, she says.

"During these times in a game, we encourage them not to give up and assure them they can still win," Summitt says. "We also give them the needed technical changes in offense or defense that may turn the game around in our favor."

Post-game comments following a tough loss or a poor performance will vary, depending upon the outcome and other factors.

"My post-game response to the players depends on our effort and execution," she says. "I try to evaluate why we lost or performed poorly and respond accordingly."

In summary Coach Summitt believes that open, honest communication within the program has a positive psychological effect on the players and staff.

Comments at halftime or late during a game in a losing cause will be positive in tone. She says it is important to encourage the players at all times and assure them that they will be successful if they keep working hard. Technical adjustments in offensive and defensive strategy are also made during this time.

Finally, post-game comments following a tough loss or poor team performance will vary, depending upon the outcome of the game and effort and execution exhibited by the players. She says that it is important to evaluate <u>why</u> the team lost or performed poorly and respond accordingly.

MEL TJEERDSMA

Northwest Missouri State University

- - - - - - - - - - - - - - -

Position
Head Football Coach

Career Record
129-59-4 (17 seasons)

Education
B.A.   Southern (SD) State College
M.A.   Northwest Missouri State University

Team and Personal Highlights

- ➢ Two-time NCAA Division II national champions.
- ➢ NAIA national championship.
- ➢ Two-time National Coach of the Year.
- ➢ Five-time American Football Coaches Association Regional Coach of the Year.
- ➢ Six-time Missouri Intercollegiate Athletic Association Coach of the Year.
- ➢ Three-time Texas Intercollegiate Athletic Association Coach of the Year.
- ➢ 16 All-American players.
- ➢ 27 first-team All-MIAA performers.
- ➢ 16 NAIA All-America selections and 11 Academic All-America picks.
- ➢ Six players drafted or signed with NFL teams.
- ➢ Member of AFCA Board of Trustees.
- ➢ Chairman, AFCA Division II All-America Committee.

MEL TJEERDSMA

Introduction . . .

Over the past seven years, the Northwest Missouri State University football program has evolved from a winless team to a national powerhouse, winning NCAA Division II National Championships in both 1998 and 1999. In addition to the two national titles, the Bearcats have won five straight MIAA championships and made five consecutive trips to the NCAA Division II Playoffs.

The architect of this dramatic turn-around is Mel Tjeerdsma (pronounced TERTS-MA). Since arriving at the Maryville, Missouri, school in 1994, and absorbing a winless season in his first year, things have skyrocketed. His 1995 team finished with a 6-5 record and a tie for second in the MIAA. In 1996, Northwest won its first MIAA Championship since 1984, sharing the title with Pittsburg State University, and quarterback Greg Teale was awarded the NCAA Post-Graduate Scholarship, a prestigious scholarship for graduate school. The team finished with an 11-2 record, losing in the quarterfinal round of the NCAA Playoffs to Northern Colorado.

In 1997, the Bearcats solidified their position as a national power, winning the MIAA championship, and advancing once again to the quarterfinals of the playoffs. As in 1996, Tjeerdsma's squad again lost to eventual national champion, Northern Colorado, to end their season at 12-1. But the best was still to come.

The 1998 season saw the completion of a worst-to-first story. After going 0-11 in 1994, Northwest set an NCAA Division II record by becoming the first team ever to go 15-0, and winning their first national title in the process.

The 1999 Bearcat team struggled to create their own identity amongst a great deal of adversity. Injuries to key players, a potentially devastating early season loss, and the unexpected death of a teammate were obstacles that Tjeerdsma's squad would have to overcome. Northwest cleared those hurdles and made a repeat trip to the NCAA Division II national championship game in Florence, Alabama. A miracle finish in the last four minutes of the game tied the score at 44-44 with 10 seconds remaining. Four overtimes later, in what some have called the greatest college football game ever, Coach Tjeerdsma had guided his Bearcats to their second consecutive National Championship with a 58-52 win over Carson-Newman College.

The 2000 team was undefeated and looking for a three-peat national championship when North Dakota State used a big third quarter to upset the

Bearcats, 31-17, in a quarterfinal playoff game. But Northwest won their fifth consecutive MIAA title, and Mel again won Coach of the Year honors.

Tjeerdsma coached at Austin College in Sherman, Texas, from 1984 to 1993, compiling a 60-38-4 record, guiding the team to three Texas Intercollegiate Athletic Association championships, and becoming the winningest coach in school history. He was TIAA Coach of the Year three times, and made two trips to the NAIA Division II Playoffs.

Mel began his college coaching career as offensive coordinator at Northwestern College in Orange City, Iowa. The Red Raiders earned four trips to the NAIA Division II Playoffs while Tjeerdsma was there, winning a national championship in 1983. He also served as head track and field coach at Northwestern, winning three Tri-State Conference titles and five consecutive NAIA District 15 indoor championships. Tjeerdsma and his wife, Carol, reside in Maryville. They have three grown children.

One of the nicest, most sincere individuals you will find in college coaching, Coach Tjeerdsma was enthusiastic when relating his winning ideas . . .

. . . on Motivation

Coach Mel Tjeerdsma doesn't waste words in defining motivation. "Motivation in athletics is getting the athlete to give his very best effort." This definition, while brief, may go beyond what others define as motivation in that it carries an implied sense of success.

Mel points to three factors essential to motivating athletes: goal setting, total preparation, and honesty.

He says, "Athletes must understand how each game and each performance relates to the entire season." "Performance" covers a lot of territory. Performance in practice, performance in the classroom, and performance in personal conduct. He considers performance and games as building blocks. When put together into a season, the goals of the season emerge.

How does preparation motivate? According to Mel, "If an athlete is totally prepared for all aspects of the contest, then he feels ready to give his best effort." Feeling that you're not prepared results in inhibition, and inhibition results in tentativeness, which can be fatal in a fast-moving game like football. Some actions must be instinctive, and the right instinctive actions result from experiences on the practice field.

Honesty plays a role in any endeavor. Mel makes it an integral part of preparation, which, in turn, relates to motivation. He says, "An athlete feels more comfortable when he knows the whole picture and all of the real possibilities before him."

Mel feels that short-term, superficial acts to motivate don't work. They don't penetrate down to the core of the athlete's make up. As an example, he cites the "Rah, Rah," attitude. He says, "You can't 'win one for the gipper' every week." Motivation has to be more lasting than just at game time. It involves everything an athlete does.

And fear doesn't work either. Mel: "Don't tell your team 'if you're not ready to play this week, you'll lose." They don't want to hear what will make them lose. They want to hear what will make them win. Maybe sometimes a combination of the carrot and the stick will work, but there has to be a carrot. The stick by itself doesn't cut it.

Finally, Mel lists threats separately from fear. A threat is something he can administer. "If you don't play up to your abilities, you'll be replaced."

Put all this together and you're right back to Mel's concise definition: "getting the athlete to give his very best effort."

. . . on Team Chemistry

Some teams have slogans like, "BIG TEAM, little me." Mel expresses the same concept in defining team cohesion: "Team cohesion is working together toward a common goal with little or no concern for individual credit. To develop team cohesion—or team chemistry—athletes must care for each other sincerely. Individuality has no place in team chemistry. Each player must be willing to give up individuality in becoming a part of the team."

Let the media create the stars. A team is no stronger than its weakest link. One missed block by a lineman can result in a running back's being thrown for a loss—maybe even a fumble. Failure to cover your zone on defense can result in a touchdown for an opponent. Carrying out your assignments that the typical fan never recognizes are just as much a part of the team effort and just as vital as the guy who carries the ball across the goal line. Every member of the team has to not only accept this reality but he must embrace it.

Mel talks about three specific parts of team chemistry:

1. Developing friendship: He says to his players, "You have to include all members of the team in your friendship, and you must demonstrate that you genuinely care for each other. You do this by getting to know as much about your teammates as you can. Know them as a person, not just a face. Know about their families. The more you know them, the closer you will become, even though there may be significant differences in your

interests. Do things together other than scheduled team activities. Do things together on your own. Go to movies, to other athletic events, work together on community projects—just hang out together—and you'll develop team chemistry."

2. Focus on the team in taking credit for accomplishments. "Don't play up individual accomplishments, at least not among yourselves," says Mel. You can't control what fans and the media do, but you'd better not forget who threw that block, or the blocker may have just the slightest sense of not being appreciated, and that's all it takes for the subconscious to allow him to let up just enough to let the defensive player through. "Perhaps the most important person in focusing on team accomplishments rather than individual accomplishments is the coach," Mel points out. He can, and must, set the tone for the whole team.

3. Mel implores his staff and team to "develop sincere trust and caring among all players, coaches, and staff." Trust, caring, team versus individual, and genuine friendship result in team cohesion and team chemistry.

◆ ◆ ◆ ◆ ◆

. . . on Discipline

To Mel, discipline is something athletes want. That goes a long way in helping develop a well disciplined team. He says, "Athletes want to know the boundaries and guidelines for their actions. I believe that discipline is necessary in every aspect of athletics."

"I don't get carried away with establishing rules, although athletes need, and want, structure. But I prefer to guide them and teach them what constitutes acceptable behavior." In doing that, Mel is teaching the athletes something they can translate to other activities, and he's teaching them something that will allow them to feel comfortable that they are doing the right thing. There are simply too many variations in life for a coach to develop specific rules that will be applicable to every variable in human behavior. But providing an athlete a sense of right and wrong and giving him boundaries and general guidelines will let him feel he knows what's the right thing to do.

"Don't have too many set rules. Every situation is different," says Mel. "We try to teach our players to deal with each situation as it comes up. I really believe in self discipline and individual responsibility. Athletes have to learn that they are responsible for their actions. We help our athletes learn to do things for themselves. Too many athletes are 'spoon fed' all through their careers, and they don't know how to take care of themselves when they get into the real world. And you must BE CONSISTENT! Treat everyone the same."

Mel believes that empty threats are a major impediment to discipline. He doesn't like threats, because they have to be carried out, once made. He also says that discipline should be individualized. "Don't punish the team for what one athlete does."

He believes that reducing playing time is a positive type of discipline. It gives those who work and don't get to play as much because of their physical limitations a chance to play, and it teaches the starter who goes beyond the rules that he isn't indispensable. Mel also thinks that early morning running is a good form of discipline. It never hurts to build additional stamina.

And Mel cautions not to let too much time pass between the unacceptable behavior and the time corrective action is taken: "Discipline must be immediate!"

◆ ◆ ◆ ◆ ◆

. . . on Mental Preparation

Mel emphasizes the importance of mental preparation by indicating that it is inseparable from physical preparation: "Mental preparation includes total preparation (physical, mental, and emotional). A team that has prepared mentally for all aspects and situations of the game and is prepared physically as well is the team that will be able to deal with any game situation."

In addressing pre-season and off-season preparation, he stresses the link between mental and physical preparation again. "If an athlete is physically prepared, he will be able to handle all of the other aspects of the off-season."

"Athletes need to know in advance what is expected of them. They need to know what pre-season activities will be like, just as they need to know what to expect in a game."

Goals are important to Mel: "Team goals for physical testing will provide guidance and motivation for individual athletes as well."

"We try to have the same approach for every game. If you put too much emphasis on one game, you're bound to have some let down afterward, regardless of the outcome." And how many upsets result for looking beyond a weak opponent or resting on your laurels right after a victory over a major opponent?

"A coach has to be honest about his approach to each game. Players need to know the importance of every game," says Mel. If the coach doesn't believe that each game is important, how can the players be expected to believe it? Mel believes in focusing on what you have control over and not worrying about what you can't control. "We try to emphasize our preparation and our performance as opposed to who our opponent is. We don't worry about the scoreboard at the end of the game. If each player gives his best effort, then each player is a winner."

Mel thinks that it's a mistake to try to make big changes in late game strategy. He says, "Be consistent. Stay with what you're prepared to do. Each player has to have trust in his coaches and his teammates. He must have NO DOUBTS. You can't be confident on 'new strategy,' so don't try things you haven't prepared for.

"Finally, put your best players in a position to make the 'big play'." If you've prepared mentally, they'll probably make it.

. . . on Mental Toughness

Mel puts it this way: "Mentally tough athletes can block out all of the distractions associated with a particular situation. In doing so, they are prepared to deal with whatever comes up." In a game like football, there are countless unexpected adverse occurrences—fumbles, missed blocks, pass interceptions etc. So the application of "whatever comes up" covers a lot of territory. Any of these happenings can test a player's mental toughness.

Mentally tough athletes exhibit some characteristics that make them stand out. "They are focused," says Mel. "They see only the tasks as hand, They are self confident, and in most cases, that self-confidence is exhibited in a way that spreads to their teammates, helping to make self-confidence a team characteristic."

"They are well-prepared. It is this preparation that makes them ready to deal with unexpected adversity. One of those adversities that the mentally prepared athlete is prepared to deal with is mistakes made by his teammates. He stays focused on what has to be done, without being distracted to analyze what just happened and cast blame."

"Most mentally tough athletes have a tremendous work ethic that extends beyond the practice field into all of his off-season activities."

Mentally tough players thrive on challenges. Mel says, "They always seem to be able to respond effectively when the chips are down."

. . . on Communication

Mel wants to challenge his team at halftime. After reviewing the technical changes that he has decided will help in the second half, he wants them to fully grasp their current situation. The first half is history. Focus on the second half, and point out that it's the only chance the players have left to influence the outcome of the game. Don't let it get away.

He says, "Once the game is over the entire game will be history. You can't do anything to change the outcome after the final gun. Remind your team of the investment they're protecting—all the pre-season practice, the progress they've made toward their own personal goals, the games already past. And, finally, remind them of their obligation to the team and to their teammates. Your players really care about each other; but sometimes, in the heat of battle, they have to be reminded that we're a team—not just a group of individual players wearing the same colors."

In a post-game locker room just after a disappointing performance, Mel says that several things are critical:

"BE HONEST! Tell your players exactly what you feel caused the problems in the game. But don't single out individuals in this meeting," according to Mel. That's for next week's practice, when you can be constructive and let them work on solutions to problems right after they learn of them. That helps them avoid a long period of dwelling on them. "Then get them to focus on the next opponent. What happened in the game just completed can't be changed, but they can surely look forward to playing better against the next opponent.

"Make sure that the players understand that you don't expect everything to work out right all the time. That's the reality of life, and what better time to get this point across than right after something went wrong and their attention is focused on what went wrong? If you gave your very best, you've accomplished your goal of giving it all you have all the time. In one sense you're a winner, and you shouldn't overlook that. If you didn't give your best effort, you are staring at what results when you don't, and you resolve to never fail to give it your best again. Knowing that you didn't give it your best isn't a very good feeling."

Mel takes advantage of situations to make sure the circumstances help him communicate. That makes communications more effective than anything a coach can say in a vacuum.

◆ ◆ ◆ ◆ ◆

SHAWN WALSH

University of Maine-Orono

Position
Head Men's Ice Hockey Coach

Career Record
399-215-44 (17 seasons)

Education
B.A.   Bowling Green State (OH) University
M.A.   Bowling Green State (OH) University

Team and Personal Highlights

- ➤ National Coach of the Year.
- ➤ Four-time Hockey East and New England Coach of the Year.
- ➤ Two-time NCAA national champions.
- ➤ Eight Hockey East regular-season titles and Hockey East tournament titles.
- ➤ 11 NCAA tournament berths.
- ➤ Seven Frozen Four appearances.
- ➤ Two Hobey Baker Award winners
- ➤ 28 All-American players.
- ➤ Eight U.S. Olympic team members.
- ➤ Two Canadian Olympians.
- ➤ 35 National Hockey League players.
- ➤ President, American Hockey Coaches Association.
- ➤ Board of Directors, American Hockey Coaches Association.

SHAWN WALSH

Introduction . . .

The arrival of Shawn Walsh to the University of Maine in 1984 signaled a resurgence and new energy to the men's ice hockey program. In the three years prior to his arrival, the Black Bears were 27-65-0. It took him only three years to guide the Black Bears into the NCAA tournament. And there has been no looking back.

Walsh followed the successful 1987 season with a banner year in 1988. The Black Bears finished the year 34-8-2, winning the Hockey East title and holding the top ranking in the country for the last eight weeks before falling to eventual national champion Lake Superior State in the NCAA semifinals. Walsh also received his first Hockey East and New England Division I Coach of the Year awards following the 1988 season.

The 11th all-time winningest active collegiate hockey coach, Walsh's squads averaged over 28 wins per season from 1989-1992, advanced to the finals of the Hockey East tournament each year (winning the league in 1989), and played in the NCAA tournament each year. In 1993, the Black Bears posted a school record for wins with a 42-1-2 mark. The winning percentage of .956 ranks among the best in college hockey history.

The 1993 season also featured a 32-game winning streak to start the season. UMaine won its last 12 games, including a dramatic win over Lake Superior State in the national title game in Milwaukee, giving Walsh his first national championship. It was the first NCAA Division I team title in UMaine school history.

The following five seasons brought NCAA tournament appearances, with a second Frozen Four finals appearance in 1995. Walsh led the 1999 Black Bears to their second NCAA Division I national championship and its sixth Frozen Four appearance in Anaheim, California, that was dominated by teams from Hockey East. After beating Boston College 2-1 in overtime in the first semifinal game, the Black Bears defeated New Hampshire 3-2 in overtime to clinch the second national championship in school history.

In addition to team excellence, Walsh's teams have produced 28 All-Americans, eight U.S. Olympians, two Canadian Olympians, and 35 National Hockey League players. He has also produced an 11-0-1 record in international competition. Twice teams that Walsh coached have won the gold medal at the U.S. Olympic Festival. He also coached the U.S. Select teams to victories in 1989 and 1993. He has also coached two Hobey Baker Award winners. The Hobey Baker Award is considered college hockey's most prestigious honor.

Walsh has also had a profound effect on the careers of his former assistant coaches, including Red Gendron (New Jersey Devils), Jay Leach (Atlanta Thrashers), Greg Cronin (New York Islanders), Bruce Crowder (Northeastern University), and Tim Whitehead (UMass-Lowell). Dave Norris, another former UMaine assistant coach, serves as the Assistant General Manager of the Vancouver Canucks.

Walsh, a White Plains, New York, native, began his coaching career as an undergraduate at Bowling Green State University, coaching the junior varsity hockey team and working with head coach, Ron Mason. In 1979, Mason and Walsh left Bowling Green to resurrect the struggling ice hockey program at Michigan State. Mason would go on to become the winningest active college hockey coach with almost 900 career victories at MSU, and Walsh would leave in 1984 for Maine.

Walsh has been active in the community, serving as the Eastern Maine Spokesman for the United Way. He annually assists with the Muscular Dystrophy Telethon, Children's Miracle Network, and speaks on the behalf of several charities throughout the community, region, and state. Shawn, wife Lynne, and their children reside in Veazie.

The high-energy coach with the contagious positive attitude was thrilled to convey his thoughts . . .

. . . on Motivation

Shawn Walsh believes motivation involves stimulating people to go beyond their normal expected outputs. "The stimulus can come from the player, motivating himself, or from someone else, but genuine motivation involves pushing beyond what the player, himself, thinks he's capable of," he says. The setting of goals is built into motivation by Shawn's definition, because going "beyond their normal outputs" defines the goal as a challenging one.

He brings goals into the picture when he discusses some of the motivational approaches he's found more effective. "You want your players to keep their 'eyes on the prize.' like keeping their minds on the NCAA Championship and what it takes to get there. Once they are focused, then a coach must be positive. I like to show a video of a great play the team made, pointing out several things we did well that made the play successful. And whenever possible I make it a point to include players who don't get a lot of extrinsic motivation, like the big scorers do."

"Taking care of 'little things' can be motivating. Some people call this discipline. But it's motivating because it helps players be successful, and success is motivating. Being consistent and 'staying the course' makes you accountable. And one thing team players are accountable to is that team name on the front of their jersey."

Conversely, Shawn points out that the video can be misused and become an impediment to motivation. He says, "Any form of public negative criticism can impede motivation. Don't point out mistakes as a means of motivating. You have to correct mistakes, but you can stress the proper technique as opposed to the mistake. So, be careful how you use the video. And, in this age, fear just doesn't work. Don't tell a player, 'if you don't do this—' followed by some threat of punishment."

"Keep your eyes on the prize, take care of the little things, and stay positive. That'll get you there," says Shawn.

. . . on Team Cohesion

Shawn defines team chemistry as "having all the players accept their own roles and the roles of other members of the team." he says, "It's being unselfish and understanding the importance of everyone in the program— not just the 'star players', but also the manager, the statistician—everyone. Egos have no place in building team cohesion. There can't be a caste system. Each person in the program is accountable for himself and to every other person in the program."

"We have team meetings each week. I think these meetings provide a mechanism for some of the best team-building we do. We are constantly assessing where WE—not where I—are now and where we are going. I strongly encourage the players to speak up in these meetings and give us their assessments about where we are, where we should be going, and what it takes to get there."

One innovation of Shawn's is his weekly "Kangaroo Courts." "They are a mixture of fun and corrective action. All the indiscretions are minor. We have monetary fines, all the way up to a quarter. The courts build cohesion. The 'offenses' can be for almost anything—something that happens in the dormitory or an apartment, something that happens with a girl friend, or even something that went wrong in a game. And guess who usually gets fined most—the coach."

One of Shawn's activities that builds team cohesion and is also motivational is his twice-a-year peer evaluation program, conducted at Christmas break and again right before playoffs.

"We give each player and each member of the staff a set of papers with every person's name (including his own), followed by sufficient space to write comments. The coaching staff's names are the first listed. Then this question is addressed for every person on the pages: 'What does he have to do physically, socially, academically, and mentally for us to win a national championship?' The evaluator even addresses the questions for the space under his own name. All staff members are given a week or so to fill out the forms anonymously and turn them in to the secretary. Just before the next road trip, one of the completed forms (not the one he filled out) is given to each person—coach, manager, player, etc.—and then the comments about each person are read, for one person at a time. For example comments from all the sheets about the head coach are read first. When a player listens to his 'peer evaluation,' he writes in his personal notebook the three most prevalent behavior patterns he needs to improve."

This process includes a lot of team building. It builds respect and trust, because the discussion is entirely in the open. It makes players sensitive to the feelings of other players. It provides a consensus of constructive criticism—probably better than one could get from any one person, even the coach. And without question, it's all about team chemistry and cohesion.

◆ ◆ ◆ ◆ ◆

. . . on Discipline

Shawn believes in simple definitions and simple rules when it comes to discipline. He says, "Behave like champions is a pretty good standard for discipline. An old coach once told me, 'Obey the law and be a gentleman.' Put those together and you have the makings of a pretty good discipline program.

"I ask my team, 'How does the Duke basketball team behave? How would someone from a national championship football team behave?' I want them to associate proper behavior with being a great team."

According to Shawn, "Make sure the disciplinary program does not hurt the team. There is no need to broadcast all of our problems to the media or to our fans, unless an indiscretion involves public conduct. For example, if I discipline a player by having him miss game time—which is good discipline in many cases—it becomes obvious that something is wrong, and the team may have to suffer for something one player did. That can be unfair. So I prefer to have players perform constructive community service, which is good for the community, good for the team, and good for the player."

"We like to involve the players in establishing rules and then in following the rules. They are much more likely to consider the rules fair if they had a hand in making them. But we like to keep the rules as general as they can be and still be understood. Rules that are too rigid can sometimes lead to a punishment that is more severe than the infraction calls for. And if the rules aren't flexible, enforcing them can embarrass the athlete, which is usually counterproductive. Leave enough flexibility to tailor the corrective action to the improper act committed."

"I like to keep disciplinary action for on-ice behavior and off-ice behavior separate. There are so many things that enter into decisions, it simply is easier to arrive at the appropriate action if I don't intertwine the two."

Sometimes Shawn does relent on his concern for having players miss game time, particularly if the infraction is already public knowledge, because it is highly effective. "Even though they may expose a problem to the public, the most effective disciplinary methods seem to be a reduction in playing time or losing ones spot in the lineup. Players work in practice to get to play in competition. They want ice time. Holding them out hits home quickly."

◆ ◆ ◆ ◆ ◆

. . . on Mental Preparation

There's no question how much importance Shawn puts on mental preparation. He says it starts the very first day he gets the team together. Shawn integrates mental preparation into other mental processes involved in training, like learning the play book. "Mental preparation is knowing the goals of the team. It's the way they behave. It's their attention to detail." He has a laundry list of things he does to help players remember the parts of the game that are not totally instinctive.

Shawn says, "I give each player a notebook and ask them to write in it reactions and thoughts about anything they think may help them in the future. Another book I give them, of course, is the play book. But I go further than just asking them to memorize the plays. I want to make sure they understand my philosophy and my style of play."

"I try to think of every off-the-ice influence that may affect our play as we prepare for a game. For example, if we're going into an arena where the crowd is loud, I play loud music during practice; and if I know the music the opponent likes to play, that's what we play, so the players are comfortable when they go into the hostile arena."

"On game day, we always follow the same format. We try to eat at the same time, we have meetings at the same time, and we talk about 'staying in the present' and stress execution over emotion."

"For playoff games, we try, again, to make everything normal and make the players comfortable. We want to make sure everybody's on the same page, and the fewer changes you have to deal with the more likely everyone will respond the same way. But I want to 'raise everyone's antenna' in the days before playoff time. I put a sign up that says, 'The playoffs are here. Our time is so dear. So have a good reason to come in here."

Shawn cautions that you can place too much responsibility on the players in the preseason: "This is clearly a tough mental time, so you need to let them experience learning the play book and the system. And to ease the stress, you want them to have fun. Varying practice routines can help. I review videotapes of scrimmages with the team and make the players accountable for what they see. We are careful not to over-practice, which can burn out players physically and mentally. I schedule two-a-days during the first part of training camp and then I cut back to just one practice a day when I sense that they are getting tired. I tell them that I'd rather they give me quality than quantity, and they usually appreciate this and really put out."

"When we're approaching important games—conference or non-conference—I emphasize that the players have to focus on the moment with no distractions, and I emphasize the importance of relaxing and good breathing. I repeat over and over that they have to focus on execution. Don't focus on emotion. 'Don't get too high. Don't get too low.'"

"I think the most important thing a coach can do in dealing with late-game strategy is to stay positive and calm. Sometimes you have to do something to loosen the players up, even in a critical moment. In such a game—maybe in overtime, or even in a national championship game—I'll call a timeout and just say to the players, 'Isn't this great!' The players will see that you are collected and smiling and they'll buy into it, loosen up, and play better."

Shawn believes in creating game-like situations in practice so that the players face as few unfamiliar situations in competition as possible. "I'll have late-game situations where we're up one, down by one, pulled goalie, etc. This helps the players react in the game instinctively. And a coach can't be tentative either. He can't be afraid to change combinations if the situation calls for it or play a 'hot guy.' He's got to get his best people on the ice. And psychology is tremendous. If you tell a player he's hot, he'll think he's hot, and he'll play well above his normal performance."

Mental preparation for hockey entails a lot of activity. That's why Shawn integrates it into other aspects of preparation. In his program, you just can't separate the mental and the physical.

◆ ◆ ◆ ◆ ◆

. . . on Mental Toughness

Shawn lists six attributes of a mentally tough athlete:

1. "He stays 'on track.'
2. He stays motivated and perseveres through thick and thin.
3. He realizes that winning is a long-term battle.
4. He has a seriousness of purpose, to do his best constantly.
5. He stays aware of what's going on and comprehends the significance of it, and
6. He grows from his experiences."

Shawn lists other traits and habits of the mentally tough. He says, "They identify areas where they need to improve and work on those weak areas, whereas some athletes tend to spend time on aspects of their game they already do well. In working to correct their weak points they exhibit creativeness in devising ways of improving. On the ice, in game situations, the mentally tough players do the fundamental things that make them good players: breath properly, control their emotions, remain coachable, bring to the coaches' attention suggested changes in strategy, retain and exhibit their self confidence. And they are—above all else—team players, placing the goals of the team above their own."

Sounds like mental toughness embodies nearly all the desired traits of a great athlete.

◆ ◆ ◆ ◆ ◆

. . . on Communication

Shawn Walsh is probably a 911 emergency operator's dream caller. He is the antithesis of what I'm told most emergency operators encounter on the other end of the line. "Calm and confident," says Shawn. "That's what I try to be in communicating with my team in a stressful situation. I may change the inflection of my voice to emphasize the more important points that I really want to get through and stick, but more important than anything else are my calmness and the fact that I expect to win. I want them to know that I look at the situation as a great opportunity for success, not an omen of failure. I'll even say, 'Isn't this great!'"

"Sometimes I'll tell a short story that relates to where we stand. For example, I'll compare our situation to that of a heavyweight boxer who withstood his opponent's countless unsuccessful attempts to put him away, and now it's his turn. So go get 'em!"

In considering post-game remarks after a disappointing performance, Shawn likes to point out Vince Lombardi's comment, "People need praise the most when they deserve it the least." He says, "The team feels bad enough when it loses. They don't need any more problems. So I like to encourage them right after the game. I like to tell them that it's not the end of the world. Instead, it's a great opportunity to learn something we can grow from. And then immediately I begin showing how we can grow. I point out a few things we could have done differently that would have made a big difference. And I stress that ours is a team effort. No one is by himself. We win as a team; we lose as a team."

Shawn might add another word to calmness and confidence: timing. He obviously is skilled at knowing when to say what. That's a big part of effective communications.

[Editor's note: Shawn Walsh died of cancer on September 24, 2001. We feel this chapter is a testimonial to his legacy.]

SCOTT WHITLOCK

Kennesaw State University

- - - - - - - - - - - - - - - - - -

Position
Head Softball Coach

Career Record
530-77-0 (11 seasons)

Education
B.A.   Piedmont (GA) College

Team and Personal Highlights

- ➢ National Coach of the Year.
- ➢ Two-time NCAA Division II national champions.
- ➢ Four-time Peach Belt Coach of the Year.
- ➢ Three-time South Atlantic Coach of the Year.
- ➢ Six NCAA tournament berths.
- ➢ Four NAIA national tournament berths.
- ➢ Seven Peach Belt regular-season titles.
- ➢ Six South Atlantic Region titles.
- ➢ Three 50-win seasons.
- ➢ Nine straight years with less than 10 losses.
- ➢ 40-game winning streak.
- ➢ 36 All-American players

SCOTT WHITLOCK

Introduction . . .

Kennesaw, Georgia, is a small, thriving community a few miles from Atlanta, and the location of Kennesaw State University. When anyone speaks of Kennesaw State University, Scott Whitlock is the next name that is mentioned. And there is a reason for that. From its infancy as a slow pitch softball program in the late 1980's and early 1990's, Whitlock has grown the Owls softball program into one of the most successful and respected programs in the country.

Recognized as one of the nation's premier head coaches, Whitlock also holds the all-time, all-division best winning percentage of .873. His teams are perennial participants in the NCAA tournament, and the school won back-to-back Division II national championships in 1995 and 1996. Nine of his teams from 1992 to 2000 finished their seasons with less than 10 losses. Two of his last three teams have won 50 or more games.

During the 2001 season, Whitlock's mastery was never more evident. Without the services of two starters, including his number one pitcher, Whitlock guided the Owls to 48 wins, their sixth NCAA tournament appearance, and a final national ranking of Number 7. In just 11 years, Whitlock has become one of the most prominent fast-pitch figures in the country, racking up numerous national awards for himself and his players.

With three All-Americans in 2001, Whitlock has produced 36 All-Americans during his tenure, including back-to-back Catcher's-of-the-Year in Audra Thomas (2000) and Blake Baskin (2001).

Known for his candor and wit, Scott has established himself throughout North America as a Softball Ambassador. Having coached several All-Star teams and running many national camps, Whitlock's knowledge, expertise, and flavorful demeanor have made him a highly-sought-after speaker and instructor.

Never one to lose his focus or train of thought, the chatty and easygoing softball coach truly enjoyed talking about winning and building success by starting his discussion . . .

. . . on Motivation

Scott Whitlock provides a rather comprehensive, yet precise, definition of motivation: "Motivation is any action or reaction that prompts one to initiate an assertive and persistent effort in pursuit of reaching a goal."

He brings to the forefront two motivational forces that are always present, yet seldom recognized for their motivational value: tradition and enjoyment. "If a coach can build a tradition of doing the right things—playing the game the right way—then every player will push to make sure he's not the first one to let the team down." And about enjoyment he says this: "This is a 'no brainer.' You can be serious about the job at hand and still enjoy doing it. Players enjoy games. That's why they come out for the team. But you want them to enjoy practice, too. They spend a lot more time in practice. So, if you can create an enjoyable atmosphere for the team to work in on a daily basis, the players will be more motivated and productive."

Two other inter-related motivational forces Scott points out are team co-ownership and team interdependency. In comparing the team and the coaches to employees and owners in a business, Scott says, "You want to make the players feel that they are partners with you, not your employees. But make no mistake, the players must always know who is in charge. The coach is the 'CEO,' and makes final decisions, but a sense of team co-ownership results in players' taking better care of tangibles and intangibles and pushing themselves for team achievement. At the same time they must know they are respected. And each player must recognize that everyone connected with the team—players, coaches, support staff--- is dependent on all others in the group. They must understand and accept that if anyone falls short, in any way, the entire team suffers. Awareness of this interdependency will motivate players to carry their weight."

Pride is the other factor Scott relates to motivation. "I like to talk with my players about the concept of 'personal pride'—in academics, athletics, and in social interactions. No player wants to be the weak link, even if she can't always be the star. Having pride in one's achievements is a tremendous motivator."

Here are some things Scott has found to impede motivation:

"Threatening a player almost always creates an adversarial atmosphere, which is always counterproductive. 'If you do this, I'll bench you,' doesn't motivate. Threats are also poor disciplinary practices. Closely related to threatening a player is making her feel guilty. 'Guilt trips' distract conscientious players and don't phase those who aren't."

"The old 'Win One for the Gipper' is just that—old and outmoded. Whether we like it or not, today's society is more sophisticated than it was in the days when these somewhat corny, emotional, and long-winded speeches by coaches stirred up players to give it their all. A lot of players would snicker at that type of talk today. But there are occasions when innovative appeals to either the sense of humor or the emotions of the team are effective."

While Scott has said that players need to respect authority, they also need to be treated with respect. Very young children—and sometimes older ones—can't be reasoned with. Their lifetime experiences have not helped them develop a sense of logic and reasoning. But college-aged girls question, either openly or privately, what they are told to do. Not recognizing this is hazardous to a coach's longevity. Scott says, "The days of blind faith in a coach are over. 'Because I said so' doesn't satisfy a player's sense of reason. When you give a player something specific to do, you'd better explain how the assignment will help the team, if it isn't abundantly obvious."

Most authorities agree that in athletic practices, there is a point in time of diminishing return. Scott says failure to make practices efficient and make sure the players understand the reasons behind each phase of practice can be a major obstacle to motivation. "If practices become 'stale,' or your team is bored with what's going on, they won't retain what you're trying to teach them. A coach must plan his practices to get the most bang for the time spent. That's part of his job, and if a player senses the coach is slacking off on his job, she may tend to slack off on hers. Quality Practices equal Success!"

◆ ◆ ◆ ◆ ◆

. . . on Team Cohesion

"When the entire team understands the importance of each individual connected with the team, finds common ground, and works together in reaching both daily and seasonal goals"—that's chemistry, according to Scott. He recommends creating situations where it's appropriate to use some of the team building drills that sports psychologists suggest for establishing trust and reliance among players.

Scott requires his team to meet together socially once a week, without coaches, in a non sports-related activity—like watching a movie or eating a meal together. "The activity doesn't have to last more than thirty minutes, but I've found that such events are fruitful in building common bonds that, in turn, lead to enhancement of good team chemistry," he says.

A section of this chapter is devoted to communications. The chapter themes overlap; communications is involved in nearly every other theme. Scott points out its importance in building team chemistry: "Some teams never build good team chemistry because they don't communicate well with their teammates. They don't have trouble talking to each other on some matters that aren't controversial, but they hesitate to talk about issues of conflict. I urge players to discuss their problems with each other and to talk TO each other, not ABOUT each other. If the lines of communication are kept open, small issues rarely turn into big problems, and chances of achieving team chemistry are enhanced."

As sophisticated as our world has become, with television and the Internet to expose us to all sorts of different philosophies, somehow young people still seem to adopt the philosophies and traditions that were common with the people they encountered daily, face-to-face, before they left home. So college may be the first time freshmen encounter people who are different, at least superficially. Scott addresses this: "All players must realize that we are all different from each other. One of the most traumatic events a young person faces is when she comes face-to-face with opinions and personal philosophies that differ from the environments where they were raised. In managing our team, we try to make this a positive experience. We never ask a person to change anything related to their deep moral convictions. We encourage them to accept others for who and what they are, to not intrude on others' personal lives, and to respect their own 'space' and let no one else abuse it."

"All of these things are essential for positive team chemistry to develop."

◆ ◆ ◆ ◆ ◆

. . . on Discipline

Scott says, "Team discipline is a code of behavior, both on the field and off the field. It must start with the inherent self-discipline that players have; but, beyond that, players must know what is expected of them—what is acceptable. They must learn to make good choices and to act responsibly. Part of discipline is acceptance of the team's standards of conduct, once they have been established. Everyone must understand the consequences of unacceptable behavior."

"When a player's conduct requires disciplinary action, the coach should respond as soon as he is fully aware of all of the pertinent facts. No action will be effective if delayed unnecessarily. The players must know that consequences always result from unacceptable behavior and that they will be swift and fair. A coach must never 'look the other way' when undesirable events occur." Of course the reason for never overlooking indiscretions is that other teammates will wonder how a coach can be fair if he doesn't react to all wrongs he knows about, regardless of the level of the indiscretion. The corrective action can be, and should be, tailored to the indiscretion.

"One way I've found effective in administering corrective action involves accountability to teammates. When players realize that their actions adversely affect teammates, two things can happen. First, the players will be more reluctant to act improperly because they respect their teammates and don't want to alienate them. Second, the players do a better job of policing themselves."

"I've also found reducing playing time is effective in motivating players to 'live within the lines.' Playing in games is what people come out for athletic teams for. Reducing playing time gets their attention in a hurry.

Finally, although it may be a last resort in dealing with a continuing problem, athletes must be aware that their scholarships can be revoked. A scholarship is a valuable asset and should go only to one deserving it."

Scott lists some approaches to discipline to avoid: "Don't threaten consequences to unacceptable conduct unless you carry out the threat. First you must be reasonable in telling your team what the consequences will be. And you must be fair in determining the circumstances under which the infraction occurred—some actions are malicious, some are unintentional. But once you've decided what is fair, you must go through with it. Idle threats of punishment only encourage players to see how far they can push the limits of behavior."

Scott says, "Parents must be notified of serious rule infractions— illegal drug use, academic probation, or a high potential for dismissal—but they should not be involved in other disciplinary matters. A coach must build a relationship with players based on mutual respect. There must be clear and unimpeded communications between the coach and the player. A part of a college student's personal growth is learning to deal with superiors in a constructive manner. Inappropriate involvement of parents makes the coach nothing more than a baby sitter."

Scott thinks social restrictions—confinement to room or apartment— don't work because they are resented, and players are tempted to figure out a way to break the confinement, which is not too difficult to achieve. He has already mentioned in the section on "Motivation" that trying to shame a player—make her feel guilty—only distracts the conscientious player and has no effect on the less conscientious ones.

He sums up discipline, "Understanding a coach's philosophy and practices results in the best type of discipline. It deters commission of unacceptable actions and reduces the need for punishment."

. . . on Mental Preparation

Scott separates mental preparation for competition into three steps:

> ➢ "Identify the task to be accomplished.
> ➢ Clear the mind of any distractions.
> ➢ Focus your thoughts and concentration on accomplishing the task."

Scott recognizes that the preseason is critical because of the fundamental training that takes place, but he also realizes that it is the most challenging stage from the standpoint of establishing and maintaining enthusiasm about the competitive season, which seems years away to the players. His approach to the preseason takes these factors into account, as he addresses them: "Sell players on the idea that preseason work is an investment in the team's future. And make sure they understand that dividends to that investment come during the season. The harder they work in preseason, the greater the dividend. To make sure they stay focused, remind the team of the investment concept every day."

"Take steps to make the atmosphere fresh at practice. Never allow your team to become bored with practice." This is particularly difficult in preseason as opposed to the competitive season, when the practices are punctuated by games, and the importance of game strategies and correction of mistakes are obvious and short in duration. Coaches are challenged to be more innovative in preseason to make practices stimulating.

Scott says, "One of the ways to keep practices lively is to integrate the team-building drills into the pre-season physical conditioning. This integrates the building of team chemistry into the development of physical skills. It can be a pleasant distraction from the daily physical grind and can be very productive."

When the competitive season finally arrives, Scott changes gears and emphasizes different aspects of the program. He likes to treat every game the same, to the extent possible: "I try to play down the home game versus the road game scenario. Instill in your players the idea that if they are prepared, skilled, and focused, they can meet any challenge, regardless of the site."

"And make EVERY game a big game. A team should be challenged to give their best effort always and to approach every game the same way. Of course, the players know that some games are bigger than others— there's no way to keep them from knowing that—but if the coach treats every game the same, then the players are not likely to tighten up in the 'big ones'."

Players expect guidance from the coach. He needs to make sure they don't hold the opponent in awe. Familiarity with the other team's abilities and tendencies removes this anxiety. Scott says, "Make a point to go over anything and everything that you might encounter in a game. Discuss special or unique challenges that a game may bring. Then simulate those situations in your preparation."

Scott thinks that one of the important factors in late-game strategies is remembering that the late-game is still a part of the game, and the opponent is the same one you've faced up until the late game. Sometimes teams can focus so much on late-game strategies that they forget the fundamentals that are important to good execution regardless of the situation. According to Scott: "Though situations may change and specific strategies may be used, the fundamental skills used should never change.

Emphasize this to the entire team and demonstrate it in practice as you simulate late-game situations. Make the players comfortable with the idea that if they employ solid fundamentals in executing the chosen strategy, they will succeed."

Preparing in practice for executing late-game strategy requires the same approach as for preparing for the entire game. Scott repeats, "Anticipate and simulate. Make it a point to go over everything your team could encounter late in a game. Teach the players how to recognize those situations they've prepared for."

"Finally, learn from failure and build on success. When late-game strategies fail, analyze the play and identify why they failed. In the very next practice, get the team's input. What did they think went wrong? Make the indicated changes and practice the new approach. This gives the team even more confidence in their ability the next time that situation occurs. And when late-game strategies succeed, make sure you point out the relationship of your pre-game plan to the successful execution." That also builds confidence, and they'll execute even better when the situation occurs again.

. . . on Mental Toughness

Scott obviously places a lot of importance on mental toughness, but he doesn't spend a lot of time defining it or describing mentally tough players. Yet his ideas may provide considerable organization for stimulating mental toughness. They can provide the basis for enhancing a player's mental toughness.

He defines mental toughness as "the capability to perform at proficient levels regardless of the setting or situation."

Scott lists four traits or characteristics of a mentally tough player that you can work to develop.

1. "Composure is paramount. A player must control her emotions and remain calm in challenging situations." If you think about it, you see how various types of mental training can build and improve this ability.
2. "Focus is necessary. A mentally tough player must have a clear idea of the situation at hand and avoid distraction from concentrating on her short-term objective."
3. "You have to have self confidence." You're composed, you're focused, now you must prepare to execute. Composure and focus should lead to the logical next essential characteristic—self-confidence.

4. "A mentally tough player is decisive. She must analyze the situation quickly and act without hesitation."

You're playing shortstop. Runners are on first and third. There is one out in the bottom of the last inning. You're leading by one run. A grounder comes to you. The factors to consider are too numerous to enumerate. You're composed, you're focused, you're ready to execute confidently, but what do you do? If you're mentally tough, you analyze the situation and act without hesitation.

. . . on Communication

The late-game strategy discussed earlier, motivation, effective team discipline, and team chemistry all have one thing in common. Success in these areas is dependent on effective communication. Scott considers three factors essential to effective communications.

Scott: "When you're behind late in the game, the coach must remain composed. A coach must always control his emotions, but in critical situations, it's absolutely essential to control them. The team needs to be calm and in a receptive state of mind for him to communicate the changes he wants to implement to have the best chance of winning. If the coach is composed, the players will be more composed and receptive to instructions."

"Once I have the players' attention, I like to recall a similar situation in another game. This helps settle them down, because people tend to fear the unknown more than they do familiar situations. So they are more comfortable and confident. Then I recall to them the strategy we used before and how we perfected it in practice after the game.

"And I think Yogi Berra's famous quotation, 'It ain't over till it's over,' should be every team's battle cry. Sometimes I become a cheer leader—maybe their biggest cheerleader—imploring them to continue to give their best efforts and never give up. A team that relaxes while winning is vulnerable. A team that quits when behind is doomed."

Scott doesn't believe in spending too much time dwelling on a poor performance after the game. "I believe in reviewing and critiquing the situation thoroughly and then telling the players to LOOK AHEAD. No one benefits from dwelling on bad days. Fortunately, there is usually another game to prepare for, so we can turn our attention to thinking victory again. No one will be effective in the future if she is preoccupied with the past.

"Don't exaggerate the importance of the loss. Be honest and fair in your critique, but be positive, whether you won or lost. If a coach treats every loss as if the world is ending, his players will begin to play not to lose instead of playing to win. We all know how destructive that can be to a team."

"Another way of turning the players' attention away from bemoaning the loss is to ask for their input to the critique. This accomplishes several things. First, it provides information the coach may not have gleaned, because being on the field gives you a different perspective from being in the dugout. It takes their mind off the loss. But at the same time, speaking out, even in a positive way, provides a means of venting emotions."

There's a silver lining to every cloud. Scott thinks there's no better time to find that silver lining than in the cloud accompanying a loss. "Identify successes, even small ones, in the midst of a disappointing day. It may be an individual breaking out of a batting slump or improved base running by the team as a whole—whatever it is—recognition of the positive things can go a long way in healing a team's wounded ego."

TERESA WILSON
University of Washington

- - - - - - - - - - - - - - - - - -

Position
Head Softball Coach

Career Record
643-325 (15 seasons)

Education
B.A.   University of Missouri-Columbia

Team and Personal Highlights

- ➤ National Coach of the Year.
- ➤ Big 10 Conference Coach of the Year.
- ➤ Three-time Pacific-10 Conference Coach of the Year.
- ➤ Two-time Pacific-10 Conference champions.
- ➤ Two-time College World Series finalists.
- ➤ Five consecutive College World Series appearances.
- ➤ All-American pitcher at the University of Missouri-Columbia.
- ➤ Inducted into the University of Missouri Athletic Hall of Fame.
- ➤ Recipient of 1984 NCAA Post-Eligibility Scholarship.
- ➤ Assistant Coach, U.S. Junior World Championships.
- ➤ Assistant Coach, USA National Team.

TERESA WILSON

Introduction . . .

Teresa Wilson transitioned herself from being an All-American pitcher and Dean's List student-athlete at the University of Missouri-Columbia to a National Coach of the Year award winner and leader of one of the highly-successful softball programs in the nation. She built the University of Washington softball program from the ground up, taking the team to five consecutive College World Series in the nine-year history of the program.

A fierce competitor, Wilson has been successful in both her playing and coaching careers. She earned national and conference Coach of the Year honors after setting numerous records as an All-American pitcher at Missouri. Also while at Missouri, she was on the Dean's List and was honored with an NCAA Post-Eligibility Scholarship in 1984. She was also named to **Who's Who Among Students in American Universities and Colleges** in 1983 and 1984.

Following a one-year stint as an assistant coach at her alma mater, Wilson accepted the head coaching position at the University of Oregon in 1986. In her four years in Eugene, her teams won 126 games. They finished the 1989 season with a 54-18 overall record, a second-place finish in the league, a fifth-place finish at the College World Series, and a final ranking of No. 4. Wilson was named the 1989 National Coach of the Year for her accomplishments. Also in 1989, she became the first person to have both played and coached in the College World Series.

She moved to the University of Minnesota in 1990, winning the Big 10 Conference Coach of the Year award in 1991 after the team finished 47-25, won the Big 10 Conference title and finished with a final national ranking of No. 15.

Her successes at Oregon and Minnesota paved the way to Seattle, where Teresa was hired to start an intercollegiate softball program from the ground up in the country's toughest softball conference. She vigorously accepted the challenge, using one season to recruit talented student-athletes, create a schedule, develop indoor and outdoor facilities, and order equipment. And stoke that competitive fire.

Her first team in 1993 completed a winning season, and the 1994 team was invited to the NCAA tournament for the first time. The 1995 team reached the Regional finals and ended up with a final ranking of No. 15 in the country after compiling a 50-23 record. The 1996 team had a banner year, going 59-9 overall and 23-4 in the Pac-10 conference. They came up one win short of a national title, but Wilson had by now put all the pieces together for the Huskies to be perennial national championship contenders.

From 1997 to 2000, Wilson's teams averaged over 50 wins per season, were ranked No. 1 in the country on several occasions, were among the national leaders in home attendance, won a Pac-10 championship, defeated arch-rivals Arizona and UCLA quite handily, appeared in the College World Series each year, and again were national runner-up in 1999.

Wilson has coached numerous All-Americans, all-conference players, and Players of the Year. Her teams have been national statistical leaders, from home runs per game to ERA (earned run average) and hitting. Her students also excel in the classroom. Her alma mater also took note of her achievements, inducting her into the University of Missouri Hall of Fame in 1995. Her expertise has also landed her on the USA coaching staffs for international competitions.

Wilson has been an active speaker at clinics around the Pacific Northwest, helping athletes make the transition from slow-pitch to fast-pitch. She has also spoken at clinics throughout the United States and Europe. The hard-working coach with a constant smile on her face welcomed the chance to discuss success strategies, beginning with her thoughts . . .

. . . on Motivation

Teresa Wilson equates motivation to "the fuel in the gas tank." And she says, "Without it, you aren't going very far. Of course, there are different types and qualities of fuel. Fortunately, college coaches work with athletes who would have never reached the college level unless they were already highly motivated."

"The source of motivation can be internal or external. Internal motivation is almost exclusively a product of ones personality traits. But it can be enhanced by knowledge, environment, circumstances, maturity or other external motivational forces. But I look for certain personality traits in identifying a new athlete's level of internal motivation."

"I have found the most coachable—motivated—athletes to be open-minded, eager to learn, and hard working. They have a high level of self respect, respect for others, and respect for the game they play. Typically, they set high standards for themselves, have a deep sense of pride, and are perseverant. Motivated athletes are objective in self evaluation of both their personal behavior and their athletic skills. They welcome feedback, love to be challenged, and have a passion for the game that motivates them to become 'students of the game' at a high level."

Teresa sees an intertwining of motivation with other characteristics addressed in this book. She says, "Internal motivation provides discipline to train hard and the desire to maintain, year after year, the strong personal qualities mentioned above. Internal motivation is often the key to performance longevity and avoidance of burnout."

"External motivation comes from outside a person. For example, watching other athletes perform miraculously on TV or a teammate having an exceptional practice or game motivates an athlete to want to raise her own level of performance to emulate them. Receiving an award for play or conduct and compliments from coaches and teammates are motivating. And sometimes even failure can motivate a player to make sure she doesn't fail again."

Has Teresa observed coaches' behaviors that impede motivation? She doesn't have to search for an answer. "Over the years, I've found yelling and screaming to wipe out motivation. In our ever-changing society, the athletes of today don't respond positively to that type of treatment. In administering discipline, firm discussions are appropriate at times, and those discussions, if carried out properly, can be motivating by making an athlete see her mistakes and want to avoid the coach's having to conduct additional discussions. But the coach should never lose her composure."

"Without a doubt the most effective forms of external motivation involve positive reinforcement. The word of praise or the pat on the back for mental, physical, emotional, or skill-related good performance still remains the most immediate and satisfying form of external motivation."

Internal motivation, as defined by Teresa, is difficult for a coach to impact, because it's "internal." But she says the coach can recognize the athlete's own response to it. "You can discern a sense of accomplishment, self discipline, and pride. The athlete assumes more responsibility and displays her feeling of ownership of the program. Once responsibility and ownership are achieved, the goal of motivation has come full-circle."

◆　◆　◆　◆　◆

. . . on Team Cohesion

Teresa believes in the power of team chemistry or the lack thereof. She says she's seen very talented teams self-destruct in the post season because of a lack of team cohesion/chemistry. She uses both terms, chemistry and cohesion, but assigns slightly different definitions to them.

"Team chemistry is what makes a team function as one unit—one heartbeat, one mindset—in the pursuit of a common goal," according to Teresa. "They don't have to be the closest friends off the field, but when they come into the locker room or step across the white line, their mission is singular. Respect for each other and unity are the driving forces to achieve their goals."

"There's a physical side to team chemistry, too. It's in timing. Softball is all about timing. Whether it's fielding a bunt, coming through a ground ball, turning a double play, a catcher's throwing to second on a steal, or a pitch breaking with perfect timing and location, the team has to be in sync. Team chemistry is not having to look up to see who you're throwing to or to actually see the outcome. You KNOW she's going to be there to execute her end of the play . Knowing that is chemistry."

Teresa gives cohesion a more literal translation—bonding and sticking together. She says, "Cohesion is the bond that makes teams stick together. It's quite a challenge to bring together 20 people from all walks of life, from all over the country, and all backgrounds and develop a cohesion that will enable them to function with unity."

"When we recruit, we consider certain positional needs—hitters, pitchers, infielders, outfielders—but we also consider personality needs. If everyone on the team had the same personality, at some point we would become unproductive. We like to bring in a mixture of personalities—vocal leaders, those who lead by example, feisty players, calm players, regulators, motivators, stabilizers, and even one or two instigators."

"We don't just wait for chemistry and cohesion to develop. We train to develop it. First we state our goals and our mission. We establish standards and discuss important characteristics, like pride, discipline, responsibility, and ownership. We work toward becoming a 'family.' In our nine seasons at Washington, the sense of family has probably been our biggest non-skill-related factor leading to success."

"In the best scenario, the team develops a unity that bonds them both on and off the field. They must develop team chemistry to achieve ultimate success. To aid in this development, we do ropes courses, sports psychology sessions where we identify personality types and preferred feedback and motivation sources for each team member. We host guest speakers on these subjects and participate in other team-building progressions and identification drills throughout the year."

There are some precautions Teresa takes. "As the year passes, we make a pact to avoid petty distractions at all costs and to remain focused on commitment to team mission, ownership—and yes, team chemistry. As the cohesion, the mission, and ownership develop, the chemistry becomes apparent—the team members feed off each other and actions and reactions are instinctive."

◆ ◆ ◆ ◆ ◆

. . . on Discipline

To Teresa, if there is a common thread that entwines all of the elements of this book, it's discipline. That's apparent from her discussion of the subject. "Discipline is a key component of internal motivation. Over the years discipline has probably been the benchmark of our program. It provides the foundation on which the program is developed. We believe that discipline transcends athletics. It's essential to success in all aspects of life. Discipline is not a part-time trait. It's a part of a person. It's who we are."

Are you convinced Teresa thinks discipline is important? And you notice she doesn't confuse discipline with punishment. Now that we know it's important and that it is integral to everything, can Teresa give us a definition? She can, and it's simple, it's straightforward, and it explains why discipline is so important. "Discipline is doing things right—even little things—all the time—on and off the field."

"We begin developing discipline with the staff calling most of the shots. Then, as the total program develops, the players assume more and more responsibility—more self-discipline and ownership. They begin to take care of all the corrective actions, except those where a coach's involvement is indicated. Believe me when I tell you how proud I am of our young ladies as they accept ownership of the program, displaying a sign of true maturity. Do you think the pride they have in recognition of this maturity is a source of motivation? Do you think developing this maturity and ownership required discipline? YOU BET IT DID!"

◆ ◆ ◆ ◆ ◆

. . . on Mental Preparation

"There is no way I can do justice to mental preparation in one chapter. We spend as much time as possible with Ken Ravizza developing our mental approach to the game. We've adopted his book, **Heads-Up Baseball** as our guide." That's how important Teresa thinks mental preparation is.

About pre-season preparation, Teresa says, "Pre-season practice lays the foundation for the rest of the season. Our players know, coming in, that success requires discipline, pride, motivation, execution, and good team chemistry. We focus on one day at a time. We don't look at the span of time from September to February; it's too long, and we'll become distracted. As coaches, we must keep practice and player development interesting and challenging. This is key to pre-season preparation."

"We divide the competitive season into three segments: the tournament schedule, the conference schedule, and post-season. During the tournament schedule, we focus on fundamentals, defining roles, and honing the game plan. But we also integrate aspects of team chemistry—singular mission and timing. You can actually feel the all-important 'one thought, one heartbeat' cohesion develop during this period, as the players' roles are defined in the context of game situations and teammates begin to see in individual players the characteristics of leadership, energy, stability, and enthusiasm. You can see the 'team personality' develop."

Teresa challenges us to define a situation more dependent on mental preparation than the conference segment of the season: "The Pac-10 Conference is a monster all its own—a 28-game schedule spanning almost 9 weeks. Every weekend is as intense as a national championship. It provides a perfect tune-up for competing in the College Worlds Series, because in each game we're playing teams that have dominated the College World Series. During this segment we turn it up a notch from the tournament season with respect to pressure, focus, and application. If we're successful, then we're mentally prepared for the two weeks of post season.

"That mental preparation means that there should be no surprises in the post-season play, because we've faced every situation we are likely to see in the post-season during the other two segments of the competitive season. The tournament schedule allowed game application of our fundamentals and chemistry, and the Pac-10 schedule provided pressure. We've seen it all, and we're prepared. So now it comes down to execution. Play the game we've developed over the past eight months."

Teresa indicates that even execution of late-game strategy depends on mental preparation during the season. She says, "Late game strategy is dictated by the situation. But mentally, your late game strategy is already in place with the earlier development of team cohesion and chemistry. My best teams were so well prepared mentally that they felt no pressure. Their mind set was that it wasn't a matter of 'whether' they would score but 'when' they would score."

That's what mental preparation did for her team.

. . . on Mental Toughness

"Mental toughness," according to Teresa, "is a topic spanning a wide range of applications. For the purpose of this presentation, I'll focus on this definition: 'Mental toughness is the ability to stick with the plan in the face of adversity'."

"In pursuit of the home run record, Mark McGwire displayed the ultimate in mental toughness—sticking with the plan in the face of adversity. Every pitcher he faced put extra effort into keeping him from hitting a home run. That was the physical part. The media deluged him with attention, and his fans hounded him with admiration. That was the mentally distracting part. But he stayed focused through all of that—mentally tough."

But you don't have to be in Mark McGwire's situation to face mentally tough challenges. Teresa explains: "Mentally tough players don't allow themselves to become upset by an umpire's call. After all, you can only hurt yourself if you do. You can't tell by looking at the mentally tough hitter whether she's 0-fer or 4-4 for the day. She doesn't lose focus based on his success. She maintains composure in difficult situations. She deals with adversity. She leads others by remaining composed and sticking with the game plan, when panic and chaos might otherwise develop."

"Developing mental toughness takes time and patience, but much can be done to achieve it. Creating the environment for learning helps. All of the characteristics of a team discussed in this chapter help. The central theme to developing mental toughness is 'believing in the process.' When the going gets tough, go back to fundamentals. Like muscle memory in a skill-related task, consistent repetition and reinforcement during pre-season and all through the competition season lead to confidence in the process."

Teresa relates the generic challenges to mental toughness to baseball and softball: "The challenges to mental toughness are pressure, failure, the feeling of being overwhelmed, distractions, and unfamiliar surroundings. Mental toughness is developed when we work through these challenges. Softball and baseball are games of failure. Every major league player experiences a batting slump at one time or another. The goal is to find the shortest route to success. The more positive the attitude, the more stable the plan, the more calculated the approach, the quicker will come the solution."

"Players have to believe in this process, and they have to believe that it's OK to 'fake it till you make it.' Role-playing can ingrain in a player the characteristics of the role she's playing. We play roles frequently—when we're about to embark on a job interview, for example. The 'fake it till you make it' practice is just successful role-playing.

"Mental toughness is developed through practice and experience just like physical skills are. The more a player faces adversity and overcomes it through practice of problem solving and persistence, the mentally tougher she gets. She feels in control. All of the characteristics addressed in this chapter have helped her to come full circle. And now she's mentally tough."

◆ ◆ ◆ ◆ ◆

. . . on Communication

John Wooden doesn't have much to learn. But he'd learn one additional thing if he read this book: he's the most referenced coach in the book, by far—and not just by basketball coaches.

Teresa's among those who refer to John Wooden: "I'm a firm believer in John Wooden's theory that you win games in practice. I don't do a lot of coaching during a game. Softball is a game of adjustments—from pitch to pitch, inning to inning, and game to game. But the adjustments made in a game must be minor ones. Attempting to make major adjustments during a game are usually unsuccessful. So, from a technical standpoint, most of my communication during a game is in making minor adjustments."

"But I communicate for other reasons. Softball is a game of momentum switches. Positive reinforcement and ability to refocus are vital to success. So occasionally I remind the team to believe in the process: refocus, 'flush.' And I use other phrases of encouragement and reminders to get back to the game plan. And all softballers, including the coach, are pitch-to-pitch 'cheerleaders' both offensively and defensively."

Teresa uses the phrase, "teaching moment" to describe a time when a player or the team is in a receptive mood. You have to take advantage of these times for most effective communications. Teresa says, "In practice, I can step on the field and stop play when a 'teaching moment' comes along, but I can't do this in a game. So post-game meetings are 'teaching moments' for me. We cover the good, the bad, and everything in between. We cover situations that occurred in the game that we hadn't covered before, while they are fresh in the players' minds. To allow the players to loosen up and to make the meetings interesting, we do high-fives for great plays we review and we go in the other direction in reviewing fundamentals. In a perfect world, we wouldn't be reviewing missed signals, poor communications etc. at mid-season. But if these things occur, there's no better time to discuss them than at the first opportunity, and that opportunity is the post-game meeting."

"I usually avoid 'outcome' discussions. When we lose, we ask ourselves, 'Did we get beat, or did we beat ourselves?' A team doesn't 'have it' every day. On the days when we don't, we point out that we're a much better team than what we showed. I don't go into much detail. What can I say to make them feel worse? Would demeaning the team help? Probably not. The coaching staff must make every effort to help the team keep things in perspective when we lose. We should learn from the loss. That will make us better. It's like a day to day practice. What did we do today to get closer to completing out mission?"

"One of my assistant coaches points out that our team philosophy is a living, breathing entity. We must adjust it from year to year as changes in personnel and other situations dictate. Getting back to the beginning of the chapter, every person on the team is motivated in a slightly different way. Don't be afraid to make minor adjustments as you go through the season. Never forget what got us to our goals before. But you can't execute any of these things that get us to our goals without effective communications."

◆ ◆ ◆ ◆ ◆

SUZANNE YOCULAN

University of Georgia

- - - - - - - - - - - - - - - - - - -

Position
Head Women's Gymnastics Coach

Career Record
580-92-5 (18 seasons)

Education
B.S.   Pennsylvania State University

Team and Personal Highlights

- ➢ Three-time National Coach of the Year.
- ➢ Three-time Georgia Coach of the Year.
- ➢ Five NCAA national championships.
- ➢ Three Undefeated seasons (NCAA record).
- ➢ 14 NCAA Regional championships.
- ➢ 11 Southeastern Conference championships.
- ➢ Six consecutive seasons—highest team average score in NCAA.
- ➢ Five Honda Award winners.
- ➢ 38 All-American selections.
- ➢ 27 Individual NCAA national champions.
- ➢ 100% graduation rate since 1988.

SUZANNE YOCULAN

Introduction . . .

Suzanne Yoculan was a New Jersey state AAU gymnastics champion when she accepted an invitation to join the Penn State University women's gymnastics team. Disillusioned with the mundane, non-challenging routines of college gymnastics, she left the team during her freshman year to become a gymnastics instructor and coach at a private gym, while completing her degree in therapeutic recreation with a dance emphasis.

Coaching became her passion, training gymnasts from two-year-olds to elite-level, Olympic candidates. Her long-held vision was that college gymnastics could be the most exciting, challenging, and beautiful of any spectator sport. When she was hired to revive a floundering women's gymnastics program at the University of Georgia, she turned college gymnastics on its ear, upgrading skills to Olympic levels and bringing former Olympians into college gymnastics.

Hired in 1983, Suzanne quickly established a totally comprehensive athletic program, utilizing her mental-physical philosophy as the core foundation. Suzanne: "Gymnastics is one of the oldest sports involving modern-day athletes. The mind/body concept involving physical training, seeking beauty, strength, and efficiency in movement began with the Greek culture. Gymnastics also develops these psychological attributes: high self-esteem, physical courage, determination/perseverance, expressiveness, reliance, and self-confidence." She also developed a procedure incorporating athletic trainers and nutrition experts for dealing with anorexia and bulimia, formerly a common malady among female college athletes. She effectively dispelled the myths of the "female athletic triad", which unnecessarily alarmed female athletes and their parents concerning severe osteoporosis as a consequence of intensive athletic training.

In her fourth year as coach, her team, which had been slated for elimination before she took over and never before qualified for the NCAA tournament, won the 1987 national championship, the first of five national titles for Yoculan. Pushing the envelope by forcing teams to adopt the dynamic and exciting skills that her gymnasts perform, her teams have dominated the sport ever since. Her teams won 67 consecutive competitions in the undefeated seasons of 1998 and 1999, defeating the second and third ranked teams a total of 18 times during that span.

Always flamboyant and an endless promoter of the sport, Yoculan has capitalized on the media's fascination with her high heels and short skirts. ESPN's Chris Marlowe called her "the most enthusiastic coach I've ever seen in any sport." She has raised the average attendance at

GymDogs' meets from 200 to 10,000, and is continually pressing national television networks for a weekly live college gymnastics telecast. She speaks nationally, has written a syndicated column and magazine articles, and appears on numerous radio and television shows. Her own cable television program, **The Suzanne Yoculan GymDog Show**, is broadcast into seven neighboring states.

The outgoing, highly-energetic coach who wants her gymnasts to experience the complete academic, social and cultural activities of a "college girl" and have a lot of fun in the process, was focused and articulate when discussing her championship thoughts . . .

. . . on Motivation

"Before you can even consider motivation, you must establish goals that go beyond any achievements an athlete has attained in the past. Setting goals, in itself, is motivating, provided the goals contain intermediate steps that lay out the map for achieving the ultimate motivating goals. Each step and the ultimate goals must be clearly defined. Then motivation results from the melding of the desire, determination, and effort with the vision of pride and fulfillment when goals are achieved." That's Suzanne Yoculan's definition of motivation.

She says, "Every year, one of our team goals is to win the NCAA National Championship, but because that goal is too far away at the beginning of the season, we have to set other specific team goals that may be even more challenging, such as target scores for each meet and going undefeated through the most difficult schedule in the college gymnastics. In gymnastics, individual goals are just as important as team goals. They include developing new and more challenging skills and improving consistency and execution. All of our goals are precisely defined and their achievement can be measured objectively and quantitatively."

Suzanne believes that you must assure every team member that you are interested in her as a person as well as a gymnast and that you believe that she can reach the goals agreed on. She is the epitome of positiveness and says, "A negative attitude is the worst handicap anyone can have."

She says that competition, itself, is motivating. "The individualistic nature of gymnastics is both a blessing and a curse—blessing because our gymnasts are self motivated, having competed all over the world in elite-level gymnastics; and a curse because coaches have to harness the motivation for individual achievement to build team motivation. Because of the individualistic nature of gymnastics, a gymnast is always competing—against teammates in daily practice and intra-squad competitions, against opposing teams in intercollegiate dual competitions, and against what seems like 'the world' in championship competitions. But perhaps the toughest competition is in bettering your own records. The pride and fulfillment of winning competitions is motivating. The 'vision' I mentioned can be a vision of standing on the awards stand at the end of the competition or flashing that championship ring. That's motivating! "

Suzanne says that, in gymnastics, technical instruction is motivating. "Gymnasts almost crave constructive criticism from skilled coaches. After all, in the past, their parents paid big bucks for coaching before they came to college, so they consider skilled instruction a tangible asset. When a coach tells a gymnast why she didn't execute a skill perfectly, and then she makes the correction he suggests, you can see the sense of satisfaction and elation in her face when she performs flawlessly on the next try. You motivate by helping athletes achieve their goals,"

Suzanne believes that "The biggest impediments to motivation are failure to set challenging and well defined goals, failure to communicate that you believe in a gymnast's ability and that you care for her, and failure to recognize and praise progress toward the achievement of goals."

◆　◆　◆　◆　◆

. . . on Team Cohesion

Suzanne says that there is no "teamwork" in gymnastics in the traditional sense, in that participants don't interact while competing. Each gymnast is a solo performer. However, because the mental part of gymnastics is central to performance, good team chemistry is absolutely essential to good team performance. "I'm certain that good team chemistry has won championships for us and lack of it has lost them. After searching for years for a definition of this elusive ingredient, I've settled on this one: Team chemistry is what makes the sum of the combined parts greater than the sum of the individual parts. Individual performance is enhanced when gymnasts are a cohesive team."

Developing team chemistry starts with recruiting, according to Suzanne. "We put as much emphasis on evaluating a potential recruit's ability to work well with others as we do on evaluating her technical skills, which are much more obvious. Our current team members are key to our evaluation. We seldom make an offer to a candidate who the gymnasts on the team don't think would fit in."

One of the factors Suzanne cites as essential in building team chemistry is an awareness of the team's diversity. "Many races, religions, geographic origins, intellects, financial backgrounds, and recreational interests are integrated into our team. My objective is to fully recognize diversity, but completely take it out of the interpersonal equation, except from the standpoint of the educational opportunities afforded by communicating with people of diverse backgrounds."

But perhaps the biggest challenge in developing team chemistry comes, not from diversity, but from something all team members have in common. "They are women," says Suzanne, "and if a coach doesn't recognize the difference between coaching men and coaching women, he's in for a heap of trouble. We don't communicate as directly. Regardless of how tough we may be mentally, we cry openly. We have feminine tastes and interests—maybe more interested in the leotards than in the opponents' average scores. I don't believe in reprimanding publicly, regardless of gender, but embarrassing a female gymnast in front of her teammates can be absolutely fatal."

"Team chemistry is built on honesty, openness and equal treatment. While there may be obvious differences in athletic abilities among our gymnasts, they are all respected for what they are as people, not athletes. If you visit one of our practices, you can't tell the walk-ons from the top gymnasts in the country. They all receive the same attention from the coaches and support staff and the same respect from their teammates."

"One of the best ways to assess team chemistry is observing the gymnasts at intra-squad competitions. They cheer for each gymnast while she is competing, but a special type of cheering and reinforcing comes into play when a gymnast is struggling, seems to have a mental block, and is frustrated. After a fall from the apparatus, she may even be crying. As the vocal support from the team gets louder and stronger, you can actually see the performing gymnast's determination and confidence build. And the cheer at the end of the routine—after she has at least partially overcome her frustration—is usually louder than it is for the gymnast who performs flawlessly. It's not just the cheer. That gymnast performing feels something, and that something is chemistry."

◆　◆　◆　◆　◆

On Discipline. . .

"Discipline is the training that makes punishment unnecessary," according to Suzanne. "And I separate discipline to perform from discipline to conform. I like to think that the word, self, is an understood modifier of discipline, because if someone else is controlling your activities, you're not exercising discipline, you're merely following instructions. A great deal of gymnastics training and academic pursuit depends on an individual's discipline to perform somewhat arduous activities on her own initiative—for example: the rigorous repetitions involved in rehabilitation from injury and the seemingly endless study required for academic excellence".

"We try to make sure that each gymnast fully appreciates the measurable benefits from arduous activities, even those that are performed under supervision. One of the changes females undergo about the age they come to college from club gymnastics is that they get heavier—they begin to look like mature women. They can't propel themselves high enough into the air and stay long enough to do the flips and twists they need to do in challenging routines unless they get a lot stronger than they were previously and have a great deal more stamina. The only way to achieve the physical attributes necessary to be a collegiate gymnast is to undergo drudgerous weight and aerobic training. We make sure we demonstrate to each gymnast that she can do better gymnastics as a result of undergoing this drudgery."

Suzanne says that college coaches must understand the nature of college students in getting them to conform to rules. "College kids think conformity 'sucks'—in their words. However, they are clever and innovative. If you can define objectives without directing team members, in detail, how to achieve those objectives, they are likely to come up with better approaches than the ones you might devise. So I much prefer general guidelines to hard and fast rules, but the guidelines must have well-understood boundaries. And a gymnast must understand that if she goes beyond those boundaries, there will be appropriate adverse consequences."

Is Suzanne always able to achieve discipline to the degree that punishment is unnecessary? "Unfortunately not. Even in the best programs, athlete behavior sometimes requires corrective action. The corrective action must be carefully thought out before it is implemented. It must have a positive result. It should not reflect a coach's anger, even though we all get angry with athletes at times. You must be predictable, consistent, and direct. Don't play games. Don't be sarcastic. It is essential that an athlete undergoing corrective action—you notice I didn't say 'being disciplined'—understands that she was told of the guidelines or rules she violated before she violated them. She must know, given the same circumstances, anyone else with a similar past record would receive the same treatment. The treatment must not be embarrassing or demeaning, and the objective of improvement must be clearly appreciated by the one undergoing the action and the other team members."

"I work to make every aspect of my program positive. Making athletes feel that discipline is positive isn't easy. But it can and should be done. When discipline truly achieves its goal, the athlete feels good about it, you feel good about it, the other coaches feel good about it, and the teammates feel good about it."

◆ ◆ ◆ ◆ ◆

On Mental Preparation. . .

Suzanne breaks mental preparation into two categories as well. She says, "In college gymnastics, mental preparation can be divided into (1) preparation of the individual for performing her routines and (2) preparation of the team to deal with the season.

"Just think about this: A gymnast has to remain mentally focused through an entire routine, which may last 50 to 100 times longer than shooting a free throw, throwing a pitch, or kicking a field goal. Mental preparation for performing routines encompasses the thought processes a gymnast goes through to block out everything except the task at hand and to develop a mental picture of every skill involved in the routine and every move in the skill."

"Preparation for performing routines is different for every gymnast. We try to enhance what they already know, if it's been successful for them. For example, Karin Lichey, who came from Cincinnati Gymnastics, prepared for balance beam by doing a lot of repetitions. She went through them on the floor, in the area near the balance beam. It's this physical activity that keeps her from 'over-thinking.' Kim Arnold did a lot of imagery—especially for balance beam. For example, her beam routine was a minute and 21 seconds. When she did the mental preparation, she'd shut her eyes and time herself as she went through the routine."

"We try to prepare the team mentally for meets by having a lot of competitions in the gym—competitions that mean something. We had a three-day beam intra-squad with nine people, and we said the top six scores are gonna compete. They were under pressure every single day. In gymnastics, you have to create a pressure situation as much as you can every day."

"In preparing for the season we focus on helping the gymnasts become well-rounded college girls, and this helps them prepare for the season. It's just a natural part of their packed schedule. But because of the reduced time in the gym, relative to prior training, it's fun. It's fun for all of us. So it's not a mental grind."

"We try to keep things as normal for our team members at each competition as we can. For home meets, the day of a meet is the same as any other day, except that the gymnasts come to the coliseum about two hours and a half before the meet."

"When we travel, again, I try to keep the team in their comfort zone. Whatever that happens to be—whether it's sleeping late and having breakfast in bed, getting up and riding the bicycle at 9 o'clock in the morning, working out—we accommodate them. I don't believe in making them all do the same thing on a meet day. The only meal we eat together is a late lunch before going to the arena. From there on, the routine is the same as at home meets."

"For the national championship meets, our routine is different, because we stay at the location of the meet several days. We arrange for sightseeing, academic study periods, and even group Internet chat sessions with our fans all over the country—arranged by our web site manager, who travels with us. We want to do things that take the girls' minds off the competitions. Three or four days is too much time to dwell on the meets. For example, at Nationals in '98 and '99, when we won back-to-back championships, I had the girls write poems on Wednesday, the day before the competition. On Thursday, the first day of competition, we shared the poems with each other. It went so well that they asked to do it again Friday. It took their minds off the competition."

Suzanne says her "pep talks" before meets vary according to the situation. "Sometime I'm a cheerleader—all hyped up, telling the team to be enthusiastic about every routine by every gymnast. At other times, I probably sound more like a counselor—low key and somewhat instructional. But one thing is common to all of my pre-meet talks. I am always up-beat, even after we've just lost someone to injury in warm-ups. We know that we can win any meet we compete in, because records are published, for individual gymnasts, on every apparatus, for every team. So I usually remind the team to "stay focused," although this is probably superfluous. Good gymnastics is staying focused."

"I'm not one who pulls out the tape of the team crying the year before, when they lost. I know that's a well publicized tactic that has worked well, but that's not me. I suppose I came close to that in 1993, after we had been ranked number one and had such a disappointing competition in '92 in Minnesota. I reflected on the year before, but not directly. I didn't mention the meet itself, but talked about, not being afraid to lose. 'Go for it! Don't hold back. Don't be concerned with what happened last year.' But by the time I was five minutes into the talk, I was standing up on the chair, really getting into it, and the whole team was crying. In the Super Six, we hit 24 for 24 routines in scoring 198.000 for the first time in college gymnastics competition and winning our third national championship."

"One year the week before a big Alabama meet, the team kept saying among themselves, 'Oh, it's just another meet—it's not different from any other meet. It's just another meet.' I felt that, underneath all of the talk about 'just another meet,' the girls were actually getting up tight, and I needed to loosen them up. Also, I didn't agree with what they were saying, because I don't feel like when you go over to Alabama, it's just another meet. It's 15 thousand people. We don't have that anywhere else. It's not 'just another meet.' It's different over there. The equipment's the same. The routines are the same. But all the outside things that factor in are not the same, and they can influence an athlete's performance. So when I went in to talk to the team before the meet, I had on a T-shirt, and on the front it said, 'Alabama/Georgia—It's just another meet.' I didn't mention the importance as I talked to them. I just went over some instructional things. But when I finished, I turned around. On the back of the T-shirt it said 'It's NOT just another meet.' It worked. They cracked up laughing—and the point was made without a lecture. We scored our highest score of the season in winning by 1.3 points, which is huge in gymnastics. So sometime I have them crying, and sometime I have them laughing."

"Again, I prepare them differently for different situations. My style of coaching—whether it's in the gym, in the competition, prior to the competition, or after a competition— is consistent in that it is instinctive. It's what I feel like needs to be done at the moment. I don't have a planned script, ever."

Suzanne points out another unusual feature of gymnastics. "Gymnastics is probably unique in sports in that nearly all of the coaching is done before the meet. I'd like to see this characteristic in other sports. Let the athletes run the team, like John Wooden did. Ideally, if a coach has taught his team all he should, he would only have to determine who's in the lineup. Everything else would be controlled by the players during a game."

"We seldom change routines during a meet, because we are seldom in a situation where we are in danger of losing. Gymnasts like performing skills that are challenging and will excite the fans. We usually keep as much difficulty in the routines as the gymnasts have shown they can master in practice. This does add some risk of having a fall or major form break, so we may take some difficulty out of a routine when the score is close. When we do, we talk with the gymnast in a somewhat 'matter of fact' way. It's about like calling a fast ball instead of a curve when there are three balls and no strikes. Taking difficulty out may be as much mental as physical. It gives the gymnast more confidence. After all, that's what it's all about."

"After each routine is completed, the gymnasts and other coaches hug and praise the performer—or console her (without saying anything, just with affectionate gestures)—and I do the same."

"A difference in my response to a routine is that I make my consolation instructional, first pointing out why she fell or made some other mistake, and then encouraging her about her next routine. Don't look back. The only place we can improve our score is in the events that lie ahead of us. But I never get on an athlete's case for making a mistake in a competition. I don't have to. She knows that she has let her team down, and she's on her own case."

"In practices, I always require a gymnast to repeat a skill on which she falls, so that she has the mental picture of doing it right when she moves on, not the mental picture of doing it wrong. And if she's 'down' at the end of the practice session, because she's had a bad practice, I call her aside and try to console her, letting her know that I believe in her and that she just had a bad day. I don't want her to leave the gym with a negative attitude. These conversations are some of the most rewarding, for both of us, of any communications we have."

◆ ◆ ◆ ◆ ◆

. . . on Mental Toughness

Suzanne likes to cite examples of displaying mental toughness. "When you fall at the beginning of your beam routine, hitting the hardwood beam with your cheek, drawing an egg-sized welt, causing excruciating pain and agonizing disappointment, and you suck it up, get back on the beam within the allowed 30 seconds, and remain focused to complete the remaining 60 seconds without another major break, that's mental toughness."

"But mental toughness is not just dealing with physical pain, though dealing with pain can sometimes require mental toughness. You display mental toughness when you are up third in the uneven bars competition, the gymnast up second fell, you know that any more falls will have to be counted, and you remain focused on each technique and each element of the routine to 'hit it.'"

"In 1991, Heather Stepp exhibited the ultimate in mental toughness. During touch warm-ups on vault at the meet in Utah, Heather over-rotated on her pike front and stuck out her arm to catch herself. She essentially destroyed her elbow. Back home in Athens, the doctors told her that she would probably never do gymnastics again. She would be lucky to have reasonable use of the elbow. Heather was absolutely devastated. She and I cried together in her hospital room. Then, the morning after her surgery, Heather asked the doctors what she could do to enhance rehabilitation. They told her that the sooner she began trying to go through the rehabilitation exercises, the faster and more complete the rehab would be. But they also told her that the earlier she began, the more severe the pain would be. Heather said, 'Let's start today.'"

"The doctors said they had never seen anyone endure so much pain voluntarily. Now get this: Heather not only regained use of the elbow, she was ready for gymnastics at the beginning of the 1992 season. Even more astonishing, she scored a school record 39.60 all-around in winning the SEC title, and she won the NCAA individual national championship on vaulting, the apparatus on which she was injured the previous year. No one was surprised when Heather won the 1992 National Honda Inspiration Award. Can you define mental toughness any better than Heather?"

But I asked Suzanne to define mental toughness in some way other than just citing examples. She answered. " See if this fits the examples above: Mental toughness is the ability to block out excruciating pain, agonizing disappointment, and immense psychological pressure, to remain focused on overcoming adversity and performing the skills in your routine up to your normal performance standards."

"Some people confuse mental toughness with being aggressive or macho. These traits are superficial; they don't tell you how mentally tough a person is. It's an inner thing. I have found that our mentally toughest gymnasts come in all sorts of external personalities. I'm known for the size of the tears that run down my cheeks when I'm emotional, whether the emotion results from a shocking disappointment or adulation over a monumental achievement. But most people think I'm mentally tough."

"My experiences tell me that one of the fundamental characteristics of a mentally tough person is that she has an inner strength derived from a strong and inalterable faith in herself —from her religion or from some other source. She is self-reliant and content with who she is. This may surprise you, but mentally tough gymnasts are considerate, compassionate and unselfish. These characteristics take their minds off selfish concerns and give them the determination to fight through adversity."

◆ ◆ ◆ ◆ ◆

. . . on Communication

Suzanne believes communication is, without question, one of the most important aspects of any team or organizational endeavor. She says, "But it's a two-way function. Feedback is essential to make sure the one being communicated to understands what the communicator intended to communicate."

She provides an illustration of communicating when your team falls behind early. "We entered the 1997 National Championships as the overwhelming favorite. During the season we attained the highest regular season average in the history of NCAA women's gymnastics—over a point higher than the second place team. We scored the highest score of any team in the preliminary rounds. But on the first event in the Super Six, the balance beam, three GymDogs fell from the apparatus, counting two falls and digging a hole that would be impossible to climb from, unless all of the major contenders counted at least one fall."

"So what do you do? First, you have to erase the past from your mind by concentrating on the future. You can't do anything about the past. Then you have to concentrate on every skill, every routine, and every event, in that order. And we did it! We won each of the other three events. That is as good as we could have done. But, unfortunately for us, no other team counted even one fall, and we came in third, 0.55 points behind the champion, UCLA."

So how do you deal with the loss? Suzanne's way: "First, put yourself in the place of the winner. How would you like to be treated if you won? Remember the Golden Rule. Would you like the other team to demonstrate sour grapes? So I told the team in 1997 that as soon as it was evident who won, they should take off running as fast as they could toward the winning team's place on the floor and congratulate them enthusiastically. We gave the meet away, but we didn't give away our class and good sportsmanship. We could at least win the sportsmanship contest, which is important. As soon as it was determined who won the National Championship, I took off across the floor first, with the team right behind me, to congratulate UCLA."

"Then we had to face our fans. They had arranged a victory party for us. They felt terrible. They had supported us all season. We needed to support them. So I told the team to go into the victory party with the biggest smiles they could put on their faces, just as big as if we had won. 'Let the fans know that you appreciate their support and that you are proud of what you achieved during the season and the way you came back and won three of the four events. That will pick them up.' And it did. Just as important, it lifted our team's spirits, too. Holding your head high after disappointment is difficult, but it's a sure-fire way to lift your spirits."

Suzanne sums up her philosophy: "One of my most ardent beliefs is that 'Winning is not everything.' You recruit right, you set goals, you train right, you stress academics, you teach good technique, you teach good sportsmanship, you teach fairness, you teach integrity, but you don't teach winning. How do you teach winning? Winning comes as a consequence of doing all of these other things well. Of course, you must want to win. And if you do all of the things you are supposed to do well all of the time, you will win most of the time."

"Remember what was written in my introduction: Gymnastics is the sport involving the body/mind concept—physical training seeking beauty, strength, and efficiency in movement—with the psychological attributes of high self-esteem, physical courage, determination/ perseverance, expressiveness, reliance, and self-confidence. Master being a good gymnast and you are a winner."

◆ ◆ ◆ ◆ ◆

THE

FINAL

ANALYSIS

The Final Analysis

As a former college basketball coach, the contents of this book proved to be an excellent resource into the myriad of organizational philosophies and strategies of the top coaches in the country. As a practicing sport psychology consultant, the book was invaluable regarding the study of psychological and behavioral techniques of team building. As my esteemed co-author, Bill Donaldson, documents in the appendix section of the book, corporate management also can benefit highly from the knowledge espoused in this book.

As a researcher, it has always been important to me to explore the connections between theory (research data) and practice. Over the years, many coaches in youth, high school, college, and professional athletics have contacted me and asked the question: "I'm doing things my way, but is it the right way?" In essence, the coaches were interested in discovering if their coaching techniques were compatible with the documented research in that area.

The purpose of this final chapter is to analyze the qualitative data from the coaches and compare/contrast this information with what the research has to say on the topic, and to attempt to answer the question posed by coaches and managers: "Am I doing things the right way?"

Allow me to qualify this announcement regarding analysis by admitting that the analysis will be far from an in-depth review of the literature. In fact, it will be quite brief. But the intent is to somewhat quantify this qualitative data and possibly motivate others to pursue research into this area of interest. Here, then, is the final analysis . . .

. . . on Motivation

What the Research Says

Motivation has been identified as an important psychological force that is needed if individuals are to successfully meet the many challenges that they encounter (Vallerand & Losier, 1999). Both coaches and athletes agree that motivation is a prime ingredient to achieve excellence (Gould, 1982).

Two elements of motivation (intrinsic and extrinsic) consume the bulk of the research on this topic (Vallerand, 1997). Simply stated, intrinsic motivation can be characterized as performing an activity because of the fun and enjoyment it brings to the individual. Similarly, extrinsic motivation can be characterized as performing an activity because there is a reward or recognition associated with it. You participate, not because it's fun, but because you'll receive something for participating. Ideally, athletes compete because of intrinsic motivation; but in reality, athletes usually compete because of intrinsic and extrinsic factors.

It has been found that coaching behavior can greatly influence an athlete's motivation level (Cadorette, Blanchard, & Vallerand, 1996; Goudas et al, 1995). One interactive style is the "control/autonomy support" dimension (Deci & Ryan, 1987; Deci, Schwartz, et al, 1981) in which coaches provide autonomy to their athletes when they allow them to make choices regarding aspects of the team. To help coaches modify this autonomy/support interactive coaching style, Pelletier and his colleagues (2000) developed a highly effective intervention program to assist swim coaches in becoming more supportive/autonomous towards their athletes.

Coaches can also influence athlete's intrinsic motivation through their coaching style and the types of instructions they give to their athletes (Pelletier, Briere, et al, 2000; Beauchamp et al, 1996). In addition, coaches can utilize scholarships to influence motivation levels of their athletes. Wagner, Lounsbury, and Fitzgerald (1989) found that athletes who received scholarships reported lower levels of intrinsic motivation than players who did not receive scholarships. In a related study, Brennan (1986) found that NCAA Division III athletes (non-scholarship) reported a higher level of intrinsic motivation than their Division I (scholarship) counterparts.

Another nonhuman social factor that can influence motivation is the motivational climate that surrounds the team (Mitchell, 1996; Theeboom, De Knop, & Weiss, 1995). Coaches and teammates help determine the type of climate that will prevail around a team. A mastery climate encourages team members to improve their skills, whereas a competitive climate leads athletes to believe they need to outperform their teammates (Roberts, 1992). One study (Kavussanu & Roberts, 1996) found that male and female participants were more intrinsically motivated in a mastery-oriented setting, rather than a competitive-oriented setting. Scholarship programs (NCAA Division I and II) would seem to cultivate both a mastery and competitive climate where the athletes utilize both intrinsic and extrinsic motivation to help them excel.

The importance of perceived competence for intrinsic motivation was highlighted in several studies (Markland & Hardy, 1997; Weigand & Broadhurst, 1998). Ryckman and Hamel (1993) found that younger athletes with high perceived physical ability rated intrinsic factors (having fun, skill development) as more important for participating in sports than athletes with low perceived physical ability. Blanchard and Vallerand (1996) reported that perceptions of coach support and team cohesion predicted a feeling of competence. Finally, achievement goal theory (Dweck, 1986, 1999; Nichols, 1984, 1989), which basically states that goals and motivation are linked to successful achievement, becomes an active participant in the motivation discussion.

In summary, motivation can be determined by, among other things, coaching style, scholarships, climate/atmosphere around a team, and setting and achieving goals.

What the Coaches Say

Motivation was defined in a variety of ways, but the central theme was always similar: Motivation is a process in which teams and individuals strive to accomplish a goal or goals.

Many coaches implied that motivation is the responsibility of the coach and student-athlete. It was also noted that motivation is rarely the sole responsibility of the coach or athlete.

Coaches were also unanimous in declaring that a positive, supportive, can-do climate was necessary for a high-achieving program. An open-door policy in which coaches and athletes converse often was also considered a motivating element of a championship program. A coaching style that was supportive and encouraged "ownership" in the team by the players was also given as a motivation factor of highly successful programs. An atmosphere in which consistent praise and a positive approach to coaching was also considered to be highly motivating to players.

The bottom line, however, for the overwhelming majority of the coaches regarding the most effective motivation method was the setting, and re-setting, of goals, both individual and team. These goals were developed by the coach and athlete in one-on-one meetings and in team settings, and were updated periodically depending upon the progress exhibited by the team and individual player. Since the majority of the programs mentioned in this book distributed scholarship monies in some form, it can be safely assumed that the student-athletes were both intrinsically and extrinsically motivated to accomplish their goals. Very rarely did a coach utilize the threat of a loss of scholarship money as a motivation technique. Loss of playing time, however, was used as a motivating method by some of the coaches. In addition, yelling and embarrassing an athlete in public were mentioned as the least effective motivation techniques.

In summary, the message being sent by the coaches in this book regarding motivation was simple and highly attainable. It stated that motivating student-athletes can be very easy if (1) you recruit and surround team members with other highly motivated teammates, (2) you set goals, (3) you as coach are highly motivated, (4) you give players control or "ownership" of the team, (5) you encourage your athletes to develop academically, socially, and spiritually as a person, and (6) you show respect for the players on and off the field.

Discussion of Research and Coaching Methods

It was highly apparent that the effective motivation methods utilized by the coaches were harmonious with the research. Every coach agreed that an open, positive, supportive, autonomy-promoting interactive coaching style worked best in helping to motivate players. One-on-one meetings along with team meetings were identified as critical motivation elements. Therefore, these findings reinforced the research of Deci and Ryan (1987) and Goudas and his group (1995).

Perceived competence was identified as influencing the level of motivation. A coaching style that promoted consistent praise in a positive, caring, and supportive atmosphere helped build confidence in the players, thus affecting motivation in the process. Therefore, the research (Markland & Hardy, 1997) and coaching practices meshed regarding perceived competence.

Scholarships were listed in the research as a nonhuman source for motivation for some athletes. Scholarship monies were available in some degree to athletes in the majority of the programs in this book. Scholarships could be classified as an extrinsic motivator since they could be viewed as a reward of some type to the players. Even though coaches could have used the threat of a loss of scholarship money as a negative motivator, no coach did. They simply didn't believe that this was the "right way" to motivate their players. Loss of playing time was used as a motivation technique by a few of the coaches. Loss of playing time was considered a positive approach by the coaches because it usually produced positive results from the players: increased intensity and focus. These actions again complemented the research (Pelletier, 2000) that positive coaching/atmosphere is a highly effective motivational approach.

Finally, since goal setting was the top motivational method utilized by our coaches, achievement goal theory (Dweck, 1986, 1999) was reinforced. Setting and achieving both team and individual goals seemed to be the foundation for motivation for these championship programs.

Final Analysis

The research on motivation and the motivation methods utilized by these championship coaches are very compatible. Coaches and managers can feel confident that "they are doing it right" when they apply the motivation methods recommended by the championship coaches in this book to their own teams.

◆ ◆ ◆ ◆ ◆

. . . on Team Cohesion

What the Research Says

Carron, Brawley, and Widmeyer (1998, pg. 213) defined cohesion as "a dynamic process that is reflected in the tendency for a group to stick together and remain united in the pursuit of its instrumental objectives and/or for the satisfaction of member needs." Historically, cohesion has been identified as **the** most important small-group variable (Lott & Lott, 1965).

The research states that there are four factors that influence team cohesion: environmental factors, personal factors, leadership factors, and team factors. Environmental factors include level of competition and the size of the team. In a study examining the level of competition, Granito and Rainey (1988) assessed the cohesion of high school and college football teams. It was hypothesized that high school teams would be more cohesive than the university team, and those exact results were found in this study.

In studying the effects of team size on cohesion, Widmeyer, Brawley, and Carron (1990) found that as roster size increased, task cohesion decreased. In a study of non-sport groups, Mullen and Copper (1994) concluded that cohesiveness is greater in small groups.

Personal factors influencing team chemistry were identified as social loafing and adherence behavior. Latane (1981) defined social loafing as the reduction in individual effort when people work in groups versus when they work alone. In their 1993 research, Karau and Williams showed that social loafing was consistent across task, gender, and culture. Their study also indicated that the presence of a relationship among group members reduced social loafing in that group.

Cohesion has also been found to be related to adherence in team sports (Prapavessis & Carron, 1997). Among other things, the Brawley (1988) study found that teams were better able to withstand negative and disruptive events if they were more cohesive.

The behavior and decision style of the team leader were critical elements regarding cohesion. Westre and Weiss (1991) found that football coaches with a higher level of training and instruction behavior, social support behavior, positive feedback, and a democratic decision style were associated with higher levels of task cohesion in athletes. Kozub (1993) found basically the same findings with basketball teams.

Finally, team factors influencing cohesion include role involvement, group norms, and collective efficacy. Role involvement is deeply linked to team unity. Brawley and his group (1987) reported high correlations between task cohesion and role clarity, role acceptance, and role performance for athletes in team sports. Research has also found that the higher the cohesion, the greater is the conformity to group norms (Shields et al, 1995). And in newer research, collective efficacy (a sense of shared confidence held by team members) and team cohesion were related. Paskevich and his colleagues (1999) found that when cohesion was higher among team members, a sense of collective confidence was also higher.

What the Coaches Say
The coaches invariably defined team cohesion much as Carron and his group did. Collectively, they once again linked team cohesion and goals. The coaches believed that the best way to build and solidify team cohesion was for the group to bind themselves together in the pursuit of common goals. And as would be expected, the coaches were unanimous in stating that team goals always held a priority over individual goals.

Another common theme woven among the variety of effective team building techniques was the concept of "family." Every championship coach in this book likened his/her team to a family structure. "Family" was also interpreted in one common way: Coaches and teammates were to treat each other respectfully and bond together much as they would with their own family members. Coaches also believed that all "family" matters would be resolved internally and not through any media outlet. The perception of family that the coaches also wanted to display to prospective recruits and their parents was the idea that the coaches would be surrogate fathers/mothers to these players, and that the "family" team members would watch over each other.

Building upon the family concept, the coaches mentioned a variety of activities that they believed would help build team unity and chemistry. A sampling includes the following: Performing community service projects; attending church services; attending other school sporting events; team meals; team movies; team unity councils; kangaroo courts; educational excursions during travel games; open-door policy with the coach; team parties; honesty as a team policy; older players mentoring younger players; Big Brothers/Big Sisters with younger players; captain's practices; personal growth seminars; promote "ownership" of the team to the players; invited speakers and audiotapes/videotapes/CD's; learning as much about their teammates on a personal level as possible; just hanging out together off the field; developing player respect for each other; and players creating and enforcing their own team rules.

Discussion of Research and Coaching Methods
Since team cohesion has been identified as **the** most important small-group variable (Lott & Lott, 1965), it should come as no surprise that our championship coaches also believe that team chemistry is vital to the overall success of their programs. All of these coaches make a concerted effort in the area of building and maintaining team cohesion.

The research regarding environmental factors like level of competition and the size of the team are inconsequential here. Since all of the programs in this book are championship-caliber, it is safe to assume that the level of competition is very similar because the leagues in which these teams play are all nationally-acclaimed as highly competitive. Team size is also inconsequential because NCAA and league rules dictate how large or small a team can be. So these two factors are a moot point regarding cohesion and the research in environmental factors.

Personal factors influencing cohesion hold relevance. Social loafing (Latane, 1981) can be interpreted to mean that some team members may not work up to their potential, hoping that, in the scheme of the team, their loafing wouldn't be noticed. You may be able to socially loaf in a larger team setting, but not a smaller one. The research (Karau & Williams, 1993) also indicated that social loafing can be reduced if there is a presence of a relationship among group members. Our championship coaches put a premium on their team members and staff committing to a "family" relationship. With a family relationship, social loafing should totally disappear or be considerably reduced.

The concept of adherence in team sports also has close ties with team cohesion. Brawley (1988) found that highly-cohesive teams were better able to withstand negative and disruptive events surrounding the team. One of our authors, Paul Giesselmann of the College of Saint Mary, alluded to this kind of situation that his team experienced.

During the 2000 NAIA national volleyball championships in which his team was competing, word was received that the mother of one of his assistant coaches had died suddenly. The team was devastated by the news. Paul quickly made arrangements for his assistant coach to return home to her family, escorted by his second assistant coach for the purpose of emotional support. That left only Paul to prepare the team for a crucial quarter-final match. His team lost the first game, but won the next three to advance to the Final Four match. Paul clearly stated that without the strong chemistry of the team, his players would never have been able to withstand that kind of disruption and still win. This is a perfect example of how the research on adherence and real-life examples complement one another.

We have already discussed how behavior and decision-making styles of the head coach can affect motivation. The same can be said regarding behavior and decision-making style affecting team cohesion. Social support and a democratic decision style (Westre & Weiss, 1991) were two critical elements that the head coach needed to demonstrate in a championship program. All of our coaches have demonstrated these team building skills plus many more. So the research and practical application again mesh nicely regarding the personal factors influencing cohesion.

Finally, team factors influencing cohesion are all relevant to our discussion. Role, conformity to group norms, and collective efficacy do, indeed, affect cohesion. Teams are composed of role players, i.e., starters, substitutes, offensive players, defensive specialists, etc. The coach and athlete discuss what role the player will assume on the team. This democratic coaching style allows for input from the athlete. But, ultimately, the head coach must make the final decision based on what is best for the team and player.

It's also no secret that a cohesive team will conform to the group norms better than a non-cohesive team. And with many of the coaches in our book giving the responsibility of developing the team rules to the players, it should be no surprise that peer pressure would keep all the players in line if they have some kind of "ownership" in the team. Finally, the concept of collective efficacy (team self-confidence) within a cohesive championship team is evident within all the programs mentioned in this book. Therefore, the research on team factors influencing cohesion (Paskevich, 1999; Brawley et al, 1987; Shields et al, 1995) and the practical examples mentioned by the coaches were compatible.

Final Analysis

Coaching practices and philosophies regarding building team chemistry and the research on group cohesion matched in many places. The coaches believe that team chemistry is a critical factor in the overall success of their programs, and they work hard to cultivate it within their teams. The team building strategies used by these coaches are innovative, yet quite basic. Coaches and managers should feel confident in promoting these team building practices with their teams. I also believe that all successful coaches and managers are already utilizing some or all of these methods within their programs and departments.

◆ ◆ ◆ ◆ ◆

. . . on Discipline

What the Research Says

Gibson (1983) stated that discipline is not a dirty word, and that discipline should not be considered synonymous with punishment. She goes on to say that discipline is the result of training by instruction, example, and love.

Much of how discipline is interpreted in the literature can be explained with theories on behavior management. Since discipline, as it relates to team settings, has a strong connection with regulating the behavior of team members toward group norms, this seems like a logical starting point.

Gill (2000) noted that reinforcement is the key to behavior modification. There are two types of reinforcement: positive reinforcement and negative reinforcement. Gill defines positive reinforcement as occurring when behaviors are reinforced through provision of something positive, i.e., praise or rewards. Negative reinforcement occurs when behaviors are strengthened by eliminating something negative.

Punishment also falls within the parameters of reinforcement theory. Punishment is any operation that decreases the strength of a behavior (Gill, 2000). Punishment can occur through the presentation of a negative element or through the withdrawal of something positive. Some experts (Kauss, 1980) advocate that teachers and coaches use positive reinforcement extensively.

Kauss (1980) recommended the following guidelines for effective reinforcement:

1.   Reinforce immediately;
2.   Maintain consistency;
3.   Respond to effort and behavior, not to performance outcome alone;
4.   Remember that learning is not entirely cumulative; it has its ups and downs;
5.   Use reinforcement to maintain desired behaviors once they are learned.

Rushall and Siedentop (1972) discussed how behavioral modification could be applied in sport, while Siedentop (1978) and Donahue and his associates (1980) cited the use of behavioral techniques to, among other things, disruptive practice behaviors and interpersonal communication within teams.

Allison and Ayllon (1980) developed a behavioral approach to coaching that coaches easily applied in tennis, football, and gymnastics. Most of the extensive, systematic research on coaching behavior indicates that effective coaches give considerable praise and encouragement, and rarely use punishment as a discipline measure (Smith & Smoll, 1997; Smoll & Smith, 1984)

To assist coaches with regard to behavior interventions, Smith, Smoll, and Curtis (1979) developed the Coach Effectiveness Training (CET) program. Smith and Smoll (1997) summarized the core principles:

1.   Positive approach. This element included the liberal use of positive reinforcement, encouragement, and sound technical instruction. Punitive and hostile responses were discouraged.

2. Mutual support. This element included the coach being a role model for the desired behaviors.

3. Involve the athletes. This element included promoting the athletes' participation in decision-making to assist in achieving compliance to team roles.

4. Self-monitoring. This element asked the coaches to seek feedback from the players and monitor the results of the program.

What the Coaches Say

When the coaches discussed discipline, the underlying themes were often adherence/compliance with team rules and punishment in some form when rules were compromised. The majority of the coaches also stated that discipline was strongly linked to self-discipline on the part of both the players and coaches. Many coaches also revealed that discipline is a vital ingredient in the overall success of a program, and that discipline should be considered a distinctive characteristic of a championship team.

The coaches were also adamant when stating that regardless of the number of rules (Their recommendation: Don't have many!), coaches must be fair, consistent, and immediate when dealing with the disciplinary problem. In some cases, the coaches requested flexibility when dealing with a specific problem. In other cases, they stated that each disciplinary matter should be dealt with on a one-on-one basis with the athlete, reinforcing the fact that each person is unique and needs to be handled in their own unique way. Coaches, however, wanted no special treatment for their "star" players.

What the coaches distinctly expressed was that when a discipline problem occurred on the team, that the coach's response was immediate, consistent, and fair. There was no waiting period involved; coaches took action immediately. We frequently read and hear many times in the media where a high-profile college athlete or an athlete from a high-profile college athletic program breaks the law, but the head coach waits until a formal report is filed or a conviction is announced before disciplining the athlete. Keep in mind that many times these actions are taken by the coaches upon the recommendation of the college's legal counsel to avoid lawsuits filed by the athlete and his/her parents or guardians. But the coaches in this book were not afraid to deal with the problem immediately and decisively if that was the action that was needed at the moment.

Consistency and fairness were also important concepts regarding the handling of discipline problems. The coaches mentioned that the team expected the same offense to be handled consistently from player to player, with no player given a "break" from the accepted punishment. Fairness pertained to the degree of punishment. Coaches said that the players expected "the punishment to fit the crime," so to speak.

The coaches also mentioned that the players should take a leading role in developing team rules and the enforcement of them. Many coaches remarked that teams should not have many hard and fast rules, but rather guidelines with well-understood boundaries. They also mentioned that the rules should be simple, that they should deal with conduct on and off the field, and they should have short-term and long-term consequences.

There was one area of disparity. A dichotomy arose within the coaching ranks concerning the punishment of the entire team when one person made a mistake during a game or practice, or just punishment for the individual for the mistake without punishing the team. It seemed like mostly male coaches took the position of punishing the entire team in some cases.

Other disciplinary methods mentioned by the coaches included loss of playing time, not dressing for a home game, attending extra study halls, tightening curfews, and being left off the travel squad.

Discussion of Research and Coaching Methods

In spite of the singular controversial issue of punishment for the entire team because of the mistake of one person, the coaches seemed comparable in their practices and what the research had to say regarding discipline.

It has been stated that effective application of reinforcement and punishment is a critical component of successful teaching (Gill, 2000). Our coaches would seem to agree with that assessment.

Kauss (1980) recommended that reinforcement be immediate and consistent. The coaches also agreed that when dealing with a discipline matter, the coach's actions should be immediate and consistent.

The coaches also met many of the guidelines that were developed in the Coach Effectiveness Training program (Smith, Smoll, & Curtis, 1979). The coaches took a positive, pro-active approach to handling the problem; they agreed that the coach should model appropriate behavior; they involved the athletes in rules-making and decision-making; and they closely monitored the effectiveness of their own team rules and penalties.

One area of disagreement seemed to be the practice of penalizing the entire team for the mistake of a single person during a game or practice. These practices can be considered the result of personal coaching choice gained through coaching experience. The responses did not seem to draw the line at gender: Some male coaches who coached both men's and women's sports agreed with the practice, while male and female coaches who coached women's sports didn't agree with the practice. What does this mean? Simply that people will utilize their own philosophies that seem to work best for them. And there is nothing wrong with that approach.

Other techniques that were mentioned as discipline methods by the coaches were loss of playing time, not dressing for a home game, extra study halls, tighter curfews, and being left off the traveling squad. These forms of negative reinforcement and punishment could be considered as a part of the teaching style of the coach (Gill, 2000).

Final Analysis

Coaches' responses and the research data on discipline seemed to once again draw many similarities. Team sports demand discipline in order to be successful, and the coaches in this book are disciples of this concept. Whereas all the coaches professed to taking a positive approach with discipline, the vast majority indicated that, at times, punishment must be doled out for the good of the individual and for the good of the team. The recommendation to our readers would be to consider all the options regarding discipline and utilize those techniques that best fit your program's philosophy. And don't be surprised when you realize that the toughest disciplinary procedures are the ones that your players recommend for the program.

◆   ◆   ◆   ◆   ◆

. . . on Mental Preparation

What the Research Says

Mental preparation is a psychological process utilized for the purpose of improving team and individual performance, and can include the use of imagery and mental practice (Feltz & Landers, 1983; Orlick, 1992; Vealey & Greenleaf, 1998). Although imagery and mental practice are related, research has shown that the two terms should be differentiated (Murphy & Jowdy, 1993). Imagery pertains more to a <u>mental process</u>, while mental practice relates to a <u>technique</u> used by individuals.

Researchers have recently improved the ability to assess imagery and mental practice as it relates to improving motor performance. One study produced similar times it took participants to physically walk to targets of varying distances and mentally imaging walking to the same targets (Decety, Jeannerod, & Prablanc, 1989). Physiological measurements of brain activity have produced evidence that similar motor pathways are activated when imaging an action as when actually performing the action (Jeannerod, 1999). Mental practice and learning have also been documented (Kohl, Ellis, & Roenker, 1992; Hird et al, 1991). But mental preparation often utilizes additional psychological skills, such as focus/concentration, relaxation, self-talk, and simulated reality. And much mental preparation takes place during team practices.

Concentration, or focus, has been the target of several studies (Boutcher, 1993; Orlick, 1992). Nideffer and Sagal (1998) believe that concentration is often the deciding factor when it comes to winning and losing in athletic competition. Brennan (1987) developed a concentration technique called a centering cue, in which the athlete combines a visual or audio cue with a positive self-talk statement.

Elements of relaxation have also been mentioned as a part of mental preparation for a team and individual. Progressive relaxation, a technique which consists of active contraction and passive relaxation of gross muscle groups, has often been utilized with guided imagery (Edgar & Smith-Hanrahan, 1992). Relaxation methods that can assist in controlling pain and uncomfortable feelings can also be helpful for mental preparation (Taylor, 1995; James, 1992).

Positive self-talk is another psychological skill that is used extensively during mental preparation for teams and individuals. Self-talk has been identified as an important resource for building self-confidence (Zinsser et al, 1998). Ways to counter negative self-talk (Ellis, 1981) and enhance confidence in athletes (Elko & Ostrow, 1991) are also effective resources for mental preparation.

Finally, simulated reality is another way of mentally preparing for competition. Collins and Harden (1998) identified simulated reality as a simulation of competition in which human actors model a desired behavior in a controlled environment. From an athletic perspective, simulated reality could be interpreted as an exercise of practicing late-game strategy in a setting controlled by the coach during team practices.

In summary, mental preparation utilizes several psychological skills to assist the player and coach in preparing for competition. Those skills can include, but are not be limited to, imagery and mental practice, concentration/focus, relaxation skills, positive self-talk, and simulated reality.

What the Coaches Say

To a person, each coach stressed the importance of mental preparation to the overall success of the team. All of the coaches also stated or alluded to the position that mental preparation for the team begins on the first day of pre-season practice, and in some cases, before that.

Another unique finding was the declaration by the majority of the coaches that physical training is highly correlated with the practice of mental preparation. The coaches believed that physical preparation (training) assisted in developing the appropriate mental frame of mind that the coaches wanted the athletes to display during practices and scrimmages, and ultimately, during games. It was the belief of the coaches that being in excellent physical condition and understanding the coach's philosophy on game preparation were critical elements in preparing the athlete mentally for the competitive season.

Some female coaches utilized the services of sport psychologists to assist the team in mentally preparing for the season. Others utilized team meetings or team orientations for new players to teach players how to mentally prepare for competition.

Many coaches mentioned the importance of goal setting as it related to preparing mentally for competition. Time management and organizational skills were also cited by the coaches as important elements of mental preparation. The use of visualization and imagery was mentioned often as another element of mental preparation.

One theme that appeared to weave itself through the discussion of mental preparation was the need of the coaches to keep the players continually informed of expectations and the updated status of the next opponent. In other words, knowledge of the opponent and a clear understanding of game and practice expectations were considered important for mental preparation. Detailed scouting reports and extensive film study of the opponent were utilized by the coaches to aid in preparing mentally for the next game.

Coaches also stressed attention to detail as another critical aspect of mental preparation. For example, the kind of crowd the team would encounter on the road (loud, hostile, etc.) and facilities (older, newer, louder, etc.) were factors that coaches found important when preparing for games.

Coaches also used scheduling as a way to prepare mentally. Some coaches tried to schedule opponents during the regular season that they would see at national competitions. Some coaches would also try to schedule events at venues in which national championships would be conducted so that the athletes could visually see what the facility looked like so that their mental pictures matched those of the venue.

Practicing late-game strategy was also a constant for the majority of the coaches. Creating scenarios and situations to practice helped build confidence in the players and trust in the coaches that when the situation arose at the end of a game, the players would be in the correct frame of mind to handle the challenge and pressure.

Some coaches also split their seasons into three segments in order to mentally prepare for competition. The split usually occurred at pre-season, regular season, and post-season intervals. Coaches believed that concentrating on a certain portion of the season, instead of the entire, long season, would help the team focus on short-term goals and would eliminate any burn-out in the athletes that can occur during a long sport season.

Finally, some coaches advocated a year-round fitness and practice regimen that exposed the athletes to a steady diet of mental preparation the entire year. Other coaches stressed the importance of keeping emotions under wraps and concentrating on execution only during games as effective mental preparation practices. Keeping all travel arrangements and pre-game activities as normal as possible were also considered important elements of mental preparation by the coaches. Keeping practice sessions fresh and fun over the course of the season (especially during pre-season practices) were also mentioned as important mental preparation practices. In other words, the coaches wanted no surprises to occur that may harm the mental preparation that the team had invested in to prepare for competition. But if some unanticipated event did occur, the coaches believed that their players would be able to handle it because of previous mental preparation practices.

Discussion of Research and Coaching Methods

Mental preparation practices and what the research had to say again were highly correlated. The coaches mentioned the use of imagery and mental practice often as important elements for mental preparation.

Concentration and focus were mentioned often by the coaches when discussing late-game strategy and execution. Relaxation methods were considered key contributors when mental preparation was mentioned. Positive self-talk was also considered critical to the coaches. And simulated reality, or practicing late-game winning strategy, was also mentioned.

Of all the psychological factors for success that have been discussed thus far, mental preparation research and mental preparation practices of the coaches seemed to be most closely linked.

Final Analysis

Mental preparation is widely accepted and embraced within the coaching profession. Coaches feel that mental preparation coupled with demanding physical training is the perfect combination to building a winning team. All of the mental preparation techniques and strategies mentioned by our championship coaches are recommended for utilization by your sport and management team. Coaches should also feel comfortable in contacting and utilizing the services of a reputable sport psychology consultant to assist with mental preparation of the team if they so choose.

. . . on Mental Toughness

What the Research Says

To coaches, mental toughness is the desired trait of a winner. Teams with mentally tough players, coaches believe, win and win consistently. Unfortunately, there is very little published research on the topic.

A study on tough-mindedness was conducted by Cattell (1965). He attempted to identify traits or characteristics of a tough-minded individual. The findings indicated that there was a relationship between tough-mindedness and athletic achievement. Coaches interpreted the results to mean that the more tough-minded players you had on your team, the better your chances for success.

The search for the components of mental toughness continued with Kubistant (1986). His choices for mental toughness traits included the ability to gain a positive experience from a negative situation, desire, specific attainable goals, trust, belief in self, relaxed, focused, and persistent. Dienstbier (1989), in a more controlled laboratory experiment, concluded that the use of coping skills, appropriate motivation methods, and consistent positive appraisals of performance lead to physiological and psychological toughness.

One individual who has written extensively on the topic of mental toughness is Jim Loehr (1982, 1986, 1993, 1994). Loehr's books are written for individuals in sports and business. He identified these mental toughness traits: mental calmness, physical relaxation, free from anxiety, energetic, optimistic, enjoy the moment, effortlessness, alertness, focus, self-confident, and in emotional control. The association between mental toughness and personality were studied by Kobasa and Maddi (1982) and Kobasa (1979).

Finally, mental toughness was linked to slump busting in sports (Goldberg, 1998). Goldberg mentioned that the way in which a person deals with emotions and the concept of failure often has much to do with establishing mental toughness in one's life.

What the Coaches Say

The coaches did a marvelous job in defining mental toughness and identifying the traits of a mentally tough individual. Some definitions mentioned sticking to game plans, blocking out distractions, overcoming obstacles, facing adversity, and the ability to handle all situations that arise during games. But one definition was so profound that it became the prototype definition that encompassed what all the coaches were thinking. Suzanne Yoculan, the women's gymnastics coach at the University of Georgia, passionately proclaimed: "Mental toughness is the ability to block out excruciating pain, agonizing disappointment, and immense psychological pressure, to remain focused on overcoming adversity and performing the skills in your routine up to your normal performance standards."

Some specific characteristics of mental toughness were mentioned often by many of the coaches. These included self-confidence, staying focused, blocking out distractions, achieving goals, fighting through adversity, and controlling emotions. Other characteristics of the mentally-tough player were the ability to block out pain and continue competing, keeping a positive attitude, being well-prepared, a never-give-up, in-your-face approach, always hustling, being a strong leader, being "in a zone", accepting responsibility for mistakes, a strong work ethic, being self-disciplined, and being decisive.

A handful of coaches remarked that mental toughness can't be coached because it is an inherent trait, a trait that the person is born with. Some coaches also indicated that coaches themselves need to be mentally tough as well as their players. It was a consensus among the coaches, however, that mental toughness can be learned and taught at practices. These practice sessions would need to simulate pressure game conditions, and the players would need to be taught how to respond appropriately. The coaches believed that making practice sessions as demanding as possible was an excellent way to develop mental toughness in their players.

In summary, the coaches all asserted that mentally tough players loved a challenge and would do whatever it takes to perform at an optimum level. The coaches agreed that this outward sign of determination and perseverance by the players helped the individual and team turn a negative situation into a positive experience.

Discussion of Research and Coaching Appraisals

What the research says and what the coaches say about mental toughness are synonymous in nature. Cattell's tough-minded player (emotionally mature, independent-minded, does not over react emotionally) exhibited the same traits as the players on the teams of our championship coaches. Many of Loehr's Ideal Performing State characteristics were present in the descriptions presented by our coaches: physically relaxed, energetic, optimistic, alert, focused, and under control.

Kubistant's mental toughness components of unwavering trust, desire, and gutsy play were also mentioned as important mental toughness traits by our coaches. Finally, Goldberg's assumptions that mentally tough individuals deal effectively with failure and control their emotions were solidified in the responses of our coaches.

The only point of contention between the coach's appraisals and what the research said lay in the area of inherent skills. Whereas some coaches believed that mentally tough individuals were born with the trait, the literature was clear in stating that mental toughness skills can be learned and developed.

Final Analysis

One reason why there is not very much research data on the concept of mental toughness may be because mental toughness has been identified as a single psychological trait containing many different characteristics, and with so many components, it is very difficult to test. The abstract concept of mental toughness is easier to comprehend when you identify behavioral traits of a mentally tough individual.

Our championship coaches were passionate when describing a mentally tough person. It was also apparent that our coaches believed that they have many mentally tough players on their teams, and that the mentally tough players were considered the leaders and role models on their teams.

Since the coaches subscribed to the idea that mental toughness skills can be taught and learned, it is imperative that coaches create mental toughness scenarios and assist their players in devising an appropriate response to these scenarios during practice sessions. Constant repetition and exposure to mental toughness situations during practice sessions can build self-confidence in the players to perform successfully at "crunch time" during competition.

One must also remember that mental toughness skills are life-enhancing skills. Coaches and corporate managers are advised to identify the mental toughness traits they wish to instill in their players and employees, and to create an environment in which these skills can be embellished. Not only will you be preparing your players and employees to handle adversity in athletics and the workplace . . . you will be preparing them for the game of life beyond the athletic fields and corporate offices.

◆ ◆ ◆ ◆ ◆

. . . on Communication

What the Research Says

Communication skills have been identified as a critical psychological tool (Weinberg & Gould, 1999). The type of response you receive from your communication to others is closely tied to how your message was interpreted by your intended audience (Bandler, 1997). John Madden, the highly-successful coach of the Oakland Raiders and currently an NFL television analyst for Fox Sports, commented that communication between coach and players can influence future communication patterns. Madden: "Communication between a coach and his players was being able to say good things, bad things, and average things. Conversely, it's being able to listen to good, bad, and average things. I tried to talk to each player. Sometimes, it was merely a quick 'How ya doin?' Sometimes it was a conversation. But by [my] talking to them every day, they didn't feel something was up when I would stop to talk to them" (Syer, 1986, pp. 99-110).

Another primary goal of all coaches is to get the team to perform optimally at all times, to get them to achieve "flow." Flow has been characterized as a special state of mind in which the perfect competitive environment has been actualized to allow for optimal performance (Csikszentmihalyi, 1990). Some commonly-heard phrases to describe this state of mind include "hot", "in a groove", "on a roll", or "in the zone." Coaches are considered a powerful source of communication for athletes when flow is trying to be achieved (Jackson & Csikszentmihalyi, 1999).

Verbal and nonverbal messages are important in the communication process. Verbal messages need to be clear and concise. Bill Parcells, a Super Bowl winner while coaching the New York Giants, has said that verbal messages must not be confusing. Parcells: "When sending a message, it's not enough to be honest and accurate. The impact of the message will hinge on who's receiving it and what they're willing to take in at that time (Parcells & Coplon, 1995, pp. 117). Sometimes messages break down because of a lack of trust between coach and athlete (Burke, 1997).

Even more critical are the nonverbal messages that people send. It has been reported that 50%—70% of human communication is nonverbal (Weinberg & Gould, 1999). Understanding how the various nonverbal messages work can improve both sending and receiving messages (Yukelson, 1998). Physical appearance, posture, gestures, body position, touching, facial expression, and voice characteristics all play critical roles in the nonverbal message (Weinberg & Gould, 1999).

Finally, active listening skills are also needed to complete a successful communication cycle between two people. It has been reported that people spend 40% of their communication time listening to the other person (Sathre, Olson, & Whitney, 1973). Active listening often involves attending to main and supporting ideas, acknowledging and responding, giving appropriate feedback, and paying attention to the speaker's total communication (Weinberg & Gould, 1999).

Some suggestions have been offered for improving active listening skills (Rosenfeld & Wilder, 1990). First, do not confuse hearing for listening. Hearing is simply receiving sounds; listening is an active process. It is also recommended that people should mentally prepare themselves to listen. For example, before an important discussion meeting with the coach, an athlete should develop a mental game plan that he/she can implement that includes listening carefully to the coach's message.

What the Coaches Say

The coaches were in total agreement that effective communication between players and coaches comprises the most important aspect of a championship program. They also stated that every psychological element discussed in this book (motivation, team cohesion, discipline, mental preparation, mental toughness) could not exist without two-way communication. Many coaches indicated that you can quickly discard game plans, offensive philosophy, defensive adjustments, and late-game strategy if communication skills between players and coaches are disjointed or interrupted. In addition, many coaches stated that an "open-door" policy and one-on-one player meetings were excellent ways to keep the lines of communication open between players and coaches.

Communication is especially critical at three junctures of a game: halftime commentary, commentary during the closing minutes of a highly-competitive game, and post-game commentary.

The vast majority of the coaches all painted the same picture of the player's locker room during halftime. Discussions were comprised of technical adjustments by the coaches to player execution problems experienced in the first half. Secondly, the coaches' comments were entirely positive in nature, and thirdly, a firm statement of reassurance by the coaches to the players to expect success in the second half was transmitted.

As to be expected, this scenario took on a different focus depending upon whether the team was winning or losing at halftime. If the team was winning, the same three elements mentioned above were delivered by the coaches. The twist to the situation involved the coach becoming more critical in his/her commentary regarding mistakes that were made during the first half. All of the coaches utilizing this technique indicated that they wanted to keep the team from becoming overconfident to start the second half, that by being a little more critical of mistakes would lessen the brashness or overconfidence the players may presently feel and get them re-focused and re-motivated to continue the momentum at the beginning of the second half. Many coaches stressed the importance of the first five minutes of the second half as critical in establishing momentum for the team.

If the team was losing at halftime, the three basic halftime elements were again delivered, but the closing commentary before the team returned to the field would focus more on a motivating theme for the players. The coaches would challenge the players to renew their goals, pride, and commitment to excellence in the second half. They would also mention similar situations the team had experienced in past games that had turned out successfully. The message would be delivered in a high-energy, animated speaking style as the team left the locker room for the playing field.

Coaching commentary during late-game strategy situations also took on a similar format. Very rarely would a time-out late in a game be used for a motivational pep talk. Instead, technical adjustments to strategy and a positive, reaffirming statement were the only communicated messages being sent by the coaches to the players.

Post-game commentary discussed by the coaches mostly addressed coaching responses to a loss or poor performance by the team. Everyone is happy after a victory.   Proper reaction to a loss is critical.   A high percentage of the coaches stated that after a loss or poor performance, their comments to the players were very brief, but pointed. The comments were brief because the coaches did not want to base their comments strictly on his/her emotional feelings at the time. They cautioned that heated emotional comments could irreparably harm the confidence of the players and chemistry of the team.

The comments were pointed only so far as the coach wanted to discuss his/her reasons for the loss. Most of the time, the reason given as a cause for the loss or poor performance were either lack of player effort or incorrect strategy execution. The vast majority of the coaches said that they would comment more to the players after analyzing the game film. The coaches were also in total agreement when they indicated that at no time should the coach spotlight any individual player as a contributor to the loss or poor performance. Some coaches, however, did indicate a willingness to confront a player during team film review the following day for a lack of effort or poor execution during the game. [Yes, the coaches insinuated that the highly-critical film sessions still found their way into their coaching regimen when the situation called for it.]

In addition, in their brief commentary after a loss or poor performance, the coaches made sure that a message of hope and continued improvement was passed along to the players. All coaches attempted to put a positive spin on the negative outcome. Some coaches called the loss an anomaly, something that usually doesn't happen, but did in this instance. But a positive message that the loss would be a tremendous learning experience for both the players and coaching staff was delivered.   The coaches also believed that effective film analysis of the game with the players assisted in mentally preparing the team for the following game.

Discussion of Research and Coaching Methods

In our final section of the book, it was not surprising to find continued agreement between the research and coaching methods. The coaches and the research all put a premium on the importance of communication to the overall success of a championship program. The research pointed out that all verbal communication needed to be clear and concise, and the coaches were totally in agreement with that statement.

Research also indicated that the communication between players and coaches had a direct impact on "flow" and optimal performance by the players. The coaches also indicated an awareness of the importance of the content of their messages being sent to their players.

Verbal and nonverbal messages were also shown to be critical communication vehicles between coach and player, with nonverbal methods (physical appearance, posture, gestures, body position, touching, facial expression, voice characteristics) playing a heavy role in communication. Coaches and the research also were in agreement regarding the importance of listening skills in the communication process.

Finally, unanimity among the coaches regarding coaching strategies employed at halftime, during late-game critical time-outs with the team, and in post-game commentary seemed to indicate that a universal coaching philosophy regarding these aspects of game coaching behavior exists among the championship coaching fraternity. And if these championship coaches all believe in this type of communication approach during these critical time periods of a game, then these methods should also be beneficial to corporate managers and supervisors as well.

Coaches have long been considered leaders and role models for communication and motivation skills by individuals in non-athletic professions and occupations. I hope that coaches are proud that they have established some successful standards of communication patterns for others to emulate, and I am thrilled that this book was a source of this dynamic information.

Final Analysis

There is no doubt that communication can arguably be selected as the major component for success in life, not just athletics. We must continue to communicate effectively with our spouses, our significant others, our children, our players, our coaching staffs, our students, our school administrators, and our supervisors, managers, bosses, and fellow employees.

Our championship coaches have developed and utilized highly effective communication models within their programs. These communication philosophies can be considered sound in their foundation. Coaches and managers should feel confident that the examples given throughout this section can be adapted to their programs and departments, and that these strategies can assist them in striving for competitive excellence in their lives.

One final note: My co-author, Bill Donaldson, has written an insightful response to the effectiveness of these six psychological factors for success on the corporate world. Please take the time to read his fascinating comments which can be found in the special appendix section of this book.

◆ ◆ ◆ ◆ ◆

REFERENCES

. . . on Motivation

Beauchamp, P.H., Halliwell, W.R., Fournier, J.F., & Koestner, R. (1996). Effects of cognitive-behavioral psychological skills training on the motivation, preparation, and putting performance of novice golfers. *The Sport Psychologist, 10,* 157-170.

Blanchard, C., & Vallerand, R.J. (1996). *Perceptions of competence, autonomy, and relatedness as psychological mediators of the social factors-contextual motivation relationship.* Unpublished manuscript, Universite' du Quebec a Montreal, Canada.

Brennan, S.J. (1986, June). *Intrinsic motivation of intercollegiate male and female athletes in team and individual sport groups.* Unpublished masters thesis, University of Nebraska-Lincoln, presented at the annual conference for the North American Society for Psychology of Sport and Physical Activity, Phoenix, Arizona.

Cadorette, I., Blanchard, C., & Vallerand, R.J. (1996, October). *Weight loss program: Effects of the fitness center and the instructor on participants' motivation.* Paper presented at the annual conference of the Quebec Society for Research in Psychology, Trois-Rivieres, Canada.

Deci, E.L., & Ryan, R.M. (1987). The support of autonomy and the control of behavior. *Journal of Personality and Social Psychology, 53,* 1024-1037.

Deci, E.L., Schwartz, A.J., Sheinman, L., & Ryan, R.M. (1981). An instrument to assess adults' orientations toward control versus autonomy with children: Reflections on intrinsic motivation and competence. *Journal of Educational Psychology, 83,* 642-650.

Dweck, C.S. (1986). Motivational processes affecting learning. *American Psychologist, 41,* 1040-1048.

Dweck, C.S. (1999). *Self-theories and goals: Their role in motivation, personality, and development.* Philadelphia: Taylor & Francis.

Goudas, M., Biddle, S., Fox, K., & Underwood, M. (1995). It ain't what you do, it's the way that you do it! Teaching style affects children's motivation in track and field lessons. *The Sport Psychologist, 9,* 254-264.

Gould, D. (1982). Sport psychology in the 1980's: Status, direction and challenge in youth sports research. *Journal of Sport Psychology, 4,* 203-218.

Kavussanu, M., & Roberts, G.C. (1996). Motivation in physical activity contexts: The relationship of perceived motivational climate to intrinsic motivation and self-efficacy. *Journal of Sport & Exercise Psychology, 18,* 264-280.

Markland, D., & Hardy, L. (1997). On the factorial and construct validity of the Intrinsic Motivation Inventory: Conceptual and operational concerns. *Research Quarterly for Exercise and Sport, 68,* 20-32.

Mitchell, S.A. (1996). Relationships between perceived learning environment and intrinsic motivation in middle school physical education. *Journal of Teaching in Physical Education, 15,* 369-383.

Nicholls, J.G. (1984). Achievement motivation: Conceptions of ability, subjective experience, task choice, and performance. *Psychological Review, 91,* 328-346.

Nicholls, J.G. (1989). *The competitive ethos and democratic education.* Cambridge, MA: Harvard University Press.

Pelletier, L.G., Briere, N.M., Blais, M.R., & Vallerand, R.J. (2000). *When coaches become autonomy-supportive: Effects on intrinsic motivation, persistence, and performance.* Manuscript in preparation, University of Ottawa, Canada.

Roberts, G.C. (1992). Motivation in sport and exercise: Conceptual constraints and convergence. In G.C. Roberts (Ed.), *Motivation in sport and exercise* (pp. 3-29). Champaign, IL: Human Kinetics.

Ryckman, R.M., & Hamel, J. (1993). Perceived physical ability differences in the sport participation motives of young athletes. *International Journal of Sport Psychology, 24,* 270-283.

Theeboom, M., De Knop, P., & Weiss, M.R. (1995). Motivational climate, psychological responses, and motor skill development in children's sport: A field-based intervention study. *Journal of Sport & Exercise Psychology, 17,* 294-311.

Vallerand, R.J. (1997). Toward a hierarchical model of intrinsic and extrinsic motivation.   In M.P. Zanna (Ed.), *Advances in experimental social psychology* (Vol. 29, pp. 271-360).
New York: Academic Press.

Vallerand, R.J., & Losier, G.F. (1999). An integrative analysis of intrinsic and extrinsic motivation in sport. *Journal of Applied Sport Psychology, 11,* 142-169.

Wagner, S.L., Lounsbury, J.W., & Fitzgerald, L.G. (1989). Attribute factors associated with work/leisure perceptions. *Journal of Leisure Research, 21,* 155-166.

Weigand, D.A., & Broadhurst, C.J. (1998). The relationship among perceived competence, intrinsic motivation, and control perceptions in youth soccer. *International Journal of Sport Psychology, 29,* 324-338.

On Team Cohesion. . .

Brawley, L.R., Carron, A.V., & Widmeyer, W.N. (1987). Assessing the cohesion of teams: Validity of the Group Environment Questionnaire. *Journal of Sport Psychology, 9,* 275-294.

Brawley, L.R., Carron, A.V., & Widmeyer, W.N. (1988). Exploring the relationship between cohesion and group resistance to disruption. *Journal of Sport & Exercise Psychology, 10,* 199-213.

Carron, A.V., Brawley, L.R., & Widmeyer, W.N. (1998). The measurement of cohesiveness in sport groups. In J.L. Duda (Ed.), *Advances in sport and exercise psychology measurement* (pp. 213-226). Morgantown, WV: Fitness Information Technology.

Granito, V., & Rainey, D. (1988). Differences in cohesion between high school and college football teams and starters and nonstarters. *Perceptual and Motor Skills, 66,* 471-477.

Kozub, S.A. (1993). *Exploring the relationships among coaching behavior, team cohesion, and player leadership.* Unpublished doctoral dissertation, University of Houston, TX.

Lott, A.J., & Lott, B.E. (1965). Group cohesiveness as interpersonal attraction: A review of relationships with antecedent and consequent variables. *Psychological Bulletin, 64,* 259-309.

Mullen, B., & Copper, C. (1994). The relation between group cohesiveness and performance: An integration. *Psychological Bulletin, 115,* 210-227.

Paskevich, D.M., Brawley, L.R., Dorsch, K.D., & Widmeyer, W.N. (1999). Relationship between collective efficacy and team cohesion: Conceptual and measurement issues. *Group Dynamics: Theory, Research, and Practice, 3,* 210-222.

Prapavessis, H., & Carron, A.V. (1997). The role of sacrifice in the dynamics of sport teams. *Group Dynamics, 1,* 231-240.

Shields, D.L., Bredemeier, B.J., Gardner, D.E., & Boston, A. (1995). Leadership, cohesion, and team norms regarding cheating and aggression. *Sociology of Sport Journal, 12,* 324-336.

Westre, K., & Weiss, M. (1991). The relationship between perceived coaching behaviors and group cohesion in high school football teams. *The Sport Psychologist, 5,* 41-54.

Widmeyer, W.N., Brawley, L.R., & Carron, A.V. (1990). Group size in sport. *Journal of Sport & Exercise Psychology, 12,* 177-190.

. . . on Discipline

Allison, M.G., & Ayllon, T. (1980). Behavioral coaching in the development of skills in football, gymnastics, and tennis. *Journal of Applied Behavior Analysis, 13,* 297-314.

Donahue, J.A., Gillis, J.H., & King, K. (1980). Behavior modification in sport and physical education. *Journal of Sport Psychology, 2,* 311-328.

Gibson, J.T. (1983). *Discipline is not a dirty word.* Brattlevoro, VT: The Lewis Publishing Company.

Gill, D.L. (2000). *Psychological dynamics of sport and exercise* (2nd ed.). Champaign, IL: Human Kinetics.

Kauss, D.R. (1980). *Peak performance.* Englewood Cliffs, NJ: Prentice-Hall.

Rushall, B.S., & Siedentop, D. (1972). *The development and control of behavior in sport and physical education.* Philadelphia: Lea & Febiger.

Siedentop, D. (1978). The management of practice behavior. In W.F. Straub (Ed.), *Sport psychology: An analysis of athlete behavior* (pp. 49-55). Ithaca, NY: Mouvement.

Smith, R.E., & Smoll, F.L. (1997). Coaching the coaches: Youth sports as a scientific and applied behavioral setting. *Current Directions in Psychological Science, 6,* 16-21.

Smith, R.E., Smoll, F.L., & Curtis, B. (1979). Coach effectiveness training: A cognitive-behavioral approach to enhancing relationship skills in youth sport coaches. *Journal of Sport Psychology, 1,* 59-75.

Smoll, F.L., & Smith, R.E. (1984). Leadership research in youth sports. In J.M. Silva & R.S. Weinberg (Eds.), *Psychological foundations of sport* (pp. 371-386). Champaign, IL: Human Kinetics.

. . . on Mental Preparation

Boutcher, S.H. (1993). Attention and athletic performance: An integrated approach. In T.S. Horn (Ed.), *Advances in sport psychology* (pp. 251-265). Champaign, IL: Human Kinetics.

Brennan, S.J. (1987). *The mental edge: Basketball's peak performance workbook.* Omaha, NE: Peak Performance Publishing.

Collins, J.P., & Harden, R.M. (1998). AMEE medical education guide No. 13: Real patients, simulated patients and simulators in clinical examinations. *Medical Teacher, 20,* 508-521.

Decety, J., Jeannerod, M. & Prablanc, C. (1989). The timing of mentally represented actions. *Behavioral Brain Research, 34,* 35-42.

Edgar, L., & Smith-Hanrahan, C.M. (1992). Non-pharmacological pain management. In J.H. Watt-Watson & M.I. Donovan (Eds.), *Pain management: Nursing perspective* (pp. 162-199). Sydney, Australia: Mosby.

Elko, P.K., & Ostrow, A.C. (1991). Effects of a rational-emotive education program on heightened anxiety levels of female collegiate gymnasts. *The Sport Psychologist, 5,* 235-255.

Ellis, A. (1981). *Rational emotive therapy and cognitive behavior therapy.* New York: Springer.

Feltz, D.L., & Landers, D.M. (1983). The effects of mental practice on motor skill learning and performance: A meta-analysis. *Journal of Sport Psychology, 5,* 25-57.

Hird, J.S., Landers, D.M., Thomas, J.R., & Horan, J.J. (1991). Physical practice is superior to mental practice in enhancing cognitive and motor skill performance. *Journal of Sport & Exercise Psychology, 13,* 281-293.

James, P.T. (1992). Cognitive therapies. In S. Tyrer (Ed.), *Psychology, psychiatry and chronic pain* (pp. 137-147). Sydney, Australia: Butterworth-Heinemann.

Jeannerod, M. (1999). The 25th Bartlett Lecture. To act or not to act: Perspectives on the representation of actions. *Quarterly Journal of Experimental Psychology, 52A,* 1-29.

Kohl, R.M., Ellis, S.D., & Roenker, D.L. (1992). Alternating actual and imagery practice: Preliminary theoretical considerations. *Research Quarterly for Exercise and Sport, 63,* 162-170.

Murphy, S.M., & Jowdy, D.P. (1993). Imagery and mental practice. In T.S. Horn (Ed.), *Advances in sport psychology* (pp. 221-250). Champaign, IL: Human Kinetics.

Nideffer, R.M., & Sagal, M. (1998). Concentration and attention control. In J.M. Williams (Ed.), *Applied sport psychology: Personal growth to peak performance* (3rd ed., pp. 296-315). Mountainview, CA: Mayfield.

Orlick, T. (1992). The psychology of personal excellence. *Contemporary Thought on Performance Enhancement, 1,* 109-122.

Taylor, S.E. (1995). *Health psychology.* Sydney, Australia: McGraw-Hill.

Vealey, R.S., & Greenleaf, C.A. (1998). Seeing is believing: Understanding and using imagery in sport. In J.M. Williams (Ed.), *Applied sport psychology: Personal growth to peak performance* (3rd ed., pp. 237-269). Mountainview, CA: Mayfield.

Zinsser, N., Bunker, L., & Williams, J.M. (1998). Cognitive techniques for building confidence and enhancing performance. In J.M. Williams (Ed.), *Applied sport psychology: Personal growth to peak performance* (3rd ed., pp. 270-295). Mountainview, CA: Mayfield.

. . . on Mental Toughness

Cattell, R.B. (1965). *The scientific analysis of personality.* Baltimore: Penguin Books.

Dienstbier, R.A. (1989). Arousal and physiological toughness: Implication for mental and physical health. *Psychological Review, 96(1)*, 84-100.

Goldberg, A.S. (1998). *Sports slump busting.* Champaign, IL: Human Kinetics.

Kobasa, S.C. (1979). Stressful life events, personality and health: An inquiry into hardiness. *Journal of Personality and Social Psychology, 37,* 1-11.

Kobasa, S.C., & Maddi, S.R. (1982). Hardiness and health: A prospective study. *Journal of Personality and Social Psychology, 42,* 168-177.

Kubistant, T. (1986). *Performing your best.* Champaign, IL: Life Enhancement Publications.

Loehr, J.E. (1982). *Mental toughness training for sports: Achieving athletic excellence.*
Lexington, MA: The Stephen Greene Press.

_____, (1986). *Mentally tough: The principles of winning at sports applied to winning in business.* New York: Evans and Company, Inc.

_____, (1993). *Toughness training for life.* New York: Plume/Penguin.

_____, (1994). *The new toughness training for sports: Achieving athletic excellence.* New York: Dutton.

. . . on Communication

Bandler, R. (1997). Neuro-Linguistic Programming: The Presuppositions of NLP™ [Online]. Available: www.purenlp.com/nlpresp.htm [April 16, 1999].

Burke, K.L. (1997). Communication in sports: Research and practice. *Journal of Interdisciplinary Research in Physical Education, 2,* 39-52.

Csikszentmihalyi, M. (1990). *Flow: The psychology of optimal experience.* New York: Harper & Row.

Jackson, S.A., & Csikszentmihalyi, M. (1999). *Flow in sports.* Champaign, IL: Human Kinetics.

Parcells, B., & Coplon, J. (1995). *Finding a way to win: The principles of leadership, teamwork, and motivation.* New York: Doubleday Dell Publishing Group.

Rosenfeld, L., & Wilder, L. (1990). Communication fundamentals: Active listening. *Sport Psychology Training Bulletin, 1*(5), 1-8.

Sathre, S., Olson, R.W., & Whitney, C.I. (1973). *Let's talk.* Glenview, IL: Scott, Foresman.

Syer, J. (1986). *Team spirit.* London: Simon & Schuster.

Weinberg, R.S., & Gould, D. (1999). *Foundations of sport and exercise psychology* (2nd ed.). Champaign, IL: Human Kinetics.

Yukelson, D. (1998). Communicating effectively. In J. Williams (Ed.), *Sport psychology: Peak performance to personal growth* (3rd ed., pp. 142-157). Mountain View, CA: Mayfield.

A CHAPTER BY A NON-COACH

ARE THE COACHES' EXPERIENCES APPLICABLE TO OTHER MANAGERS?

My co-author, Bill Donaldson, spent over 40 years as a manager in manufacturing and in scientific research. In talking to him about the applicability of the coaches' assessments for six psychological factors to industrial, business, and academic managers, Bill told me, " I wish I'd been able to review their chapters when I was managing various types of activities in industry and government". So I said, "Why don't you do a chapter using the same format the coaches used to illustrate what you're telling me?"

Bill took me up on my suggestion. I think his treatment will remove any doubt that all sorts of managers can profit from reading the coaches' chapters.

. . . on Motivation

There are differences in the motivation of athletes and the motivation of industrial employees, performing what can be monotonous jobs. The self motivation for college-level athletes is already at a high level when they begin college. Athletes who reach the intercollegiate competitive level have gone through a screening process that only highly motivated players can pass. Conversely, a major motivating factor for many industrial workers is their paycheck. Some would not be working—particularly mothers of small children, and I single them our because they are involved in my first anecdote—if they didn't need that paycheck in order to make ends meet. The paycheck is motivating to work, but not necessarily motivating to excel. But nearly all athletes are highly motivated to excel by the love of the game and the challenge of competition. There is no pay check. Many are not on scholarship. So while the coach may not have as tough a job in motivating athletes as the industrial supervisor has in motivating employees, the manager in business and government can learn a lot from the coaches.

There is a strong, almost inherent, level of motivation among some people, even in repetitive industrial jobs. Why? When I was with the DuPont Company in Virginia, the process control laboratories for a large nylon manufacturing plant came under my direction. There were about 200 technicians (all women—and that's another story) in the laboratories. They were all paid the same base hourly rate, with some adjustment for longevity, and promotions to higher-paying jobs were based primarily on seniority. There was no incentive pay for higher output or better performance, although the laboratory manager was evaluated on the efficiency of the laboratory. So he had a lot to gain by increasing performance.

In the mid 1960s we were just beginning to use computers in quality control—not PCs; the old punched-card monsters. We began tabulating, for the first time, the number of measurements each technician performed in a given time period and also the accuracy and precision of her measurements. Surprisingly, in general, the technicians who performed the largest number of measurements also were the more accurate workers. And the fastest ones performed almost twice the number of measurements the slowest ones performed. I would have thought that the faster a technician worked, the less precise her results would be. But it was the other way around.

Then, through a questionnaire, we made a subjective analysis that helped explain this observation. The more productive and more accurate workers were also those who appeared, from the survey, to be happier in their jobs; even though the fastest workers were paid slightly more than half what the slower and less accurate workers were paid for the same output. It certainly wasn't money that was motivating them. The more productive workers had developed, over a period of time, an intrinsic level of self motivation. The process was also self perpetuating: the more motivated—the higher the work output, the higher the work output—the happier the worker, the happier the worker—the more motivated she was. No doubt some of the performance was related to inherent ability to do the job—not just motivation. But this is a striking example of the importance of motivation—the most motivated workers twice as productive as the least motivated ones.

Now, how do you get the increased output process started for the less motivated employees? Where in the motivation-increased output-increased happiness cycle do you focus? It seems logical that you focus on motivation.

But how do you motivate the poorer performers? The employees belonged to a local labor union, and their contract would not allow a financial incentive based on output or quality. So we had to motivate the slower workers by using many of the things the coaches mention in this book: (1) Work individually with each employee to set challenging, but attainable, goals for improvement. (2) Provide instructions about the significance of each step of each procedure and give them pointers on their techniques that will improve their performance. Knowledge and training are motivators according to some coaches. They usually increase interest, and interest motivates. (3) Hold individual discussions to tell the technicians how they are performing—relative to their past performance, not relative to other employees' performance. (4) Praise them for their progress, and let them know that you're interested in their progress, that you appreciate it, and that you believe in them. The self-motivated, happier employees usually show more initiative in interacting with their supervisor. The poor performer, unmotivated employee may be overlooked and feel left out. (5) Above all, maintain a positive attitude. These are all things that one coach or another suggests for motivating athletes.

Getting this process started requires a lot of time and thought, but the potential rewards are substantial. And of course, those rewards should be shared by the employer and the employees—even if it must be shared as a group. For example, if increased efficiency eventually brought in increased profits, part of the profits should go to increased compensation for the employees. As a group—a team—they brought home a victory. They should also "bring home the bacon."

◆   ◆   ◆   ◆   ◆

. . . on Team Cohesion

I know of no story more illustrative of the power of teamwork than the story of our "multispectral identification team" at the Environmental Research Laboratory in Athens, GA. The broad assignment of the group in which this team was established was to identify and measure trace concentrations of organic chemical pollutants in water and other environmental media. Perhaps many of you have heard of gas chromatography-mass spectrometry (GC-MS) in detecting and measuring prohibited drugs in athletes' body fluids. It's a commonly used technique in which the GC separates the trace chemicals into pure compounds, and the MS identifies them by comparing their mass spectra—"fingerprints"—to mass spectra of the compounds of interest—in this case unauthorized drugs.

But there are over ten million organic compound (contrasted with the few drugs measured), and libraries of mass spectra (fingerprints) contained a small fraction of the compounds that might be found in the ambient environment. We kept coming up with compound after compound whose spectrum we couldn't match, and therefore we could not identify them. In some cases the mass spectometrist (a highly specialized scientist) could figure out the likely identity of a compound without matching it with a fingerprint, but usually the mass spectrum was not sufficiently informative about the compound to identify it unless its spectrum was on file. Other scientists (e.g., molecular spectroscopists) worked with other instrumentation, such as infrared spectrometers (IR), and nuclear magnetic resonance spectrometers (NMR). Their spectra could identify compounds too, IF the compound's spectrum was in their "fingerprint library." But we ran into the same problem with other techniques that occurred with the GC-MS with so many possible compounds.

Now each different spectroscopic method provided a different type of information. Some helped tell the molecular mass of the compound or its fragments. Another provided information on the way the atoms were grouped, and another showed how the atoms were bonded together. With all of the information together (and I've simplified just how many different types of spectral information there were) if a scientist were a specialist in all types of spectroscopy, he could piece together the identity of the unknown compound. But, because of the level of specialization of the spectroscopists, no one person had the knowledge to develop all the different types of spectra, interpret them, and piece together the information.

The solution to this problem is obvious—have the specialists work as a team, each individually providing the information he is capable of and jointly interacting to provide the chemical structure of the unknown compound. One of the coaches defined team chemistry as "what makes the sum of the combined parts greater than the sum of the individual parts." I can't think of a better example of this axiom than what we needed to do here: get these specialists working together as a team. Individually they were ineffective. As a team they would be significantly more effective than they were working separately.

Unfortunately highly specialized scientists can be prima donnas—they frequently are. Each thinks his specialty is more important than any other. They publish in different journals from specialists in other fields. Each dislikes publishing jointly, unless the authors' names are listed in a manner indicating he is the lead scientist. As a result, no one in the entire world had ever successfully put together a "multispectral identification team."

College coaches face the prima donna problem when they bring together a group of players, each of whom was the star of his team in high school. Each one must learn what role he can play on his new team and learn to appreciate the roles of the other players. The team's strategies can't be built around every player on the team.

Many of the same solutions used by the coaches were part of our efforts to get these highly individualistic scientists to work together as a team. I first took the information each individual scientist had provided and reviewed it with each of the other scientists, separately. Each one was comfortable and still totally in charge, because he was the only scientist in the meeting. Each began to see how he could use the information from the others, combined with his own, to identify the compound—playing separate "roles," if you will. Each was elated. Each was still in charge. He thought of the others as subordinates.

I then began having them meet together. Working together was much faster, because the power of multiple iterations came into play. As they began to identify more and more compounds faster and faster they realized the value of working together. They began to really see why I'd called them a "team." Then we had to broach the problem of publication, attainment of their individual goals. Actually we pulled a slick trick. If we had three spectroscopists working together, we'd publish three papers, in three different journals, with three different senior authors, publishing in a journal that focused on his specialty. Each scientist was increasing his rate of publication too.

Clearly each scientist's career was advanced because he collaborated with the others. Perhaps the most fascinating aspect of this program was to see and hear the disbelief expressed by the peer reviewers for the program from prestigious research universities. They, themselves, were leaders in their own fields of specialization, and they were astounded that we were able to get the scientists working so cooperatively.

Scientific managers could profit from studying the different coaches' approaches to development of team chemistry. Interdisciplinary research can be a powerful tool if no one is concerned about who gets the credit. Indeed interdisciplinary research is quite common in many successful scientific accomplishments. But it requires teamwork, team cohesion, and team chemistry—no pun intended.

A lot of coaches orchestrate social interactions among team members, away from the practice or competition area, as an aid in building team cohesion. I've observed, over the years, that many female employees feel robbed of the opportunities non working women have to interact with other women in groups during the daytime. There are some occasions that bosses should be sensitive to—baby showers, bridal showers, etc. As more than one coach pointed out: there are differences between women and men. These are "woman things." If the work schedule will allow it, let those who want to attend such activities do it "on company time"—even at the workplace. Group get-togethers, away from the work place, for special occasions—the spring picnic, Christmas etc.,—are team-building activities that work in industry as well as with the athletic team. But the industrial groups are more diverse—in terms of age, economic background, and educational levels—than even the members of an athletic team are. Don't overlook this diversity in planning such activities.

Coaches are quick to point out their different approaches to building team cohesion. Perhaps one factor in these differences is finding the most effective level of conformity, an objective discussed in the next section.

◆ ◆ ◆ ◆ ◆

. . . on Discipline

Crawford Greenwalt was the manager of the Manhattan Project, the mammoth scientific project that developed and built the atomic bomb during World War II. It is considered one of the most outstanding managerial feats in the history of the world. After the war Dr. Greenwalt returned to the DuPont Company to become its president. I recall his saying something to the effect that in managing people effectively, you should require the minimum feasible level of conformity. Allow people to "do their own thing" to the greatest extent that is feasible. Too much conformity inhibits initiative and innovation. On the other hand, too little conformity may invite chaos. Just what that minimum feasible level should be brings quite a few different answers from the coaches.

I think you would get different answers from business managers as well. The different environments, different backgrounds of people, different work activities require different sets of rules or guidelines. The coaches' ideas on discipline reflect these differences in athletics. For example, some coaches require their athletes to get up the same time every morning on a road trip, while others allow the players freedom to get up whenever they want to, as long as they are on time for their first assignment of the day. They may both be right for their respective teams.

The two extremes in conformity are: (1) the military, where strict adherence to rules and regulations can be justified in training people to respond instinctively to commands in combat and (2) the higher academic world, where expanding knowledge suggests challenging traditional wisdom. In between those extremes, the athletic world may be closer to the military, and the business world may be closer to the academic setting. But there many shades of conformity in between.

If you stop to consider it, businesses, government, and athletics are rife with conformity. But how many rules are really necessary. I can think of a few—maybe: (1) Safety procedures must be adhered to. (2) People must get to work and meetings on time. (3) Official correspondence must be on the appropriate letterhead. (4) The phone should be answered in a pleasant, informative, and accommodating manner. Question the reasons for each rule. The reasons for these seem quite forthcoming. If they aren't, then maybe I'm being too restrictive.

Safety is something that pays dividends, not only in terms of reduced loss of time from injuries, but also in enhanced morale. People want to feel safe, and they want their employers to be concerned for their safety. But the rules seem to get awful picky sometimes. Athletes lose incentive if they think their coaches are not concerned with their safety. And of course an athletic team is usually impacted more when an athlete is injured than the manufacturing plant is when an employee is injured. As restricting and uncomfortable as much of the protective equipment may be, most athletes soon learn to appreciate it.

Nearly every large company has a safety policy and safety rules. Most claim that they put "safety first." But for many of them, it's just lip service. The DuPont Company meant business with its safety program. So when I joined the federal government, after years with the DuPont Company, I brought with me my concern for safety. When a new employee came into my organization, I met with him and his immediate boss. Early in our "get acquainted" talk, I posed the question, "What's the most important thing about your job?" This usually caught the new employees off guard, so they were slow in answering. The answers were usually something like, "to identify all the significant pollutants in the world" or "find the most important influences on global climate." Then I would say, "The most important thing about your job is for you not to get hurt." It let the employee know that I meant business about safety, and it let him know that I was saying the same thing to his boss. It made him realize that wearing safety glasses in an area designated for such was not an option. He remembered what I said, because it surprised him.

Every coach has a few things—like the laboratory supervisor's safety policy—that are not an option with him. He has to decide which practices are optional and which are not. He also should distinguish between rules, which leave no room for exercise of judgment, and guidelines, which prescribe to the athlete the exercising of judgment to achieve a specified objective. Each has its place.

In reviewing the coaches' comments on discipline, I believe all of them agree on one requirement: athletes must be on time for practices, meetings, travel etc. The same is true for employees. But some employers have established "flex-time" programs in which employees are allowed some flexibility in setting their schedules, within specified limits. Such a practice is highly valued by most families in which both parents work. But one of the stipulations in flex-time programs is that you still have a schedule, although it may be different from someone else's, and you must still adhere to it. The reasons for conforming to schedules are well understood. I don't need to review them. But the reasons for other mandated practices of conformity should stand up under scrutiny. Rules and restrictions that don't stand up, should be altered or removed.

As some coaches have indicated, the athletes should play a role in setting guidelines and rules. Let me tell you of a case where that worked for me. It may be difficult for people to fathom that in the 1970s, professional women and female clerical workers always wore skirts or dresses to work. Then, in some places women began wearing pants suits to work. It had been generally understood in the organization I worked for that pants suits were not proper attire for professional women and female clerical workers.

I knew the question was bound to come up, and sure enough it did. Both of my secretaries confronted me with the question. Although my first inclination was to almost laugh it off—it was no big deal. But my better judgment told me that I had to handle the question seriously, because it seemed important to the secretaries. So I scheduled a meeting for the three of us to discuss the appropriateness of pants suits in the office. I could not afford to be arbitrary, but I didn't have a real solid basis for prohibiting pants suits. They were not unsafe—perhaps even safer than skirts. They were not considered indecent. They wouldn't affect getting to work on time. The question really fell into the category of not requiring conformity.

At our meeting I first expressed my appreciation for the secretaries' bringing the question to me rather than just wearing the pants suits and challenging me. That showed respect for my interest in maintaining proper decorum and demeanor in our office and their interest in the same thing. We analyzed the question critically. It seemed that all three of us were searching for something to base a decision on. Finally we got around to my question to each secretary, "What is the next step in pursuing your career goal?" Fortunately for me the answer was the same from both: to become the Laboratory Director's secretary. What should you do to get there—perhaps emulate his current secretary? Does she wear pants suits? The Laboratory Director's secretary was a long-time career secretary, devoted to doing her job in a professional manner. She was a spinster. The secretaries suggested, themselves, that they should not wear pants suits to work until the Director's secretary wore them. I commended them for their judgment. It was their decision.

Less than two months later, the two secretaries came into the office and suggested that I go down to the Director's office and check out his secretary's attire. You guessed it; she was in a pants suit. Apparently the Director couldn't come up with a good reason for conforming to a long-held practice either.

One coach defined discipline as "the training that makes punishment unnecessary." Another quoted Coach John Wooden: "Discipline yourself, and others won't need to." Discipline is often considered just punishment. But "punishment" is the eighth definition of discipline in my dictionary. The first seven deal with training, order, obedience, a system of rules, etc. But punishment is certainly a part of the discipline system. The same common-sense criteria apply in administering punishment in coaching as apply in the business world. Of course the first steps are to make sure you know the facts and you give the employee an opportunity to explain his version of whatever happened. The one being punished must have been fully aware of the rules he broke—preferably of the reasons behind them. The punishment must be uniform—the same punishment for anyone who broke the same rules under the same circumstances. It must be done without any show of animosity. It must not be demeaning. Statements by the one prescribing the discipline must not be sarcastic. Every effort should be made to make the process a positive, if not pleasant, experience for all concerned.

A well-thought-out discipline program—not just rules, regulations, and punishment—can enhance performance in business and athletics. Indeed, it is essential. But "well-thought-out" is the operative term, and that presents a significant challenge to the manager and the coach.

◆ ◆ ◆ ◆ ◆

. . . on Mental Preparation

Does one have to prepare mentally to go to work? I'm not talking about the training he's gone through to be able to do his job. Does he have to get in the proper "state of mind" to do his job. In athletics, much of the mental preparation is associated with competition—just on the game day. But in business every day is game day. So maybe mental preparation is something we need to consider for workers in the business world.

In athletics much of the mental preparation is going through the same routines before the game starts or before one shoots a free-throw or mounts the balance beam. I think if we examine the typical worker's practices in business, we'll find he goes through just about the same routine every day when he arrives at the workplace. He may go by the coffee shop and get a cup of coffee. Or he may routinely chat with a coworker about the previous night's television show, a problem at home, or the football game coming up.

Whatever he does prior to starting his job, he should be allowed a reasonable time to do it. It's his mental preparation for the job. He has to get other distractions out of his mind, so he can concentrate on his work, just like the free-throw shooter has to concentrate on that free throw. The worker can't just start off cold without that routine of mental preparation. He has to adjust to the workplace environment every time he leaves it for a while. It may be equated to the athlete's stretching before warm-ups.

The only advice I have for supervisors is to let the worker get prepared mentally before you approach him with a business-related task.

Now, is the beginning of the work day the only time a supervisor should be concerned about mental preparation? No, there is at least one other time. That's when a supervisor needs to discuss a sensitive or important problem with an employee. One of my associates once told me it's essential that an employee be in a "receptive state of mind" when discussing a problem. If you have time, you may want to schedule a meeting with him several hours or a day in advance. He may wonder what you want to talk about. If it's appropriate, by all means let him know. After all, you've had time to prepare for the talk. He should have time too; it's only fair. If you can't schedule a meeting in advance, try to establish a pleasant mood by discussing something you know he'll want to discuss. If you have to criticize something he's done wrong, start off the conversation by recognizing something he's done well. Then introduce the topic of concern. These techniques are part of mental preparation.

Is there a place for imagery in the business world? Suppose you're going to have an important meeting or going to make a presentation to a group of people—or maybe just one person. Do you go over it mentally? Of course you do. Do you picture a conversation that may take place or anticipate questions you may get? You may want to practice a little imagery in anticipation of any important interaction. It may keep you from reacting in the wrong way spontaneously, by being mentally prepared.

And finally, as the boss—or coach—you, yourself, must be in a positive state of mind for discussions, whether with subordinates, with your peers, or with your boss. What mental preparation techniques do you go through to get yourself into a positive state of mind? Your state of mind can have a significant effect on the outcome of your interactions.

◆ ◆ ◆ ◆ ◆

. . . on Mental Toughness

Adversity is not limited to athletics. Workers face adversity every day. A family member may be critically ill at a time when an important meeting is taking place, but you need to stay focused. You may work a year on an important paper for publication in a scientific journal, and it's rejected with harsh criticism from a peer reviewer, but you've got to rework it with a positive attitude. Lightening knocks out the power to your incubator housing a biological experiment that's been going on several months and is near completion, but you can't just let it go, if preliminary results appeared to be promising. You are passed over for a rare promotional opportunity for a person you know is less qualified, but you won't have a chance at the next one if you give up. Or you may work for the "worst boss in the world" and have to face him and suffer the consequences of his decisions every day. Do these things sound familiar? They are things you can't avoid. You have no control over their happening. But you do have control over how you respond. This is where mental toughness comes in.

The coaches have some excellent guidance on mental toughness. They say don't look back. What's passed has passed. You can't change the past. You can influence the future.

Distinguish between options and things that are not options. Just as you don't look back at the past, you don't dwell on options you don't have, regardless of how attractive they may be.

Keep a positive attitude. This is not always easy but it's an option you do have available.

Of the options you have available, analyze them carefully and as objectively as you can. Then make a plan.

Execute your plan with all of your ability.

And don't give up, regardless of what happens. This is another option you have. You can give up, or you can keep fighting. The mentally tough employee never gives up.

And what's the mentally tough worker like? He's like the mentally tough athlete. He has a positive attitude. He's considerate of others. He's confident in himself. And he won't give up.

◆ ◆ ◆ ◆ ◆

. . . on Communication

In the scientific arena the most intelligent scientist in the world will be a failure if he can't communicate the results of his research effectively. His product is the written word, and that's all most of his peers know about him—what he writes. In the business world, written communication is important, but oral communication may be more important, because there are more face-to-face communications and telephone communications than there are written communications, although E-mail is changing that rapidly.

There are many books on effective communications. I could not even begin to discuss just the more important aspects of them, but I can skim the surface.

I'm not sure where to put this admonition. It would fit many places in this chapter. Let me begin with a personal experience. When I first became a supervisor with the DuPont Company, one of my superiors was lecturing to a group of new supervisors. While he was talking about communicating he became passionate as he said, "Never, never, never, never, never lie!" This was a supervisor at the Savannah River Laboratory. Because of his passion about telling the truth, I assumed that everyone who worked for the company felt that way. In fact, during the 11 years I worked at Savannah River, I can't recall that a supervisor ever attempted to mislead me. I just assumed that all of the managers told the truth all the time. One supervisor in another organization had lied about an important issue, and he was told,

"Your assignment for the foreseeable future is to look for another job and provide periodic reports of your progress." So when someone asked me what I thought was the most important characteristic of a good manager, I didn't even consider "being truthful;" I thought it was a given. I answered, "Intelligence." I said that because I'd never encountered a boss who did not tell the truth—all the time.

After I moved to Virginia with the same company, I encountered a brilliant boss. In fact, I think one of the reasons I accepted the offer of transfer from the Savannah River Laboratory, a place I thoroughly enjoyed working, was because I was so impressed with the man who would become my boss, when he interviewed me. He was intelligent. He was flamboyant and exciting to be around. Working with him would be stimulating, because he had big plans. And he was so convincing when he told me how I was just the person he'd been looking for over the course of several years. I took it for granted that everything he said was the truth, because he was a manager in the company whose management I had come to trust and respect over the years.

I won't go into details, but if asked today what I consider the most important characteristic in a good boss, without hesitation my response would be, "Honesty." "Fairness" would probably come second, before "intelligence." I've made one observation about both honesty and fairness. If the top person in the organization has a problem with either of these characteristics, chances are that their behavior will ultimately be reflected in the behavior of their subordinates as well. Do coaches feel a responsibility as role models?

Now that I've put so much importance on being honest, let me add that you should be skeptical of anyone who tells you that being honest is easy. To be honest, you sometimes have to tell people things you know they don't want to hear. And it means that you must reveal things about yourself that you're ashamed of. And to do either of these things in a manner that is constructive and positive adds challenge to the task. But my admonition to anyone is to be honest in all of your communications, and then—and only then—do your best to make your communications constructive.

The coaches address what they say at halftime in games. A manager has lots of "halftimes" in dealing with his workers. Every time you reach a decision point or an evaluation point you have a "halftime." Plan your discussion periods and follow a routine format, like some coaches do at halftime. This approach keeps you on target, and helps avoid overlooking something. And remember that "halftime" discussions are for motivation as much as they are for evaluation. Don't be stingy with the "attaboys."

You have more time to communicate with your employees and make adjustments before halftime than the coach does in a competition. So, when you have a periodic performance interview—"halftime discussion"—with an employee, he shouldn't be surprised by anything you tell him. If you wait until performance appraisal time to try to help him correct a problem, you've let him down—letting him exacerbate the problem while waiting to correct it. So, if you've already tried to help him, you're now evaluating his progress on a matter you are already trying to help him resolve. This will likely be a positive step. But whatever the situation, be honest about it. And be positive about it. Tell him you believe in him. That's what the coaches do.

Finally, communication is not merely talking or writing. A communication is not completed until the recipient has responded in a way that assures you that he understands what you intended to communicate to him. Make sure he plays it back to you, in a manner that assures you he knows what you wanted him to learn. Don't hesitate to ask him if he understands, and make sure he feels free and to ask for clarification when he doesn't understand. Never show impatience with his questions, no matter how trivial or stupid they may seem. If he feels you are impatient or if he feels you will judge him to be stupid if he asks too many questions, he will not ask questions he should, and you will have failed to communicate with him. You both will suffer the consequences.

Communications is the essence of good coaching and the essence of good management.

◆ ◆ ◆ ◆ ◆

Summary

As I complete this analysis of the *6 Psychological Factors for Success*, it becomes clearer than ever to me that the factors are equally important in athletic and business-world performance. Indeed they are important in all aspects of ones life.

I join many others who extol the values of team sport participation. The most important role coaches play is impacting the lives of their athletes at the most psychologically impressionable and formative period of their lives. If a process of dealing with these psychological factors is ingrained in the characters of athletes as a result of their participation in team sports, this character enrichment will be one of the most significant assets the athlete ever acquires.

ABOUT THE AUTHORS

STEVE BRENNAN is the founder and president of Peak Performance Consultants, Inc., an international firm specializing in motivation, education, and performance enhancement strategies catering to student-athletes, coaches, educators, and business people.

A former high school and college teacher and coach, he holds masters degrees in Educational Administration and Sport Psychology, and a doctorate in performance and health psychology.

In addition to *6 Psychological Factors for Success*, Steve is the author of eight books and has written chapters in two others. He has research materials at the Naismith Basketball Hall of Fame and the International Center of Investigation and Documentation of Basketball in Madrid, Spain.

Steve has been included in the *World Sport Psychology Sourcebook*, *World Sport Psychology Who's Who*, *Who's Who in American Education*, *Two Thousand Notable American Men*, *Who's Who in the World*, and the *International Who's Who of Business Entrepreneurs*.

Currently, Steve is the executive director of The Recruiters Institute™, the director of The Recruiters Library™, the founder and president of The Center for Performance Enhancement Research & Education™, and founder and executive director of the Midwest Youth Coaches Association. He has been a performance consultant with the Kansas City Royals baseball organization, and has experience as a basketball analyst on the Creighton University Radio Network.

Steve and his wife, Lorna, serve as members of the Board of Directors of the Drake University Parents Association. They have three children and live in Omaha, Nebraska.

BILL DONALDSON is a freelance writer who has spent over 40 years directing scientific researchers with the E.I. DuPont Company and the U.S. Environmental Protection Agency. He says most of the psychological principles in coaching talented athletes are equally applicable in managing people in business, industry, and government, especially in melding interdisciplinary research teams. This interest is the basis for his interest in contributing to this book.

It is not surprising, then, that topics for his current writing fall into two categories not normally linked: environmental management and intercollegiate athletics. Bill's forthcoming book on women's college gymnastics, *Higher Than Yoculan's Heels and Hemlines: Soaring in College Gymnastics*, will be the first book published on this sport that is soaring in popularity. University of Georgia Coach Suzanne Yoculan, who is featured in the book, is a chapter author in *6 Psychological Factors for Success*.

Bill and his wife, Barbara, have two children and three grandchildren. They live in Athens, Georgia.

THE MENTAL EDGE BOOKSTORE
Preferred Customer Order Form

BOOKS

6 Psychological Factors for Success: America's Most Successful Coaches ...

A national best-seller! A collection of top coaches from across the United States. Each coach is highlighted in sections on motivation, team cohesion, discipline, mental preparation, mental toughness and communication. A valuable addition to every coach's library!

Retail: $29.95

Basketball Resource Guide (Second Edition)

The most comprehensive resource medium for the sport of basketball. Includes listings for audio-visual tapes, books, magazines, research studies and more ... The consummate book for the basketball junkie!

Retail: $20.00

NOTE: Third Edition available on computer disk. Inquire first.

The Mental Edge: Basketball's Peak Performance Workbook (3rd Edition)

The best mental training book for basketball on the market today! A step-by-step manual teaching mental preparation and training for coaches and athletes. Chapters include goal setting, visualization, stress management, concentration and more ...

Retail: $29.95

Psychology of Winning Notebook

The complete notes from Steve Brennan's highly-acclaimed Psychology of Winning Clinic. Topics include motivation, discipline and mental toughness. So organized, it's just like sitting at the clinic itself!

Retail: $20.00

Golf Psychology Workbook

The core text of Steve Brennan's Golf Psychology Workshop for the Competitive Golfer. An in-depth exploration of the mental side of golf for someone who takes the game seriously. It could help you drop a few strokes from your game!

Retail: $23.00

(Please reproduce for additional copies)

ORDER FORM

Book	Quantity	Unit Price	Total
6 Psychological Factors for Success	_____	$29.95	_____
Basketball Resource Guide	_____	$20.00	_____
The Mental Edge	_____	$29.95	_____
Psychology of Winning Notebook	_____	$20.00	_____
Golf Psychology Workbook	_____	$23.00	_____
Postage/Handling (Continental U.S. only)		$4.95	_____
(Canada & Foreign only)		$30.00	

_____   TOTAL AMOUNT DUE:

Send to: Name _____

Address _____

City/State/Zip
_____

Country _____

All monies in U.S. currency only. Make check payable to:
Peak Performance Publishing
and mail to:
Peak Performance Publishing
14728 Shirley Street
Omaha, Nebraska 68144 USA